Macbeth

Macbeth
Moment by Moment

by William Shakespeare

Annotated by Carmen Khan and Jack Armstrong

**THE PHILADELPHIA
SHAKESPEARE PRESS**

Scotland in Macbeth's time - 1059 A.D.

Why This Book?

We are stage practitioners. After three decades and sixty productions, (including fifty of Shakespeare and six of *Macbeth*),
we have learned some things about how to perform this play.

We are also theatre educators. After working with thousands of
students in hundreds of schools, we have learned some things
about what works in the classroom. And the main thing we
have learned is this: The best way to experience this play (or
any play) is to perform it.

So we created this book to share some of what we've learned
about performing *Macbeth*. It is for anybody who speaks this
play out loud, whether it's a two-minute scene in a middle
school classroom in front of three classmates, or a college production, or on a professional stage in front of an audience of
thousands.

Although we have extensive notes in this edition on *what* the
character is saying, that is not our primary focus. Rather, our
focus is on *why* they are speaking. "If it were done when 'tis
done, 'twere well it were done quickly": In this moment, is
Macbeth suffering from moral scruples? Is he shrinking from
violence? Is he calculating the consequences? Before you can
speak the speech well, you have to know the answer to this
question. At The Philadelphia Shakespeare Theatre we have
found that, in order to stage one of these plays, we must first
spend months poring over the script, moment by moment, to
ferret out what Shakespeare intended — to answer the question "why". In this edition we share the fruits of those efforts,
to give other students a head start on the "why"; to help you
experience for yourself the awesome power and richness of
Shakespeare's work. That's why we call it **Macbeth Moment
by Moment.**

Class Discussion

One question we've been asked about this book is: By pro-
viding interpretation, aren't we robbing you of discovering the
play for yourself? More specifically, given that this book is pri-
marily intended for students, are we preventing fruitful class
discussions by answering all the questions for you? Our answer
is: Definitely not! Rather, this book helps students get past the
preliminary questions and go straight to the eternal questions
that *Macbeth* shines such a bright light on: free will; corruption;
ambition; courage vs. foolhardiness; caution vs. cowardice —
fundamental issues for which nobody has ever found a final
answer, but which we all must grapple with. This book is coach-

ing. Good athletes have good coaches and great athletes have great coaches. With this edition our aim is not to read the play for you, but to provide some great coaching to help you read it at a higher level.

And of course, after seeing our evidence, you can decide for yourself what you think is happening in *Macbeth*. This book is intended as guidance, not doctrine. Although it is the fruit of years of collaboration with dozens of actors and designers, it is still a work in progress. After dozens of productions and thousands of hours of study, we are still students; still reaching to comprehend Shakespeare's legacy. We can never quite catch up. But we have loved spending our lives trying. In fact, if you have a comment or suggestion, please email us: info@philadelphiashakespearepress.com.

The Page Layout

On the left-hand pages of this book is the actual script. (We adhere closely to the First Folio. There's more on that below.) We have numbered every line of dialogue, to help match the notes on the right to the lines on the left. Also, we have divided each scene into subscenes: Generally, when actors enter or leave the stage, one dramatic question ends and another begins. That's how Shakespeare organized his stories. So we separate the subscenes in the script (e.g. 1.3.a, 1.3.b, 1.3.c, etc.).

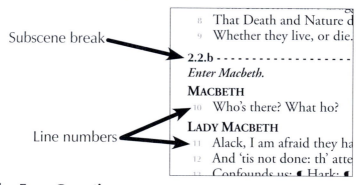

The Four Questions

The right-hand pages have four parts. These correspond to the four questions we address for every moment of the play: What are they saying? Why are they saying it? What is the drama of the scene? Why is the scene in the play? To illustrate, let us walk through the beginning of this speech (1.7.a, page 38):

> If it were done, when 'tis done, then 'twere well
> It were done quickly: if th'Assassination

Could trammel up the Consequence, and catch
With his surcease, Success: that but this blow
Might be the be all and the end all. Here,
But here, upon this Bank and Shoal of time,
We'd jump the life to come.

1. The "What" Column: What is the speaker saying?

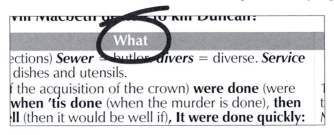

In the "What" column are extensive notes on what the character is saying. We define obscure or changed words (like "trammel" and "surcease"), we supply the missing words, we unpack the imagery (like "we'd jump the life to come" means we would jump into the deep water of that future), and decipher the sentence structure, so that you can do more than just get past the line: so that you can navigate for yourself what it says, word for word; truly appreciate the intricate wordplay of Shakespeare's poetry. And the real test: so that you can speak the speech out loud, as if it were your own words, for every single word.

2. The "Why" column: Why does the speaker say this?

The "What" column, explained above, is just the beginning. If you're going to speak the words out loud, you need to know not just what you are saying, but why you are saying it.

No character in a Shakespeare play is ever just creating verbal fireworks for the sheer joy of it. Characters on stage (like people in real life) say things because they need something. So in order to really understand the play, we have to know what they need. Let's look again at "If it were done". This speech is often interpreted as a moral dilemma — Macbeth struggling with his conscience. But closer reading reveals that he is doing something else. He has already decided he would accept the moral consequences of murdering Duncan if he knew it would make him king. What Macbeth is worried about in this passage is rather the practical problem of how to do it without subjecting himself in turn to the same treatment.

3. The "Drama" Heading: What is the *question* of this scene?

> **1.7.a A room in Macbeth's castle at Inverness. In**
>
> **Purpose: 1. To heighten our eagerness to see if h murder. For a second time, Macbeth decides to c positions Macbeth to be persuaded by his wife ir End ..., p.192).**
>
> **Drama: Will Macbeth decide to kill Duncan?**
>
> What

Again, it is important to remember that for our purposes these plays are scripts to be performed, not literature to be read. Shakespeare created them under the ever-present threat that his boisterous and impatient audience would get bored, abandon the Globe and slog through the mud to a competing theatre, or perhaps a bear-baiting at the Rose around the corner. He knew that the way to prevent them getting bored was to make sure there was always a question they couldn't stand to leave unanswered. Will the Witches persuade Macbeth? Can they be trusted? Will Macbeth kill Duncan? Will he get away with it in the end? Shakespeare kept his audience hungrily hanging on the outcome of not just one, but many such questions. That is what "drama" is. **Violence is not drama. Suffering is not drama. Joy is not drama.** Real drama can always be posed as a question. And Shakespeare was the consummate master of drama. In our experience, virtually every scene in every Shakespeare play, no matter how brief, either poses a question to keep the audience hanging, or provides the answer to such a question. In the scene discussed above, for example, the drama is, "Will Macbeth decide to kill Duncan?"

Note: This is a specific kind of question. In the Drama heading, we ask only, What is the dramatic question the audience hopes to see answered? We do not include literary questions, such as "Why does Lady Macbeth break down?" or "Why does Macbeth grow tyrannical?" Those questions can provide very illuminating discussion, but they are not the drama of the scene.

4. The "Purpose" Heading: Why is this scene in the play?

> 1.a A room in Macbeth's castle at Inverne
>
> **Purpose:** . To heighten our eagerness to s
> murder. For a second time, Macbeth decide
> positions Macbeth to be persuaded by his v
> Endnote 5, p.192).
>
> Drama: Will Macbeth decide to kill Duncar

Shakespeare's poetry is so rich and satisfying that it is tempting to believe the poetry is all there is to see. And since most of Shakespeare's plays are based on stories from Holinshed, Ovid, Plutarch, or even a competitor playwright, it seems natural to view the story itself as unimportant – as a fill-in-the-blank mannequin upon which Shakespeare lovingly draped his majestic wordplay.

But in our view, the poetry alone is only a part of Shakespeare's creation. It is the architecture of the story that gives the poetry its power. "Life's but a walking shadow", taken by itself, is beautiful language. But it is only within the context of the play – after Shakespeare has led us step by step through Macbeth's downward trajectory into living Hell – that we can really feel it resonate in our deepest being.

Shakespeare did not simply take Holinshed's story and add poetry. He radically pruned, rearranged and added, until the original is scarcely recognizable. Shakespeare was a story alchemist, turning forgettable base metal into immortal gold.

Another indicator of the importance of Shakespeare's story architecture is the problem of translating a play into another language: In translation, the intricate wordplay is lost. Only the plot, the unforgettable characters and the imagery survive. And despite that loss, Shakespeare is still one of the most important literary figures in Azerbajian, India, Poland, Russia. Half the world's children study Shakespeare. This is a measure of the power of his storytelling. And that's what this edition is about: Shakespeare's storytelling. We try to unpack and reveal the framework of the story that underlies the script.

To summarize, every right-hand page in this book has four parts: 1. The "What" column (What is the speaker saying?); 2. The "Why" column (Why is the speaker saying it?); 3. The "Drama" heading (What is the question the audience wants to see answered?); and 4. The "Purpose" heading (Why is this scene in the play?). If we can answer those four questions for every line and every scene, then we can really speak the play.

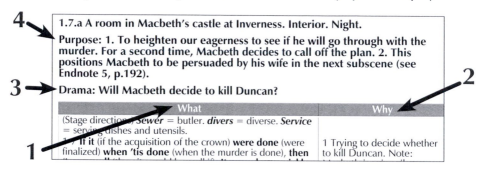

4

1.7.a A room in Macbeth's castle at Inverness. Interior. Night.

Purpose: 1. To heighten our eagerness to see if he will go through with the murder. For a second time, Macbeth decides to call off the plan. 2. This positions Macbeth to be persuaded by his wife in the next subscene (see Endnote 5, p.192).

3 → Drama: Will Macbeth decide to kill Duncan?

2

What	Why
(Stage directions: **Sewer** = butler. **divers** = diverse. **Service** = serving dishes and utensils.	
If it (if the acquisition of the crown) **were done** (were finalized) **when 'tis done** (when the murder is done), **then**	1 Trying to decide whether to kill Duncan. Note:

1

Evidence-Based Shakespeare

There are many good ways to approach directing a play. Our way is not to try to add layers of meaning, but to dig down and find the meaning that is already there. In our view, Shakespeare had something quite specific in mind when he wrote these plays. Unfortunately, neither he nor his actors kept notes on his directing, so we are left with a detective's puzzle, to decode his intentions for ourselves. But if we look closely enough at a scene, there is usually clear evidence of precisely what Shakespeare intended (Note: We said "usually", not "always"). We call it **"evidence-based Shakespeare"**.

In 1.7.b ("When you durst do it, then you were a man"), Lady Macbeth can be played as a nag or a seductress or a dominatrix, who wears her husband down until he relents. But we believe this is one of the theatre's great "aha" moments: the moment when she has the idea of framing the chamberlains for the murder of Duncan. Now, instead of seeing Macbeth slowly ground down, we see his world completely rearranged at a stroke by the power of an idea. In our opinion, that's more dramatic. And the script supports this interpretation: Before this moment, Macbeth is set against the murder; afterwards, he is all for it. And besides, a Lady Macbeth who wins over her husband with a great idea is so much more compelling than one who nags him. And a clear-eyed and dauntless Macbeth, who can only be swayed by a better path to his goal, is so much more effective than one who can be nagged into changing his mind.

When faced with competing interpretations, we ask only, **Which interpretation makes the better story based on the evidence?** *Macbeth* has a number of seemingly ambivalent passages which, like this one, have inspired a lot of debate over the centuries. We discuss some of those passages, and the reasons for our choices, in the Endnotes.

Iambic Pentameter

There are dozens of poetical devices of which Shakespeare was master. Most of that knowledge is beyond the scope of this book. But the student cannot speak this text aloud well without understanding the "scansion" – how the line "scans" – the rhythm of stressed and unstressed syllables. And in particular, understanding iambic pentameter.

An "iamb" is two syllables, with the first unstressed and the second stressed. For example, "be**gone**", or "a **word**". Shakespeare wrote most of his plays (and hundreds of poems), in lines of verse, five iambs per line, hence "iambic pentameter" (penta = Latin for five; meter = Latin for measure). When speaking the lines, it doesn't flow quite right until you've worked out the ten syllables. Here's an example so you can see what we mean, from 1.7.b, page 42 (the stressed syllables are in bold type):

> But **screw** your **cour**age **to** the **sticking-place**,
> And **we'll** not **fail:** when *Duncan* **is** asleep

But you will immediately see that many lines don't fit into this neat scanning. Shakespeare also used meter and rhythm to indicate the character's state of mind. Often, when Shakespeare wanted us to see a character balanced and calm, he wrote perfect iambic pentameter (like the line above, in which Lady Macbeth is full of conviction). Other times, when Shakespeare wanted to show a character in an unbalanced or agitated state, he gave them lines that don't scan perfectly. For example, here is Macbeth in 5.5.a, page 174:

> **Life's** but a **walking Shad**ow, a **poor Play**er

Also, some characters speak in plain prose, like the Porter in 2.3.a, page 58: "Here's a knocking, indeed: If a man were Porter of Hell Gate, he should have old turning the Key". The stakes are low, so the Porter does not use the heightened language of poetry.

It is important to learn the regular beat of iambic pentameter so that you can detect the variations and understand better the speaker's character and state of mind.

Reordered Sentences

Shakespeare sometimes employed unusual sentence order, to emphasize certain words or to improve the scansion. In those cases, we reorder it in the notes to help understand the meaning. For example, in 4.1.b on page 122, for "Thyself and Office deftly show", our note says, "Reordered: deftly (quickly) show yourself and your Office (function)".

Forwards

Occasionally you will see the word **FORWARD** in the "Why" column. A "forward" plants a question in the audience's mind, that we are eager to see answered. For example, at 1.3.b line 53, Banquo asks Macbeth, "Why do you start, and seem to fear things that do sound so fair?" It gets us wondering. Why is Macbeth's reaction so different from Banquo's? We will see that question answered later.

Turns

A **TURN** is a point in the story when a dramatic question is answered. In a well-crafted drama (like this one), it usually happens at one crisp moment of decision, rather than morphing slowly from one state of mind to the next. In the scene we've just been discussing, when Macbeth says, "Bring forth Men -Children only" (in 1.7.b on page 42), he has made a decision. The question, "Can Lady Macbeth persuade Macbeth to murder Duncan?" is answered. She has persuaded him.

New Drama

Another feature of dramatic turns is, they usually lead to a new question; a new drama. In the example above, the new question is, "Can he get away with it?" Sometimes a new dramatic question is posed in the middle of a scene. When this happens, you will see **NEW DRAMA** in the Why column.

Resolution

When a long-standing dramatic question finally gets answered, we put **RESOLUTION** in the notes. A **TURN** is a resolution that simultaneously poses a new question.

Beats

Peppered throughout the script, you will see pilcrows (paragraph marks): "¶". We use these to demarcate beats in the text – the points at which a character is finished with one idea and begins another.

The First Folio
Shakespeare did not keep copies of his scripts. During his life, a number of printers published "quarto editions" of his plays. A "quarto" was a book made by printing four pages to each side of a standard 18"x24" press sheet, folding into quarters ("quartos"), and cutting. Some quartos were strictly what we would now call bootleg editions: somebody sneaked pen and paper into the theatre, scribbled notes, went home and filled out those notes into a more-or-less complete copy of the play, and published it. Moreover, it may well be that over the course of successive productions, Shakespeare tinkered with his scripts. So even in his lifetime there was no single correct version. In 1623 (seven years after Shakespeare's death) two of his actors, John Heminge and Henry Condell, assembled their notes from thirty-six of Shakespeare's plays and published what has come to be known as the "First Folio" (a folio was twice the size of a quarto). They were working from prompt books and from memory, so the Folio unfortunately has some obvious errors.

In the four hundred intervening years, generations of scholars have struggled to correct the Folio – compare the various editions, amend the errors, and reconstruct what they think was Shakespeare's original.

But with a few exceptions (which are noted), we have decided to use the First Folio almost verbatim, errors, idiosyncrasies and all (specifically, the "Applause" facsimile, by Doug Moston). Our reasoning is that, for all their scientific methodology, the amendments made by Shakespeare scholars are by definition speculative. The Folio, for all its shortcomings, is the closest thing we will ever have to an authoritative edition.

Spelling
The one area where we depart from the Folio is the spelling. Spelling has changed so much since Shakespeare that the original spelling is a real impediment to reading. So we have standardized to modern spellings. For example, we changed "'Gainft my Captiuitie" to "'Gainst my captivity", and we changed "inuifible" to "invisible".

Other Notes on the Folio Text

- For proper names, we used Shakespeare's spelling. Where he used different spellings for the same name, we standardized to the one he used most often. Thus Byrnam, Byrnan, Byrnane, Birnane, and Byrnane are all rendered Byrnam. Malcolme as Malcolm. Donalbaine as Donalbain. MacDuff as Macduff.
- We kept capitalization of key words, e.g. "To make them Kings, the Seeds of *Banquo* Kings". We believe these are guidance on how to perform the line.
- We kept italics (same example).
- We kept elisions (dropped letters) to maintain scansion. In Shakespeare, "damned" is often pronounced as two syllables: "dam ned"; "damn'd" is one. So we kept "damn'd" when called for.
- We changed "dy'de" to "died", since that matches the original pronunciation.
- We combined "for ever", "my self" and "to morrow" into the modern "forever", "myself" and "tomorrow".
- For "colour", "clamour", "honour", etc., we have used the British spelling. Shakespeare (or at least Heminge's typesetter) used both "-or" and "-our". Since both modern spellings are correct, we chose the one more favored by Shakespeare.
- We capitalized after questions, e.g. "But how, of Cawdor? The Thane of Cawdor lives"
- We added apostrophes for possessives, e.g. "Kingdomes" to "Kingdom's".
- We've inserted pilcrows ("¶") to demarcate beats, as explained above.
- We've moved most stage directions to the left (in the Folio some appear within dialogue).
- We spelled out the speakers' names above each speech (in the Folio, the name is abbreviated at the beginning of the line).
- We standardized the character headings (e.g. "Duncan" instead of "King").
- We added the "Dramatis Personae" section, a tradition dating to 17th century editions.
- We added brackets around in-line stage directions, e.g. "[Reading]".
- We have included some stage directions that have been inserted by tradition since the 16th century. Here's an example, from 1.3.d, page 20:

> [*aside*] Glamis, and Thane of Cawdor:
>
> The greatest is behind. ¶ [*to Rosse and Angus*] Thanks for your pains.
>
> [*to Banquo*] Do you not hope your Children shall be Kings,
>
> When those that gave the Thane of Cawdor to me,
>
> Promis'd no less to them.

What We Don't Do

There are libraries full of books of Shakespeare scholarship on valuable topics which we do not attempt to address.

Historical information: What was Shakespeare's source material? What other authors contributed to the plays attributed to Shakespeare? What devices did Shakespeare borrow from Marlowe or Jonson? In what way was this script influenced by the machinations of London's Master of Revels, or the succession of the throne in 1603 from Queen Elizabeth to King James? How have performances of the play changed over the generations since Shakespeare's day? These questions are important, but are beyond the scope of this book.

Rhetoric: What is onomatopoeia? Chiasmus? Anaphora? Shakespeare was a master of these and dozens of other poetic devices, which he used constantly to increase the power of his language. This is yet another vast and fascinating field of study which we do not attempt to enter. Our focus is on the story structure, so we leave the exploration of rhetoric to other experts. The American Shakespeare Center in Virginia, for example, has superb print materials and workshops on Shakespeare's rhetoric.

The Philadelphia Shakespeare Theatre

In 1994, Carmen Khan was invited to become Artistic Director of the Red Heel Theatre, dedicated to producing "the little-known classics" of the Jacobean era. Following a lifelong dream, she changed the focus and the name of the company, and we became The Philadelphia Shakespeare Theatre. Along the way we instituted matinee performances for school students, the Artist-in-Residence Program, the Shakespeare Tour, the Classical Acting Academy (which trains early-career professionals in Shakespeare), the Summer Shakespeare Camp, and the Shakespeare In The World lecture/performance series featuring renowned Shakespeare scholars.

Our plays and programs have been critically acclaimed in the local and national press, and have received countless Barrymore, Phindie, and Falstaff awards and nominations. The City Council of Philadelphia has formally adopted a Special Resolution for Excellence honoring our contribution to Philadelphia's educational and cultural landscape.

From our years of working with students of every possible background, one lesson stands clear: The very best way to experience Shakespeare is to perform it. When the students actually get up and speak the play out loud in front of their peers, retention, vocabulary, leadership, and social dynamics jump to another level. This book is created with that truth in mind. It's here to help you get on your feet and "speak the speech trippingly on the tongue" (as Hamlet says).

Acknowledgements

This edition is (1) a collaboration and (2) a work in progress. It stands on the shoulders not just of the Bard, but of twenty generations of Shakespeare scholars. Annalisa Castaldo, Professor of English at Widener University, has provided particularly insightful steering on many important topics. In working out the drama, we have recalled the lessons of Robert McKee's *Story Structure* class countless times. We owe some of our fundamental concepts to David Ball's *Backwards and Forwards*. Nancy Doyle proofread this book and made thousands of corrections. For the actual text of the script, we are indebted to Douglas Moston's facsimile edition of the *First Folio*. For the "what" column, we have leaned heavily upon *A Shakespeare Glossary*, by C.T. Onions, the *Shakespeare Lexicon and Quotation Dictionary*, by Alexander Schmidt, and the *Oxford English Dictionary*. Other resources we have kept always handy are the *Folger Macbeth*, edited by Barbara A. Mowat and Paul Werstine, www.*Shakespeare-Navigators.com*, by Philip Weller, *Internet Shakespeare Editions*, edited by Anthony Dawson at the University of Victoria, and the *Arden Macbeth*, edited by Kenneth Muir. Teachers Emily Cohen, Sherry Forste-Grupp, Stacey Carlough and Dolores Verdeur test-drove this book with their students, and provided invaluable feedback, all arranged and documented by our Education Director, Rebekah Wilcox. Bud Carlson was our Virgil, guiding us through the complex world of creating a publishing company. And of course, none of this could have happened without the amazing artists, supporters and administrative staff with whom it has been our privilege to live and work for the last quarter-century.

And by no means do we consider this work complete. After four hundred years, we are still trying to catch up with Shakespeare. We welcome your questions and comments.

Carmen Khan and Jack Armstrong, 2017

The Tragedy of

Macbeth

DRAMATIS PERSONAE

DUNCAN, King of Scotland
BANQUO, a Thane of Scotland
MACBETH, Thane of Glamis
LADY MACBETH
FLEANCE, son to Banquo
MACDUFF, a Thane of Scotland
LADY MACDUFF
LENOX, a Thane of Scotland
ROSSE, a Thane of Scotland
ANGUS, a Thane of Scotland
MENTETH, a Thane of Scotland
CATHNES, a Thane of Scotland
SEYTON, an officer attending on Macbeth
SEYWARD, Earl of Northumberland
YOUNG SEYWARD, his son
BOY, son to Macduff
THREE WITCHES
HECATE
CAPTAIN
English DOCTOR
Scottish DOCTOR
SOLDIER
PORTER
OLD MAN
SERVANT
GENTLEWOMAN attending on Lady Macbeth
THREE APPARITIONS
THREE MURDERERS
Lords, Gentlemen, Officers, Soldiers, Murderers and Messengers

Dramatis Personae: This cast list does not appear in the Folio. It has been added by tradition since the 17th Century. This version is adapted from the Variorum Shakespeare, by H.H. Furness of Philadelphia, 1873.

ACTUS PRIMUS. SCENA PRIMA.

Thunder and Lightning. Enter three Witches.

FIRST WITCH

1 When shall we three meet again?
2 In Thunder, Lightning, or in Rain?

SECOND WITCH

3 When the Hurley-burley's done,
4 When the Battle's lost, and won.

THIRD WITCH

5 That will be ere the set of Sun.

FIRST WITCH

6 Where the place?

SECOND WITCH

7 Upon the Heath.

THIRD WITCH

8 There to meet with *Macbeth*.

FIRST WITCH

9 I come, *Gray-Malkin*.

ALL

10 *Padock* calls anon:
11 Fair is foul, and foul is fair,
12 Hover through the fog and filthy air.

Exeunt.

SCENA SECUNDA.

Alarum within. Enter King [Duncan], Malcolm, Donalbain, Lenox, with attendants, meeting a bleeding Captain.

DUNCAN

1 What bloody man is that? He can report,
2 As seemeth by his plight, of the Revolt
3 The newest state.

1.1 A heath — an open place. Exterior. Night.

Purpose: To establish the basic danger of this story: the Witches intend to use subterfuge to undermine right and wrong.

Drama: 1. Who are these witches? 2. What are they going to do to Macbeth?

What	Why
Actus Primus. Scena Prima = Latin for First Act. First Scene.	1 Gathering their evil resources for a plot against Macbeth.
3 **Hurley-burley** = commotion. 4 **When the Battle's lost, and won**: when one side has lost and the other side has won. As they speak, Macbeth is engaged in a heated battle to save Scotland.	4 **FORWARD**: What battle?
5 **ere** = before.	
7 **Heath** = treeless plain, usually covered in gorse (a low, prickly shrub) and heather (a low, prickly flower). Much of Scotland is heath.	
	8 **There to meet with *Macbeth*: FORWARD:** Who is Macbeth, and what do they want with him?
9-10 *Gray-Malkin* and *Padock*: Tradition held that witches had 'familiars', or animal spirits who assisted their magic. Gray-Malkin was a gray cat, Padock a poisonous toad. 10 **anon** = soon.	Implied stage direction: She has heard a cat meow. 10 Implied stage direction: she has heard her toad croak.
11 **Fair is foul**: what appears lovely is actually evil. **foul is fair**: perhaps what appears evil is actually good, or perhaps foul play is allowed, or both. 12 **fog and filthy air**: Their workplace is where it's hard to see clearly	11 Explaining their strategy. **FORWARD**: What is their fascination with fog? As we will learn later, fog is a metaphor for the state of mind they intend to create. They will use fake news to sow chaos and bring down the government.
(Stage directions) *Exeunt*: Latin for 'they exit'.	

1.2.a A camp near Forres. Exterior. Day.

Purpose: 1. To show how brave, loyal and loved Macbeth is. 2. To show Duncan is a just and generous ruler (see Endnote 1, page 190).

Drama: 1. Can the Captain convey his important information before he faints or dies from blood loss? 2. Who won the battle?

What	Why
(Stage directions) *Alarum* = blast on a war-trumpet. **within** = offstage. 2 **as seemeth by his plight** = as it seems because of his wounds. 3 **newest state** = latest news. His bleeding wounds indicate he's just been in the fighting, and can give us the latest news.	1 Seeking information that is of life-and-death importance.

*break in text
from 1 idea
to another

MALCOLM

4 This is the Sergeant,
5 Who like a good and hardy Soldier fought
6 'Gainst my Captivity: ⸙Hail brave friend;
7 Say to the King, the knowledge of the Broil,
8 As thou didst leave it.

CAPTAIN

9 Doubtful it stood,
10 As two spent Swimmers, that do cling together,
11 And choke their Art: The merciless *Macdonwald*
12 (Worthy to be a Rebel, for to that
13 The multiplying Villainies of Nature
14 Do swarm upon him) from the Western Isles
15 Of Kernes and Gallowgrosses is supplied,
16 And Fortune, on his damned Quarrel smiling,
17 Show'd like a Rebel's Whore: ¶ but all's too weak:
18 For brave *Macbeth* (well he deserves that Name)
19 Disdaining Fortune, with his brandish'd Steel,
20 Which smok'd with bloody execution
21 (Like Valour's Minion) carv'd out his passage,
22 Till he fac'd the Slave:
23 Which nev'r shook hands, nor bade farewell to him,
24 Till he unseam'd him from the Nave to th' Chops,
25 And fix'd his Head upon our Battlements.

DUNCAN

26 O valiant Cousin, worthy Gentleman.

CAPTAIN

27 As whence the Sun 'gins his reflection,
28 Shipwracking Storms, and direful Thunders:
29 So from that Spring, whence comfort seem'd to come,
30 Discomfort swells: Mark King of Scotland, mark,
31 No sooner Justice had, with Valour arm'd,
32 Compell'd these skipping Kernes to trust their heels,
33 But the Norweyan Lord, surveying vantage,
34 With furbish'd Arms, and new supplies of men,
35 Began a fresh assault.

DUNCAN

36 Dismay'd not this our Captains, *Macbeth* and *Banquo*?

What	Why
5-6 **fought 'Gainst my Captivity** = saved me from capture.	4 **This is the Sergeant:** Recognizing his savior. Note: This gives credibility to the Captain.
7 **knowledge of the Broil** = news of the battle.	7 Asking the Captain for news.
8 **As thou didst leave it** = As it stood when you left.	
9 **Doubtful it stood** = the outcome was in doubt.	9 Trying to stay conscious long enough to adequately convey how Macbeth saved the day.
11 **choke their Art:** Picture two drowning swimmers, each in his panic to get above water incidentally choking the other (preventing his art of swimming).	
12 **Worthy to be** called **a Rebel, for to that** = since.	
13 **Nature** = human nature. His **Villainies** (defects) **do swarm upon him** like flies.	
14 **Western Isles** = The Hebrides, a group of islands off the northwest coast of Scotland.	
15 **Kernes and Gallowgrosses** = Irish soldiers and horsemen, serving as mercenaries. (**Gallowgrosses** is often changed to Gallowglasses in modern editions.)	
16 **Fortune** (the goddess of good luck) **smiling on** (favoring) **his damned Quarrel** (his unholy rebellion). ('quarrel' is changed from Folio 'quarry'.)	
17 **Rebel's Whore:** the goddess Fortune appeared to be (**show'd like**) sleeping with the rebellious enemy. **All** = all the things in Macdonwald's favor.	18 **FORWARD:** who is this 'brave Macbeth'?
19 **Disdaining Fortune** = Ignoring the losing tide of battle. **brandish'd Steel** = swinging sword.	
20 **smok'd:** its coating of fresh hot blood steamed in the chill air.	
21 **Valour's Minion** = bravery's favorite. **carv'd out his passage** = cut his way through the enemy.	
22 **the Slave:** Macdonwald (He's not actually a slave. Shakespeare uses the term as an insult).	
23 **nev'r shook hands:** did not stop to talk.	
24 **unseam'd him** (ripped him open like a pillow at the seams) **from the Nave to th' Chops** (from navel to jaws).	
25 **fix'd his Head upon our Battlements** = cut off his head and stuck it on a spike on our wall	
26 **valiant Cousin:** brave Macbeth.	26 Wondering at Macbeth's bravery.
27-30 **As** (in the same way as) **whence** (from the direction where) **the Sun 'gins his reflection** (the Sun begins to see his reflection; i.e. the East), **Shipwracking Storms, and direful Thunders** (that's also the direction storms come from)**: So** (in the same way) **from that Spring** (from that source, the victory over Macdonwald), **whence comfort seem'd to come** (from which we expected relief), **Discomfort swells:** (bad news grows; it allowed Norway to attack).	
30 **Mark** = listen.	
31-32 **No sooner** (as soon as) **Justice had, with Valour arm'd** (the Goddess Justice, using Macbeth's valor as her weapon, had), **Compell'd these skipping Kernes** (forced these easily-deterred Kerne mercenaries) **to trust their heels** (to run away).	
33 **surveying vantage** = seeing an opportunity.	
34 **furbish'd** = refurbished.	
36 **dismay'd not this** = did this not dismay.	36 **FORWARD:** who is Banquo?

CAPTAIN

37 Yes, as Sparrows, Eagles;
38 Or the Hare, the Lion:
39 If I say sooth, I must report they were
40 As Cannons over-charg'd with double Cracks,
41 So they doubly redoubled strokes upon the Foe:
42 Except they meant to bathe in reeking Wounds,
43 Or memorize another *Golgotha*,
44 I cannot tell: ¶ but I am faint,
45 My Gashes cry for help.

DUNCAN

46 So well thy words become thee, as thy wounds,
47 They smack of Honour both: ¶ Go get him Surgeons.

Exit Captain, attended.

1.2.b -
Enter Rosse and Angus.

48 Who comes here?

MALCOLM

49 The worthy *Thane* of Rosse.

LENOX

50 What a haste looks through his eyes?
51 So should he look, that seems to speak things strange.

ROSSE

52 God save the King.

DUNCAN

53 Whence cam'st thou, worthy *Thane*?

ROSSE

54 From Fife, great King,
55 Where the Norweyan Banners flout the Sky,
56 And fan our people cold.
57 *Norway* himself, with terrible numbers,
58 Assisted by that most disloyal Traitor,
59 The *Thane* of Cawdor, began a dismal Conflict,
60 ¶ Till that *Bellona's* Bridegroom, lapp'd in proof,
61 Confronted him with self-comparisons,
62 Point against Point, rebellious Arm 'gainst Arm,
63 Curbing his lavish spirit: and to conclude,

What	Why
37-38 **As Sparrows,** frighten **Eagles; Or the Hare,** (frightens) **the Lion:** in other words, not in the least.	
39 **sooth** = truth.	
40 **over-charg'd with double Cracks** = with double the usual amount of gunpowder.	
41 **doubly redoubled** = attacked four times as hard.	
42-44 **Except** (whether) **they meant to bathe in reeking Wounds** (to bathe in the blood spraying from wounds), **Or memorize another** *Golgotha* (or make another memorial as famous as Golgotha, where Christ was crucified), **I cannot tell** (I cannot tell which).	
	44 **I am faint**: implied stage direction: literally fainting.
46 **So well thy words become thee, as thy wounds** = Your words are as honorable as your wounds.	46 **TURN**: Success. The Captain has delivered his message. Duncan is well pleased. **Exit Captain, attended** does not appear in the First Folio. It was soon added in subsequent editions.

1.2.b Purpose: 1. To show that Duncan is generous and humble (which later makes Macbeth's crime so much worse. See Endnote 2, page 190). 2. To show that Rosse is loyal and capable. 3. To make Macbeth Thane of Cawdor, thus fulfilling the Witches' prophecy.

Drama: The question is still, Who won the battle?

What	Why
49 A *Thane* was a Scottish nobleman.	49 Recognizing him.
50 **What a haste looks through his eyes** = You can see through his eyes to the haste in his mind.	
51 **that seems to speak things strange** = he looks as if about to speak of unknown things ('strange' meant not 'unusual', but 'unknown', as in 'stranger'.)	51 Alerting to possible bad news.
52 **God save the King**: a standard greeting for the King.	52 Kneeling, or bowing.
53 **Whence cam'st thou** = where did you come from? n.b.: Whence = from where. Hence = from here. Thence = from there.	
54 **Fife**: a county in the southeast of Scotland, home of Macduff. Later home of Malcolm and successive kings.	
55-56 **Where the Norweyan Banners** (Norwegian flags) **flout the Sky** (offend the Scottish sky by their unwelcome presence), **And fan our people cold** (and chill our people with their flapping).	55 Reporting important, wonderful news.
57 *Norway* himself = the King of Norway. **terrible numbers** = a terrifyingly large army.	
59 **dismal Conflict** = terrible battle.	
60-63 **Till that** *Bellona's* **bridegroom** (until Macbeth, worthy to be husband of Bellona, goddess of war), **lapp'd in proof** (clothed in blood, proving his valor), **Confronted him with self-comparisons** (confronted Cawdor with one who compared equally to himself), **Point against Point** (sword's point against sword's point), **rebellious Arm 'gainst Arm** (Cawdor's rebellious arm against Macbeth's arm), **Curbing** (reining in like a horse) **his lavish** (insolent) **spirit.**	

64 The Victory fell on us.

DUNCAN

65 Great happiness.

ROSSE

66 That now *Sweno*, the Norway's King,
67 Craves composition:
68 Nor would we deign him burial of his men,
69 Till he disbursed, at Saint *Colme's* Inch,
70 Ten thousand Dollars, to our general use.

DUNCAN

71 No more that *Thane* of Cawdor shall deceive
72 Our Bosom interest: ¶ Go pronounce his present death,
73 And with his former Title greet *Macbeth*.

ROSSE

74 I'll see it done.

DUNCAN

75 What he hath lost, Noble *Macbeth* hath won.

Exeunt.

SCENA TERTIA.

Thunder. Enter the three Witches.

FIRST WITCH

1 Where hast thou been, Sister?

SECOND WITCH

2 Killing Swine.

THIRD WITCH

3 Sister, where thou?

FIRST WITCH

4 A Sailor's Wife had Chestnuts in her Lap,
5 And mounch'd, & mounch'd, and mounch'd:
6 'Give me', quoth I.
7 'Aroynt thee, Witch', the rump-fed Ronyon cries.
8 Her Husband's to Aleppo gone, Master o' th' *Tiger*:
9 But in a Sieve I'll thither sail,
10 And like a Rat without a tail,
11 I'll do, I'll do, and I'll do.

What	Why
	65 **Great happiness: TURN.** Now we know Duncan has won.
67 **Craves composition** = asks to be ransomed. It was customary for captured nobles to be held for ransom, rather than imprisoned or executed.	67 Putting the icing on the cake.
68 **Nor would we deign** (allow) **him** to bury his men.	
69 **disbursed** = paid. **Saint *Colme's* Inch** = Island of St. Columba, or Inchcolme, a tiny island in the Firth of Forth (a bay in eastern Scotland). Macbeth charged Sweno ten thousand dollars to bury his dead on the island. A firth is a long bay, where a river opens to the sea.	69 **Inch**: Folio has 'ynch'
70 **our general use**: Macbeth generously contributed Sweno's ransom to the government's coffers, rather than keeping it for his own private enrichment.	
71-72 **No more** (never again will) **that *Thane* of Cawdor shall deceive our Bosom interest** (deceive me in regard to my most vital interest).	71 Pronouncing judgment. The King is also judge.
72 **present death** = sentence of death, to be carried out immediately.	
73 **with his former Title greet *Macbeth*** = go to Macbeth and say, 'Hail Thane of Cawdor', i.e. relay that I give Cawdor to him.	73 **FORWARD**: what will happen when Macbeth becomes Thane of Cawdor?
	74 **I'll see it done:** Pledging obedient service.
75 **What** (the thanedom – the lands belonging to whoever holds the title Thane of Cawdor, which) **he** (Cawdor) **hath** (has) **lost, Noble *Macbeth* hath won.**	75 Honoring Macbeth with a great prize. This will double Macbeth's lands, revenues and power.

1.3.a A heath near Forres. Exterior. Dusk.

Purpose: To show the audience what Macbeth doesn't know: the Witches' intent is only to sow mayhem and grief.

Drama: 1. What are they planning? 2. Will they succeed in summoning the dark spirits they need to ensnare Macbeth?

What	Why
	1 Gloating together over the delicious mischief they've caused.
5 **mounch'd** = munched.	4 Taking a sensuous delight in savage revenge. The woman refused to give her a chestnut, and in response the Witch is going to shipwreck her husband, so that he won't be able to return home for a year and a half!
6 **Give me** = give me some.	
7 **Aroynt** = be gone. **rump-fed** = perhaps fed on tender rump meat, and thus spoiled? or fat-rumped? **Ronyon** = scab, a standard term of abuse.	
8 **Aleppo**: a city in Syria; i.e. to the far end of the world. **Master o'th' Tiger** = captain of the ship Tiger.	
9 **Sieve** = flour sifter. This was a standard item of witch equipment, like the broom. **thither** = to there.	
10 **like** = shaped like. **a Rat without a tail**: perhaps because the witch has no tail, when she transforms into a rat she still won't? Or perhaps because witches can't transform perfectly?	
11 **I'll do**: I'll do him in; or do him over.	

SECOND WITCH

12 I'll give thee a Wind.

FIRST WITCH

13 Th' art kind.

THIRD WITCH

14 And I another.

FIRST WITCH

15 I myself have all the other,
16 And the very Ports they blow,
17 All the Quarters that they know,
18 I' th' Shipman's Card.
19 I'll drain him dry as Hay:
20 Sleep shall neither Night nor Day
21 Hang upon his Penthouse Lid:
22 He shall live a man forbid:
23 Weary Sev' nights, nine times nine,
24 Shall he dwindle, peak, and pine:
25 Though his Bark cannot be lost,
26 Yet it shall be Tempest-toss'd.
27 Look what I have.

SECOND WITCH

28 Show me, show me.

FIRST WITCH

29 Here I have a Pilot's Thumb,
30 Wrack'd, as homeward he did come.

Drum within.

THIRD WITCH

31 A Drum, a Drum:
32 *Macbeth* doth come.

ALL

33 The weird Sisters, hand in hand,
34 Posters of the Sea and Land,
35 Thus do go, about, about,
36 Thrice to thine, and thrice to mine,
37 And thrice again, to make up nine.
38 Peace, the Charm's wound up.

What	Why
12 **I'll give thee a Wind**: I'll conjure a wind to help you wreck him.	12 Enthusiastically joining in the destruction of this family.
	14 Also joining the plot, with gusto.
15 **I myself have all the other** = I control all the other winds. 16 **And the very Ports they blow** = and I control the wind in all the ports. 17 **Quarters**: quarters of the compass — north, south, east, west. 18 **Shipman's Card** = compass card — the rotating disk in the compass with N, S, E & W on it. 19 **drain him** = sap away his blood.	15 Relishing the malicious details of the plan.
21 **Penthouse Lid** = eyelid (it hangs over the eye like a pent roof). 22 **forbid** = banned (from shore); or perhaps under a curse. 23 **Weary Sev' nights, nine times nine** = 81 weary weeks (at sea). 24 **dwindle** = wither away. **peak** = grow listless. **pine** = languish. 25 **Bark** = ship. **cannot be lost**: apparently the Witches were not permitted to kill, but only to torment. 26 **Tempest-toss'd**: thrown around by the storm's wind and waves.	
30 **Wrack'd** = shipwrecked.	
	31 **A Drum**: implied stage direction. A drum sounds offstage.
33 **weird** = fateful. The modern meaning of 'unusual' did not evolve until the 19th century. **weird Sisters** = the three fates. 34 **Posters** = travelers as swift and omnipresent as post-riders (precursors of mail couriers). 35 **Thus do go, about, about**: perhaps there is a dance to accompany the chant?	
	36 **Thrice to thine**: casting a spell.
38 **wound up**: coiled like a spring and ready.	38 **FORWARD**: what will the charm do?

1.3.b -

Enter Macbeth and Banquo.

MACBETH

39 So foul and fair a day I have not seen.

BANQUO

40 How far is 't call'd to Forres? ¶ What are these,
41 So wither'd, and so wild in their attire,
42 That look not like th' Inhabitants o' th' Earth,
43 And yet are on 't? ¶ Live you, or are you aught
44 That man may question? You seem to understand me,
45 By each at once her choppy finger laying
46 Upon her skinny Lips: you should be Women,
47 And yet your Beards forbid me to interpret
48 That you are so.

MACBETH

49 Speak if you can: what are you?

FIRST WITCH

50 All hail *Macbeth*, hail to thee *Thane* of Glamis.

SECOND WITCH

51 All hail *Macbeth*, hail to thee *Thane* of Cawdor.

THIRD WITCH

52 All hail *Macbeth*, that shalt be King hereafter.

BANQUO

53 Good Sir, why do you start, and seem to fear
54 Things that do sound so fair? ¶ I' th' name of truth
55 Are ye fantastical, or that indeed
56 Which outwardly ye show? ¶ My Noble Partner
57 You greet with present Grace, and great prediction
58 Of Noble having, and of Royal hope,
59 That he seems rapt withal: to me you speak not.
60 If you can look into the Seeds of Time,
61 And say, which Grain will grow, and which will not,
62 Speak then to me, who neither beg, nor fear
63 Your favors, nor your hate.

FIRST WITCH

64 Hail.

1.3.b Purpose: This is a major plot point. All the preceding was the necessary background for this moment, and this moment sets the whole story in motion (see Endnote 3, page 191).

Drama: Will the Witches ensnare the men?

What	Why
39 **So foul** (referring to the battle) **and fair** (referring to the victory); or perhaps he refers to the contradictory weather as well?	39 Sharing the burden and the joy with his friend. Note that he echoes the Witches with '**foul and fair**'.
40 **How far is 't call'd** = how far is it? **Forres** = where Duncan's palace is. **What are these** (creatures)?	40 Tiring. Then (after ¶), startling at the Witches. (**Forres**: 'Soris' in Folio. The typesetters in Shakespeare's England used 'f' and 's' interchangeably).
41 **wither'd** = old. **wild in their attire** = with wild clothes on.	
42 **That look not like th' Inhabitants o' th' Earth** = that don't look like mortals (maybe they are supernatural).	
43-44 **on 't** = on it (the Earth). **Live you** = are you alive? **are you aught That man may question** = are you anything that can be spoken to?	43 Bravely addressing the fearful apparitions.
45 **each at once** = all at once. **choppy** = chapped; disfigured.	45 Implied stage direction: They are hushing Banquo.
46 **you should be Women** = you look like women.	
47-48 **your Beards forbid me to interpret** (won't let me believe) **That you are so** (that you are women).	
	49 **what are you:** Diplomacy having failed, Macbeth jumps in with another tactic: command.
	50 **All hail:** Flattering and enticing.
	52 **that shalt be King:** Enticing him with an alluring but incomplete nugget of information. **FORWARD:** Will Macbeth become king? How?
53 **start** = startle; jump in surprise.	53 This is an implied stage direction: **Why do you start** means that Macbeth has reacted powerfully to 'King'. Note: A more innocent mind might not react with 'fear' at the prospect. **FORWARD:** Why does Macbeth start?
55-56 **fantastical** = a fantasy of the brain. **that indeed Which outwardly ye show** = what you appear to be.	
57 **present Grace:** he's already Thane of Glamis.	
58 **Noble having** = Cawdor. **Royal hope** = King.	
59 **withal** = with it.	
60 **the Seeds of Time:** Imagine that the events of the future are great trees, and current events are the seeds that will grow into those trees.	
62-63 **neither beg, nor fear Your favors, nor your hate** = neither beg your favors (blessings) nor fear your hate (curses).	62 **Speak then to me:** demanding his share of the prophecy. Demanding a true and unbiased report. Note: Unlike Macbeth, Banquo eschews both flattery and handwringing.
	64 **Hail:** Deciding to deceive Banquo, too.

SECOND WITCH

65 Hail.

THIRD WITCH

66 Hail.

FIRST WITCH

67 Lesser than *Macbeth*, and greater.

SECOND WITCH

68 Not so happy, yet much happier.

THIRD WITCH

69 Thou shalt get Kings, though thou be none:

70 So all hail *Macbeth,* and *Banquo*.

FIRST WITCH

71 *Banquo,* and *Macbeth*, all hail.

MACBETH

72 Stay you imperfect Speakers, tell me more:

73 By *Sinell's* death, I know I am *Thane* of Glamis,

74 But how, of Cawdor? the *Thane* of Cawdor lives

75 A prosperous Gentleman: and to be King

76 Stands not within the prospect of belief,

77 No more than to be Cawdor. Say from whence

78 You owe this strange Intelligence, or why

79 Upon this blasted Heath you stop our way

80 With such Prophetic greeting?

81 Speak, I charge you.

Witches vanish.

1.3.c -

BANQUO

82 The Earth hath bubbles, as the Water has,

83 And these are of them: whither are they vanish'd?

MACBETH

84 Into the Air: and what seem'd corporal,

85 Melted, as breath into the Wind.

86 ¶ Would they had stay'd.

BANQUO

87 Were such things here, as we do speak about?

88 Or have we eaten on the insane Root,

89 That takes the Reason Prisoner?

What	Why
67 **Lesser than** *Macbeth*, **and greater**: You will be less than Macbeth in one way, but greater in another way. 68 **Not so happy, yet much happier**: less happy in one way; more happy in another. 69 **get Kings** = be the father of kings.	69 **Thou shalt get Kings**: Tantalizing. **FORWARD**: How will this come about? 70 **Macbeth, and Banquo**: Promising greatness to both. 72 **Stay**: Demanding more (Implied stage direction: The Witches have started leaving.)
72 **imperfect** = incomplete. 73 *Sinell*: Holinshed spelled the name of the historical Macbeth's father 'Finell'. Another example of confusing 'F' and 's'. Finell was the Thane of Glamis, so when he died, his son Macbeth inherited the title. 75 Cawdor is **a prosperous Gentleman.** 76 **Stands not within the prospect of belief**: Imagine standing on a hill overlooking the valley containing all that can be believed. 'King Macbeth' isn't there. 77 **No more than to be Cawdor**: For me to become king is **no more** believable than for me **to be** Thane of **Cawdor** 78 **owe** = own. **strange** = supernatural. 79 **blasted** = wind-blasted. **stop our way** = block our way.	
	81 **I charge you:** threatening them. The Witches defy his threat by vanishing.

1.3.c Purpose: To draw a contrast between Macbeth and Banquo. Banquo expresses doubt about the Witches' trustworthiness; Macbeth, by deflecting the issue, shows that the Witches have awakened a latent impulse that he must hide.

Drama: 1. Can they figure out if the Witches were real? 2. Can Macbeth hide his real reaction?

What	Why
82 **the Earth hath bubbles, as the Water has**: They came from the ground as a bubble comes from water, then popped. 83 **whither** = to where. n.b.: whither, hither, thither = towards where, towards here, towards there. 84 **corporal** = bodily; tangible. 85 **Melted, as breath** = disappeared like breath-fog.	83 Looking for the Witches. 84 Marvelling. 86 **Would they had stay'd**: hungering for more. 87 **Were such things here**: puzzling it out. Offering a possible explanation.
88-89 **the insane Root** (the root-derived drug that makes people insane, probably hemlock or henbane), **That takes the Reason Prisoner** (and controls the mind).	

MACBETH

90 Your Children shall be Kings.

BANQUO

91 You shall be King.

MACBETH

92 And *Thane* of Cawdor too: went it not so?

BANQUO

93 To th' self-same tune, and words: who's here?

1.3.d -

Enter Rosse and Angus.

ROSSE

94 The King hath happily receiv'd, *Macbeth*,

95 The news of thy success: and when he reads

96 Thy personal Venture in the Rebel's fight,

97 His Wonders and his Praises do contend,

98 Which should be thine, or his: ¶ silenc'd with that,

99 In viewing o'er the rest o' th' self-same day,

100 He finds thee in the stout Norweyan Ranks,

101 Nothing afeard of what thyself didst make

102 Strange Images of death. As thick as Hail,

103 Came post with post, and everyone did bear

104 Thy praises in his Kingdom's great defense,

105 And pour'd them down before him.

ANGUS

106 We are sent,

107 To give thee from our Royal Master thanks,

108 Only to herald thee into his sight,

109 Not pay thee.

ROSSE

110 And for an earnest of a greater Honour,

111 He bade me, from him, call thee *Thane* of Cawdor:

112 In which addition, hail most worthy *Thane*,

113 For it is thine.

BANQUO

114 What, can the Devil speak true?

What	Why
	90 **Your Children shall be Kings:** calling attention away from his own share in the prophecy, to mask how important it is to him. Perhaps laughing.
	91 **You shall be King:** joining the 'laughing', but also probing Macbeth for his real feelings.
	92 **And *Thane* of Cawdor:** 'laughing' more to demonstrate he doesn't care.
93 **To th' self-same tune, and words** = exactly the same. Macbeth's line, 'went it not so?' sounded like he was talking about a song. So Banquo responds in kind.	They both, to avoid the gravity of the situation, speak of the Witches as if they were singing a playground song.

1.3.d Purpose: 1. To vividly highlight the special position in Duncan's favor that Macbeth has won (and which he must forego if he murders Duncan). 2. To move Macbeth a step closer to murdering Duncan by confirming the first part of the Witches' prophecy. 3. To cement the contrast between Macbeth and Banquo: Macbeth is ensnared by the Witches; Banquo is not.

Drama: 1. Can Banquo distract Rosse and Angus from getting suspicious of Macbeth's strange behavior? 2. And most important, this initiates an overarching drama until 2.1: Will Macbeth decide to kill Duncan?

What	Why
94 **hath happily receiv'd** = is happy at receiving, or hearing.	94 Announcing the King's message. Congratulating.
96 **Thy personal Venture in the Rebel's fight** = the risk you took personally in the fight against the rebels.	
97-98 **His Wonders** (Duncan's state of wonder) **and his Praises** (and his praises of you) **do contend** (are arguing), **Which should be thine, or his** (whether the victory belongs to you or to himself). **silenc'd with that**: fresh news silenced his musing over the previous.	
99 **In viewing o'er** (reviewing) **the rest o' th' self-same** (very same) **day.**	Vividly elaborating Macbeth's astounding achievements, the seemingly endless string of messengers, each praising Macbeth higher than the last.
100 **He finds thee** (he finds out you were) **in the stout Norweyan Ranks** (among the formidable ranks of Norwegian soldiers).	
101 **Nothing afeard** (not afraid) **of what thyself didst make** (of the human carnage you yourself made with your sword).	
102 **Strange Images of death:** contorted piles of dead bodies.	102 **Hail:** Folio has Tale. We think this was a typo.
103 **post with post** = messenger after messenger.	
104 **Thy praises in his Kingdom's great defense** = praises of your service in great defense of his kingdom.	
	106 **We are sent:** delivering the King's official message.
108-109 **Only to herald thee into his sight, Not pay thee** = not to pay you, as might have been expected, but to summon you to see him, presumably to offer greater thanks than mere money.	
110 **earnest** = down payment.	
111 **bade** = instructed.	
112 **addition** = addition to your name: Now you are 'Macbeth, Thane of Glamis, and Thane of Cawdor'.	
	114 **What, can the Devil speak true:** reacting to this stunning confirmation of the Witches (said privately, to Macbeth only: The prophecy is not to be shared with Rosse).

MACBETH

115 The *Thane* of Cawdor lives:

116 Why do you dress me in borrowed Robes?

ANGUS

117 Who was the *Thane*, lives yet,

118 But under heavy Judgment bears that Life,

119 Which he deserves to lose.

120 Whether he was combin'd with those of Norway,

121 Or did line the Rebel with hidden help,

122 And vantage; or that with both he labour'd

123 In his Country's wrack, I know not:

124 But Treasons Capital, confess'd, and prov'd,

125 Have overthrown him.

MACBETH

126 *[aside]* Glamis, and *Thane* of Cawdor:

127 The greatest is behind. ¶ *[to Rosse and Angus]* Thanks for your pains.

128 ¶ *[to Banquo]* Do you not hope your Children shall be Kings,

129 When those that gave the *Thane* of Cawdor to me,

130 Promis'd no less to them.

BANQUO

131 That trusted home,

132 Might yet enkindle you unto the Crown,

133 Besides the *Thane* of Cawdor. ¶ But 'tis strange:

134 And oftentimes, to win us to our harm,

135 The Instruments of Darkness tell us Truths,

136 Win us with honest Trifles, to betray 's

137 In deepest consequence.

138 ¶ *[to Rosse and Angus]* Cousins, a word, I pray you.

MACBETH

139 *[aside]* Two Truths are told,

140 As happy Prologues to the swelling Act

141 Of the Imperial Theme. ¶ *[to Rosse and Angus]* I thank you Gentlemen:

142 ¶ *[aside]* This supernatural soliciting

143 Cannot be ill; cannot be good.

144 If ill? why hath it given me earnest of success,

145 Commencing in a Truth? I am *Thane* of Cawdor.

146 ¶ If good? Why do I yield to that suggestion

147 Whose horrid Image doth unfix my Hair,

148 And make my seated Heart knock at my Ribs,

What	Why
115 **lives** = is still alive.	115 Using his justifiable surprise at being named Thane of Cawdor to mask his greater surprise that the first part of the prophecy has come true.
116 **borrowed Robes**: 'Thane of Cawdor' in which you dress me belongs to someone else.	
117 He **Who was the *Thane*, lives yet** (is still alive).	117 Explaining how it's possible.
118 **heavy Judgment** = death sentence.	
120 **combin'd** = combined his army with Norway's.	
121-122 **line the Rebel with hidden help And vantage** = secretly helped Macdonwald.	
122-123 **labour'd In his Country's wrack** = worked to shipwreck his country.	
124 **Treasons Capital** = crimes of treason meriting capital punishment. **confess'd and prov'd** = confessed by him and proven against him.	126 *[Aside]*, *[To Rosse and Angus]* , etc. These stage directions are not in the Folio, but inferred from the text.
127 **greatest**: the crown. **is behind** = follows. Picture three messengers arriving one after another: 1 Glamis, 2 Cawdor, 3 crown.	127 **Thanks**: remembering they are there. Covering.
	128 **Do you not hope**: angling for Banquo's complicity.
129 **those** = the Witches. **gave the** (title) ***Thane of Cawdor**.	Note: Macbeth seems to believe that the Witches, more than merely predicting Macbeth's good fortune, created it.
130 **no less** = no less than to be kings.	
131 **trusted home** = trusted fully.	
132 **enkindle**: fan the ember of idea into the flame of reality.	
133 **strange**: new, hence not necessarily trustworthy.	
134 **to win us to our harm** = to trick us into self-harm.	134 Warning Macbeth not to trust the Witches.
135 **Instruments of Darkness** = evil spirits.	
136-137 **Win us** (win our trust) **with honest Trifles** (with trivial truths), **to betray 's** (to betray us) **in deepest consequence** (in the most consequential matters).	136 FORWARD: Now that Macbeth has been won with an honest trifle (Cawdor), will he be betrayed in deepest consequence?
138 **Cousins**: The Thanes were all cousins, descended from earlier kings.	138 **a word, I pray you**: distracting them from noticing Macbeth's strange behavior.
139 **Two Truths**: i.e. Glamis & Cawdor.	139 Fighting with himself: trust or don't trust?
140-141 **happy Prologues** (promising foretastes) **to the swelling Act** (to the climax) **of the Imperial Theme** (to the grand finale - my coronation). Likening the fulfillment of his royal destiny to a symphony.	141 **I thank you**: remembering he's not alone, covering.
142 **soliciting** = enticement.	
143 **ill** = leading to a bad end.	
144-145 **If ill?** (if malignant), **why hath it given me earnest** (down payment) **of success, Commencing in** (by beginning with) **a Truth** ('Hail Cawdor')	
146 **yield to** (allow myself to fantasize about) **that suggestion** (the idea of murdering Duncan).	
147 **unfix my Hair** = make my hair stand on end.	
148 **make my seated** (my ordinarily fixed) **Heart knock at** (beat so hard it knocks against) **my Ribs.**	

149 Against the use of Nature? Present Fears
150 Are less than horrible Imaginings:
151 My Thought, whose Murder yet is but fantastical,
152 Shakes so my single state of Man,
153 That Function is smother'd in surmise,
154 And nothing is, but what is not.

BANQUO

155 Look how our Partner's rapt.

MACBETH

156 *[aside]* If Chance will have me King,
157 Why Chance may Crown me,
158 Without my stir.

BANQUO

159 New Honours come upon him,
160 Like our strange Garments, cleave not to their mould,
161 But with the aid of use.

MACBETH

162 *[aside]* Come what come may,
163 Time, and the Hour, runs through the roughest Day.

BANQUO

164 Worthy *Macbeth*, we stay upon your leisure.

MACBETH

165 Give me your favour:
166 My dull Brain was wrought with things forgotten.
167 ¶ Kind Gentlemen, your pains are registered,
168 Where every day I turn the Leaf,
169 To read them.
170 ¶ Let us toward the King: ¶ *[to Banquo]* Think upon
171 What hath chanc'd: and at more time,
172 The *Interim* having weigh'd it, let us speak
173 Our free Hearts each to other.

BANQUO

174 Very gladly.

MACBETH

175 Till then enough:
¶ *[To all]* Come friends.
176
Exeunt.

What	Why
149 **Against the use of Nature** = contrary to its usual nature. **Present Fears**: e.g. enemies with swords.	
150 **less than horrible Imaginings** = less scary than the horrible fantasies of the mind.	
151 **My Thought, whose** (in which) **Murder** (of Duncan) **yet is but fantastical** (is still just a fantasy).	151 **FORWARD**: This is the first mention of murder. What murder is he talking about?
152 **Shakes so my single state of Man** = makes my entire person shake so much.	
153 **That** my ability to **Function is smother'd** (is stopped) **in surmise** (by this obsessive imagination).	
154 **nothing is** (nothing exists for me), **but what is not** (except that which doesn't yet exist, i.e. Duncan's end and my coronation).	
	155 **our Partner's rapt**: excusing his friend's distraction.
156 **If Chance will have me King** = If the goddess of Chance, or Fortune, wants me to become King.	156 IDEA! Flooding with relief. I don't have to kill Duncan to become King. I can just wait for it to happen on its own!
157-158 **Why Chance may Crown me** (fate can make me king) **Without my stir** = without me doing anything.	
160 **strange Garments** = new clothes. **cleave not to their mould** = don't fit well.	160 Inventing an excuse for Macbeth's strange behavior: He's not used to being Cawdor.
161 **But with the aid of use** = until with use they are broken in.	
162 **Come what come may** = whatever happens.	162 Summoning his courage to survive the rest of the day.
163 **Time, and the Hour, runs through the roughest Day** = even the roughest day must end.	163 **roughest Day**: Remember, this and the Witches' apparition came after they had already fought two battles earlier today. Politely recalling Macbeth to the present.
164 **stay upon your leisure** = wait until you are ready.	
165 **favour** = pardon.	165 Turning his attention to Rosse and Angus, thanking them properly.
166 **wrought with things forgotten** = agitated with forgotten tasks.	
167-169 **your pains** (your efforts on my behalf) **are registered** (are written in my book of memory) **Where every day I** will **turn the Leaf** (turn to that page) **To read** (to remember) **them**	
171 **chanc'd** = happened. **at more time** = later.	171 Again courting Banquo's complicity.
172-173 **The** *Interim* **having weigh'd it** = meanwhile having considered it. **speak Our free Hearts** = speak freely of what's in our hearts.	**FORWARD**: We want to be there to hear that conversation.
	174 **Very gladly**: glad for another chance to urge Macbeth to caution.

Scena Quarta.

Flourish. Enter King [Duncan], Lenox, Malcolm, Donalbain, and Attendants.

DUNCAN

1 Is execution done on *Cawdor*?

2 Or not those in Commission yet return'd?

MALCOLM

3 My Liege, they are not yet come back.

4 ¶ But I have spoke with one that saw him die:

5 Who did report, that very frankly he

6 Confess'd his Treasons, implor'd your Highness' Pardon,

7 And set forth a deep Repentance:

8 Nothing in his Life became him,

9 Like the leaving it. He died,

10 As one that had been studied in his death,

11 To throw away the dearest thing he ow'd,

12 As 'twere a careless Trifle.

DUNCAN

13 There's no Art,

14 To find the Mind's construction in the Face:

15 He was a Gentleman, on whom I built

16 An absolute Trust.

1.4.b -

Enter Macbeth, Banquo, Rosse, and Angus.

17 O worthiest Cousin,

18 The sin of my Ingratitude even now

19 Was heavy on me. Thou art so far before,

20 That swiftest Wing of Recompense is slow,

21 To overtake thee. Would thou hadst less deserv'd

22 That the proportion both of thanks, and payment,

23 Might have been mine: only I have left to say,

1.4.a A room at Forres. Interior. Night.

Purpose: To foreshadow Macbeth's trajectory: Cawdor, like Macbeth, betrays Duncan. But in contrast, Cawdor apologizes and dies honorably; Macbeth will go down steadfast in his crimes.

Drama: Can they understand why Cawdor betrayed them?

What	Why
1 **Is execution done** = Has Cawdor been executed?	1 Making sure there will be no further mischief from Cawdor.
2 **Or** have **not those in Commission** (those men commissioned with the task) **yet return'd** to inform us?	
3 **Liege** = lord.	4 Marvelling at the difference between Cawdor's disgraceful rebellion and his graceful apology. This is another clue to the wisdom Malcolm will show as king: He can punish a traitor without hating him.
5 **frankly** = honestly.	
7 **set forth** = proclaimed.	
8-9 **became him** = looked good on him. **Nothing in his Life became him Like the leaving it** = He did nothing in life as well as the way he left it.	
10 **As one that had been studied in his death** = As though he had studied how best to die (in other words, he was not afraid to die).	
11 **dearest** = most valuable. **ow'd** = owned.	
12 **As 'twere** = as if it were. **careless** = worthless.	
13-14 **There's no Art to** (no science able to) **find the Mind's construction** (find what's happening in someone's mind) **in the Face** (by studying his face).	13 Teaching them the lesson he has just learned.
	15 Note the irony: Duncan 'built an absolute trust' on the old Cawdor, who turned traitor, and immediately in walks the new Cawdor – the new traitor. Note that Duncan's downfall is that he is too trusting. Later we will see that Malcolm shares his father's generosity, but is circumspect.

1.4.b

Purpose: 1. To heighten the poignancy of Macbeth's betrayal: The more Duncan loves Macbeth, the more bitter his treachery. 2. To push Macbeth towards the murder: The threat of being supplanted by Malcolm increases Macbeth's urgency to act now.

Drama: Will Macbeth accept Duncan's largesse, and wait for chance to 'crown him without his stir'?

What	Why
18-19 **The sin of my Ingratitude even now Was heavy on me** = I have thanked you so inadequately that it's a sin. It was just now (**even now**) weighing heavily on me.	18 Thanking Macbeth - finding it impossible to thank him enough.
19-21 **Thou art so far before** (you are so far ahead), **That swiftest Wing of Recompense** (that thanks flying fastest) **is slow, To overtake thee** (struggles to catch up to you).	
21-23 **Would** (I wish) **thou hadst less deserv'd** (you deserved less) **That** (so that) **the proportion both of thanks, and payment** (the proportion of thanks and payment, measured against your deserving) **Might have been mine**: I wish I could pay you enough that you would owe me, rather than me still owing you.	

24   More is thy due, than more than all can pay.

MACBETH
25   The service, and the loyalty I owe,
26   In doing it, pays itself.
27   Your Highness' part, is to receive our Duties:
28   And our Duties are to your Throne, and State,
29   Children, and Servants; which do but what they should,
30   By doing everything safe toward your Love
31   And Honour.

DUNCAN
32   Welcome hither:
33   I have begun to plant thee, and will labour
34   To make thee full of growing. ¶ Noble *Banquo*,
35   That hast no less deserv'd, nor must be known
36   No less to have done so: Let me enfold thee,
37   And hold thee to my Heart.

BANQUO
38   There if I grow,
39   The Harvest is your own.

DUNCAN
40   My plenteous Joys,
41   Wanton in fullness, seek to hide themselves
42   In drops of sorrow. ¶ Sons, Kinsmen, *Thanes*,
43   And you whose places are the nearest, know,
44   We will establish our Estate upon
45   Our eldest, *Malcolm*, whom we name hereafter,
46   The Prince of Cumberland: ¶ which Honour must
47   Not unaccompanied, invest him only,
48   But signs of Nobleness, like Stars, shall shine
49   On all deservers. ¶ From hence to Inverness,
50   And bind us further to you.

MACBETH
51   The Rest is Labour, which is not us'd for you:
52   I'll be myself the Harbinger, and make joyful
53   The hearing of my Wife, with your approach:
54   So humbly take my leave.

DUNCAN
55   My worthy *Cawdor*.

What	Why
24 **More is thy due, than more than all can pay** = What I owe you is not only more than I can pay, not only more than all can pay, but more than even that.	
25-26 **The service, and the loyalty I owe, In doing it, pays itself** = serving you loyally, by merely doing it, gives me joy, which is payment enough.	25 Humbling himself before his King.
27 **Your Highness' part** = your job as King. **receive** = accept.	
29 **Which** (our duties) **do but** (do no more than) **what they should.**	
30 **safe** = Securely dedicated.	
33 **begun**: i.e. by making you Cawdor. In other words, that was only the beginning of what I intend to do for you.	
35-36 **nor must be known** (nor must we allow it to be believed) **No less to have done so** (that you have deserved less than Macbeth).	
36 **enfold** = hug.	
39 **The Harvest is your own** = Whatever I achieve is yours.	39 Humbling himself before the King. Note the contrast between Macbeth's exaggerated, flowery obeisance and Banquo's simple homage.
40 **plenteous** = abundant.	40 Crying with happiness.
41-42 **Wanton** (undisciplined) **in fullness** (because they are so full)**, seek to hide themselves** (seek to disguise their 'wantonness') **In drops of sorrow** (in tears; as sadness).	
43 **you whose places are the nearest** = you who are nearest the crown.	
44 **establish our Estate upon** = name as my successor (royal 'we').	44 Note: Ancient Scotland did not follow the English tradition of the throne passing from father to son, so Macbeth had reason to expect to be Duncan's heir. The title 'Prince of Cumberland' indicated the next in line for the crown.
45 **hereafter** = from now on.	**TURN**. Macbeth expected to
47 **Not unaccompanied**: Malcolm will have company in this honor, i.e. the other Thanes. **invest him** = clothe him.	hear his own name as heir. This causes him to abandon the 'chance may crown me' idea, and return to the plan to murder
48 **signs of Nobleness** = titles.	Duncan. **FORWARD**: How can
49 **all deservers** = all those who played a part in this victory. **From hence** = from here (we will go). **Inverness**: Macbeth's home.	Macbeth become king if Malcolm is heir apparent?
50 **bind us further to you**: By granting them titles, he intends to strengthen their loyalty.	
51 **The Rest is Labour, which is not us'd for you**: Resting is an effort when not devoted to your service; or perhaps, Now that the talk is done, what remains is the work, which is not suitable for the King to do himself. (He is not 'used to' it.)	51 Jumping to serve the King.
52-53 **Harbinger** = announcer. **make joyful The hearing of my Wife, with your approach** = make my wife's ears joyful with the news of your approach.	
	55 **My worthy Cawdor**: saying goodbye, with honors.

MACBETH

56 *[aside]* The Prince of Cumberland: that is a step,
57 On which I must fall down, or else o'erleap,
58 For in my way it lies. ¶ Stars hide your fires,
59 Let not Light see my black and deep desires:
60 The Eye wink at the Hand; yet let that be,
61 Which the Eye fears, when it is done to see.
Exit.

DUNCAN

62 True, worthy *Banquo*: he is full so valiant,
63 And in his commendations, I am fed:
64 It is a Banquet to me. ¶ Let's after him,
65 Whose care is gone before, to bid us welcome:
66 ¶ It is a peerless Kinsman.
Flourish. Exeunt.

SCENA QUINTA.

Enter Lady Macbeth alone with a Letter.

LADY MACBETH

1 *They met me in the day of success: and I have learn'd by the*
2 *perfect'st report, they have more in them, than mortal*
3 *knowledge. When I burnt in desire to question them further,*
4 *they made themselves Air, into which they vanish'd. Whiles I*
5 *stood rapt in the wonder of it, came Missives from the King, who*
6 *all-hail'd me 'Thane of Cawdor', by which Title before, these*
7 *weird Sisters saluted me, and referr'd me to the coming on of*
8 *time, with 'hail King that shalt be'. This have I thought good to*
9 *deliver thee (my dearest Partner of Greatness) that thou might'st*
10 *not lose the dues of rejoicing by being ignorant of what Greatness*
11 *is promis'd thee. Lay it to thy heart, and farewell.*

12 Glamis thou art, and Cawdor, and shalt be
13 What thou art promis'd: ¶ Yet do I fear thy Nature,
14 It is too full o' th' Milk of human kindness,
15 To catch the nearest way. Thou wouldst be great,
16 Art not without Ambition, but without
17 The illness should attend it. What thou wouldst highly,

What	Why
56 **step** = obstacle.	
57 **On which I must fall down, or else o'erleap** = which I must either trip on or leap over. Either I will be blocked by Malcolm or I must somehow leapfrog him.	
58 **Stars hide your fires**: Don't shine on this, but let it stay hidden.	58 **Stars hide your fires**: praying to the dark spirits. In this passage, Macbeth is saying, please let me do this murder, but not see or feel the effects of having done it. In other words, let me enjoy the reward but not pay the price.
59-61 **see** = shine on. **The Eye wink at the Hand** = Let my eye not see what my hand does: Picture him closing one eye so he can't see his hand. **yet let that** (the murder) **be** (come to be), **Which the Eye fears, when it is done** (when the murder has been done) **to see.**	
62 **he** = Macbeth.	62 Note: Banquo must have been praising Macbeth to Duncan.
63 **in his commendations, I am fed** = Hearing him praised is like a banquet to me.	
64-65 **Let's** (go) **after him, Whose care is gone** (whose care for us has prompted him to go) **before, to bid us** (to prepare a) **welcome.**	
66 **It** = Macbeth.	

1.5.a A room in Macbeth's castle at Inverness. Interior. Day.

Purpose: 1. To show that Lady Macbeth's royal ambition is even more single-minded than her husband's. This will become poignant later, when we see the difference in how the two cope with having achieved the throne through murder. 2. To give Macbeth another big push toward going through with the murder.

Drama: Can she craft a message that will overcome his scruples?

What	Why
1 **They** = the Witches. **the day of success** = the day we won the battle.	1 Reading a letter from Macbeth describing his encounter with the Weird Sisters and their prophecy. Note: the letter reiterates things we already know. Shakespeare is making sure everybody in the audience is aware of the prophecy. Also note: The swiftness with which both Macbeth and Lady Macbeth embrace the crown prophecy seems to indicate they have already dreamed together of him becoming King.
2 **perfect'st report** = most reliable source. Because they foretold his receiving the Cawdor title, it proves their prophesying can be trusted.	
5-6 **Missives** = messages. **who all-hail'd me, 'Thane of Cawdor'** = who said, 'all hail, Thane of Cawdor'.	
6-8 **by which Title before, these Weird Sisters saluted me** = which the Weird Sisters had already called me. **referr'd me to the coming on of time** = indicated what was to come.	
8-10 **This news have I thought good to deliver thee ... that thou might'st not lose the dues of rejoicing** = so that you might not lose the rejoicing that is due you.	
	9 **dearest Partner of Greatness**: note how he characterizes their marriage – as a partnership whose ambition is political stature.
11 **Lay it to thy heart** = keep it secret, like a letter hidden in your bodice.	12 **Glamis thou art:** Having finished reading, she is now speaking her mind.
13 **I fear** the weakness in **thy Nature.**	12 Preparing her arguments. **'shalt'**: notice that she is already demanding that he do what she knows he will be reluctant to do. Also, she is saying that, since it's foretold, there's no point resisting, since it's already fact.
14 **too full o' th' Milk of human kindness** = too gentle, like a mother with her baby.	
15 **nearest** = quickest. **wouldst** = want to.	
17 **illness** = the disease of mind necessary to drive you to violate your conscience. **highly** = the high position you desire.	17 Note: she couches her criticism in praise.

18 That wouldst thou holily: wouldst not play false,
19 And yet wouldst wrongly win.
20 Thou'dst have, great Glamis, that which cries,
21 'Thus thou must do', if thou have it;
22 And that which rather thou dost fear to do,
23 Than wishest should be undone. ¶ Hie thee hither,
24 That I may pour my Spirits in thine Ear,
25 And chastise with the valour of my Tongue
26 All that impedes thee from the Golden Round,
27 Which Fate and Metaphysical aid doth seem
28 To have thee crown'd withal.

1.5.b -

Enter Messenger.
29 What is your tidings?

MESSENGER
30 The King comes here Tonight.

LADY MACBETH
31 Thou'rt mad to say it.
32 Is not thy Master with him? who, were 't so,
33 Would have inform'd for preparation.

MESSENGER
34 So please you, it is true: our *Thane* is coming:
35 One of my fellows had the speed of him;
36 Who almost dead for breath, had scarcely more
37 Than would make up his Message.

LADY MACBETH
38 Give him tending,
39 He brings great news.
Exit Messenger.

1.5.c -

40 The Raven himself is hoarse,
41 That croaks the fatal entrance of *Duncan*
42 Under my Battlements. ¶ Come you Spirits,
43 That tend on mortal thoughts, unsex me here,
44 And fill me from the Crown: to the Toe, top-full

What	Why
18 **holily** = without crime. **Play false** = deceive.	18 She is saying, 'you are better than me, but in this instance, my illness – evil – is a virtue'.
19-21 **wouldst wrongly win**: You would be glad to have the ill-gotten gains, but don't want to get your hands dirty. **Thou'dst have** (you would like to have), **great Glamis** (great Macbeth, Thane of Glamis**), that** (the crown) **which cries, 'Thus thou must do',** (you must kill Duncan) **if thou have it** (if you want to get the crown).	
22-23 **that which rather thou dost fear to do, Than wishest should be undone**: It is not that you would wish the murder to be left undone but rather that you fear to do it.	
23 **Hie thee hither** = hurry here.	
24 So **that I may pour** with my words **my Spirits** (my bravery) **in** your mind through **thine Ear.**	24 **FORWARD**: Will we see her pour her spirits in his ear?
25-28 **And chastise** (beat down) **with the valour** (bravery) **of my Tongue All** the weakness **that impedes thee** (blocks you) **from the Golden Round** (crown), **Which Fate** (as reported by the Sisters) **and Metaphysical aid** (and the supernatural help they command) **doth seem To have thee crown'd withal** (do seem to have crowned you with).	

1.5.b Purpose: To impart urgency and immediacy to the plan. It's no longer 'someday'. Now it's 'tonight'!

Drama: Can the Messenger get her to believe the King is truly coming tonight?

What	Why
29 **tidings** = news.	
31 **mad** = crazy.	31 Rebuking him for lying. It's too good to be true.
32-33 **thy Master** = Macbeth. **who, were 't so** (if it were true), **Would have inform'd for preparation** (would himself have come to tell me to prepare).	
35 **had the speed of** = was faster than.	
36-37 **almost dead for** lack of **breath, had scarcely more** (scarcely more air in his lungs) **Than would make up his Message** (than needed to utter his message).	
38 **Give him tending** = tend to him.	

1.5.c Purpose: To bring the murder of Duncan one big step closer to reality.

Drama: Can she succeed in blocking out her humanity; silencing her scruples?

What	Why
40 **The Raven himself is hoarse**: This news is such a dramatic omen that the raven — harbinger of death — is hoarse with croaking.	
41 **fatal** = both fated and deadly.	42 **Battlements**: Note that she doesn't say 'doors' or 'eaves' but the part of the castle made for violence. **Come you Spirits**: praying to the devil and his minions.
43 **that tend on mortal thoughts**: that come with thoughts of death. **unsex me** = amputate my female gentleness.	

45 Of direst Cruelty: make thick my blood,
46 Stop up th' access, and passage to Remorse,
47 That no compunctious visitings of Nature
48 Shake my fell purpose, nor keep peace between
49 Th' effect, and it. Come to my Woman's Breasts,
50 And take my Milk for Gall, you murd'ring Ministers,
51 Wherever, in your sightless substances,
52 You wait on Nature's Mischief. Come thick Night,
53 And pall thee in the dunnest smoke of Hell,
54 That my keen Knife see not the Wound it makes,
55 Nor Heaven peep through the Blanket of the dark,
56 To cry, 'Hold, hold'.

1.5.d -

Enter Macbeth
57 Great Glamis, worthy Cawdor,
58 Greater than both, by the all-hail hereafter,
59 ¶ Thy Letters have transported me beyond
60 This ignorant present, and I feel now
61 The future in the instant.

MACBETH
62 My dearest Love,
63 *Duncan* comes here Tonight.

LADY MACBETH
64 And when goes hence?

MACBETH
65 Tomorrow, as he purposes.

LADY MACBETH
66 O never,
67 Shall Sun that Morrow see.

What	Why
45-46 **make thick my blood, Stop up th' access and passage to Remorse** = Make my blood so thick that it blocks the veins and prevents remorse from getting in. 47 **compunctious visitings of Nature** = natural moral hesitations. 48 **Shake** = dislodge. **fell** = deadly. **keep peace** = make peace. 49 **Th' effect** (the achievement of Duncan's death) **and it** (my fell purpose). 50 **take my Milk for Gall** = Turn my milk to gall. The product of the gall bladder (bile) was believed responsible for bitterness. **murd'ring Ministers** = spirits of murder. 51 **sightless substances** = invisible other-worlds. 52 **wait on Nature's Mischief** = wait to do mischief against Nature. 53 **pall** = a cloth to cover a coffin from view. **dunnest** = darkest. Also, a dun is a fort. 54 **keen** = sharp. 55 **Nor Heaven peep through the Blanket of the dark** (nor let God see through the dark what we do).	49 **FORWARD**: Will we see this gruesome image come to life? 53 Like her husband, she prays not only that others won't be able to see the murder, but that she herself won't be able to see it.

1.5.d Purpose: To heighten our suspense over the question, will he go through with it? Macbeth has decided for and against the murder by turns. In this scene he wavers.

Drama: Can she overcome his resistance?

What	Why
	57 **Great Glamis**: flattering him.
58 **the all-hail hereafter**: She's referring to the Witches saying 'All hail, Macbeth! that shalt be King hereafter'. 60-61 **ignorant present** = the present, which doesn't yet know that you are King. **I feel now The future** (in which you are King) **In the** (in this present) **instant.**	60 Negating his anticipated qualms by arguing that, since it's fated, it's already done. 62 **My dearest Love**: this shows the 'before' of their relationship: She is the center of his world. 63 *Duncan* **comes here Tonight**: opening a discussion of how to handle the opportunity. Note that he does not say, 'Let's kill him'. 64 **when goes hence**: circling the issue they both know is in the forefront of each other's mind.
65 **as he purposes** = as he plans. 66-67 **never, Shall Sun that Morrow see** = The sun will never rise on a tomorrow in which that happens.	65 Again avoiding a commitment. 67 Cajoling him.

68 ¶ Your Face, my *Thane*, is as a Book, where men
69 May read strange matters. To beguile the time,
70 Look like the time, bear welcome in your Eye,
71 Your Hand, your Tongue: look like th' innocent flower,
72 But be the Serpent under 't. ¶ He that's coming,
73 Must be provided for: and you shall put
74 This Night's great Business into my dispatch,
75 Which shall to all our Nights, and Days to come,
76 Give solely sovereign sway, and Masterdom.

MACBETH
77 We will speak further.

LADY MACBETH
78 Only look up clear:
79 To alter favor, ever is to fear:
80 Leave all the rest to me.
Exeunt.

SCENA SEXTA.

Hautboys, and Torches. Enter Duncan, Malcolm, Donalbain, Banquo,
Lenox, Macduff, Rosse, Angus and Attendants.

DUNCAN
1 This Castle hath a pleasant seat,
2 The air nimbly and sweetly recommends itself
3 Unto our gentle senses.

BANQUO
4 This Guest of Summer,
5 The Temple-haunting Martlet does approve,

What	Why
68-71 **Your Face, my *Thane*, is as a Book, where men May read strange matters** = Men may read dark thoughts in your face (e.g. furrowed brow, frown) as clearly as words in a book. **To beguile** (deceive) **the time** (the people around us), **Look like the time** (conform your appearance to what people expect); **bear welcome in your Eye** (smile), **Your Hand** (fond handshake), **your Tongue** (warm greetings).	68 **Your Face, my *Thane*, is as a Book**: implied stage direction. Macbeth is so fraught that it's obvious on his face. Bullying or manipulating him into submission by assuming she's already won the argument, and moving on to implementation.
71-72 **look like th' innocent flower, But be the Serpent under 't:** Hide your evil pur-pose beneath an innocent smile, like a snake hiding under a flower.	
72-73 **He that's coming, Must be provided for** = double meaning: We must prepare a feast fit for a King, and we must also prepare to murder him.	
73-76 **put This Night's great Business** (the murder plan) **into my dispatch** (into my charge), **Which shall to all our Nights, and Days to come** (to our future), **Give solely sovereign sway, and Masterdom** (devote itself exclusively, as servant to master). Put me in charge, because my only concern will be ensuring our future on the throne.	73 Rallying him with a reminder of the payoff. **FORWARD**: What is she planning? 77 **We will speak further**: Not completely closing the door, but refusing to promise. **TURN**: She has failed to persuade him. He hasn't decided yet.
78 **look up clear**: Don't look at the floor with a clouded face.	78 This is an implied stage direction. Macbeth is scowling at the floor.
79 **To alter favor ever** (to change to a dark facial expression at all) **is to** (arouse) **fear.**	

1.6.a Outside Macbeth's castle at Inverness. Exterior. Day.

Purpose: To heighten anticipation of the murder by the sharp contrast between what Duncan thinks he is entering (a warm welcome in the safe and lovely home of friends) and what we the audience know he is entering (the house of murder).

Drama: 1. (from the guests' perspective) This is the happy conclusion of a difficult journey. 2. (from the audience's perspective) Duncan is walking blithely into a deadly trap! Can she fool Duncan that her welcome is sincere?

What	Why
(Stage directions) ***Hautboys*** = oboes. From the French 'hautbois' (literally, 'high wood'), which is pronounced 'ohbwah'.	
1. **seat** = the land on which the castle 'sits'.	1 Sharing his relief and gratitude that they have arrived at an oasis after a hard journey.
2-3 **nimbly** = easily. **sweetly**: It smells of flowers. **recom-mends itself Unto our gentle senses** = says to the gentle portion of our senses that this is a good place to be.	
4 **Guest of Summer**: they fly south for winter.	4 Seconding and amplifying Duncan's favorable assessment.
5 **Temple-haunting**: They like to nest in high buildings, such as temples. **Martlet** = martin, a small bird that often nests in buildings. **approve** = prove it's a good place; or approve of the place.	

dramatic irony:
- audience knows something actors don't

irony:
- actual vs. expected (contrast ~~of~~ between)

6 By his loved Mansionry, that the Heaven's breath
7 Smells wooingly here: no Jutty frieze,
8 Buttress, nor Coign of Vantage, but this Bird
9 Hath made his pendent Bed, and procreant Cradle,
10 Where they must breed, and haunt: I have observ'd
11 The air is delicate.

1.6.b -

Enter Lady Macbeth.

DUNCAN

12 See, see, our honour'd Hostess:
13 ❡ The Love that follows us, sometime is our trouble,
14 Which still we thank as Love. Herein I teach you,
15 How you shall bid God-yield us for your pains,
16 And thank us for your trouble.

LADY MACBETH

17 All our service,
18 In every point twice done, and then done double,
19 Were poor, and single Business, to contend
20 Against those Honours deep, and broad,
21 Wherewith your Majesty loads our House:
22 For those of old, and the late Dignities,
23 Heap'd up to them, we rest your Hermits.

DUNCAN

24 Where's the Thane of Cawdor?
25 We cours'd him at the heels, and had a purpose
26 To be his Purveyor: but he rides well,
27 And his great Love (sharp as his Spur) hath holp him
28 To his home before us: ❡ Fair and Noble Hostess
29 We are your guest tonight.

LADY MACBETH

30 Your Servants ever,
31 Have theirs, themselves, and what is theirs in compt,
32 To make their Audit at your Highness' pleasure,
33 Still to return your own.

DUNCAN

34 Give me your hand:
35 Conduct me to mine Host we love him highly,
36 And shall continue, our Graces towards him.
37 By your leave Hostess.

Exeunt.

What	Why
6-10 **loved Mansionry** = loving homebuilding. **Heaven's breath Smells wooingly here** = The air here is breath from heaven, and its scent is alluring. **Jutty** = projecting part of a wall. **frieze** = horizontal strip of sculpture built into the top of a wall. **Buttress** = wall support. **Coign of Vantage** = jutting corner built to enable defenders to look along the wall. **pendent** = hanging. **procreant Cradle** = nest for raising young. **haunt** = congregate.	6 Confirming Duncan's assessment: Banquo has observed that wherever the air is sweetest, martlets congregate and nest. There are martlets all over the castle, confirming his idea.

1.6.b Purpose: 1. To cross another threshold (literally) on the path to the murder. 2. To paint a picture of Lady Macbeth before the murder, successfully hiding her treachery.

Drama: 1. Who can out-thank whom? 2. Can Lady Macbeth 'look like th'innocent flower but be the serpent under't'? (see Endnote 4, p. 191).

What	Why
	12 **honour'd Hostess**: thanking her and apologizing for imposing.
13-14 **The Love that follows us** (people who love us), **sometime is our trouble** (sometimes give us trouble), **Which still we thank as Love** (but we are thankful for the trouble since it's a sign of the love). **Herein** = with this lesson. 15 **yield** = bless.	13 In other words, I recognize how much trouble I am causing by imposing on your hospitality, but please think of it as a measure of how much the King loves your husband. 16 **thank us for your trouble**: playfully joking.
17-23 **All our service** (all we do for you) **In every point twice done, and then done double** (if doubled, then doubled again), **Were poor, and single Business** (would be as if we had barely done one little thing for you), **to contend Against** (when measured against) **those Honours deep** (profound), **and broad** (widely known), **Wherewith** (with which) **your Majesty loads our House** (heaps onto our family), both **For those of old** (existing honors, i.e. Glamis) **and the late** (recent) **Dignities** (Cawdor) **Heap'd up to them** (piled on top), **we rest your Hermits** (we remain people whose job is to pray for you all day).	17 Out-thanking him. Note that she is exaggerating her welcome, doing her best to mask her murderous intention.
25-26 **cours'd him at the heels** = followed him like hunting dogs (coursers) on a deer's heels. **purpose To be his Purveyor** = intention to announce his arrival, like a salesman (purveyor) presenting his wares. 27 **his great Love** (for his wife). **sharp as his Spur** = speeding him along like kicking a horse with a spur. 30-33 **Your Servants** (i.e. us) **ever** (always) **Have theirs** (their servants), **themselves, and what is theirs** (their possessions), **in compt** (in an account), **To make their Audit at your Highness' pleasure** (to be reckoned whenever you like), **Still to return your own** (to be paid to yourself). In other words, we are all in an account book of things that belong to you.	24 Putting her at ease by showering her with honor. 30 Redoubling her flattery.
35 **Conduct me** = bring me. 36 **continue, our Graces** = bestow more honors. 37 **By your leave** = With your permission (I will go ahead).	34 **Give me your hand**: bringing the game of mutual flattery to a gentle end. 36 **TURN**: Success. Duncan is not alarmed, and enters the house fully trusting.

SCENA SEPTIMA.

Hautboys. Torches.
Enter a Sewer, and divers Servants with Dishes and Service over the
Stage. Then enter Macbeth.

MACBETH

1 If it were done, when 'tis done, then 'twere well,
2 It were done quickly: if th' Assassination
3 Could trammel up the Consequence, and catch
4 With his surcease, Success: that but this blow
5 Might be the be all, and the end all. Here,
6 But here, upon this Bank and Shoal of time,
7 We'd jump the life to come. ❡ But in these Cases,
8 We still have judgment here, that we but teach
9 Bloody Instructions, which being taught, return
10 To plague th' Inventor. This even-handed Justice
11 Commends th' Ingredience of our poison'd Chalice
12 To our own lips. ❡ He's here in double trust;
13 First, as I am his Kinsman, and his Subject,
14 Strong both against the Deed: then, as his Host,
15 Who should against his Murderer shut the door,
16 Not bear the knife myself. ❡ Besides, this *Duncan*
17 Hath borne his Faculties so meek; hath been
18 So clear in his great Office, that his Virtues
19 Will plead like Angels, Trumpet-tongu'd against
20 The deep damnation of his taking off:
21 And Pity, like a naked New-born-Babe,
22 Striding the blast, or Heaven's Cherubin, hors'd
23 Upon the sightless Couriers of the Air,
24 Shall blow the horrid deed in every eye,
25 That tears shall drown the wind. ❡ I have no Spur
26 To prick the sides of my intent, but only
27 Vaulting Ambition, which o'er-leaps itself,
28 And falls on th' other.

— soliloquy —

1.7.a A room in Macbeth's castle at Inverness. Interior. Night.

Purpose: 1. To heighten our eagerness to see if he will go through with the murder. For a second time, Macbeth decides to call off the plan. 2. This positions Macbeth to be persuaded by his wife in the next subscene (see Endnote 5, p.192).

Drama: Will Macbeth decide to kill Duncan?

What	Why
(Stage directions) **Sewer** = butler. **divers** = diverse. **Service** = serving dishes and utensils.	
1-7 **If it** (if the acquisition of the crown) **were done** (were finalized) **when 'tis done** (when the murder is done), **then 'twere well** (then it would be well if), **It were done quickly: if th' Assassination Could trammel up** (could snare) **the Consequence** (the crown), **and catch With his surcease** (with his death), **Success: that but** (if no more than) **this blow** (the murder of Duncan) **Might be the be all, and the end all** (might be the end of it). **Here, But here** (then right at this very moment), **upon this Bank and Shoal** (shallow spot) **of time, We'd jump the life to come.** If we knew there would be no ongoing complications, we'd kill Duncan now, as a swimmer jumps from the bank into water he knows is deep.	1 Trying to decide whether to kill Duncan. Note: Macbeth is primarily concerned in this speech not with whether it is right to kill Duncan, but whether he can get away with it.
7-10 **But in these Cases** (in situations such as this) **we but teach Bloody Instructions** (we merely teach how to murder), **which being taught, return To plague th' Inventor** (which instructions, once taught, will be used to kill the teacher). By killing the king to replace him, I'm only teaching the next man to kill and replace me.	8 **We still have judgment here**: As becomes clear in the following lines, he doesn't mean moral judgment (killing Duncan is a sin), but strategic judgment (killing Duncan won't achieve the desired result).
10 **even-handed Justice** = fair: Picture Justice dealing equally to both sides, one with each hand.	
11 **Commends** = prescribes. **Ingredience** = contents. **Chalice** = ceremonial cup.	
14 **Strong both** (that I am his kinsman and his subject are both strong arguments) **against the Deed.**	14 In addition to the practical dangers, his conscience is another argument against the murder.
17 **Hath borne his Faculties so meek** = has been so humble in using his powers as king.	
18 **clear** = free of corruption. **in his great Office** = in discharging the duties of his great office.	
18-20 **his Virtues Will plead like Angels, Trumpet-tongu'd against The deep damnation of his taking off**: Word of his virtues will sound loud as trumpeting angels denouncing the deep damnation of his murderer.	
21-25 **Pity** (pity for the innocent Duncan), **like a naked New-born Babe, Striding the blast** (riding astraddle the wind), **or Heaven's Cherubin** (baby angels), **hors'd Upon the sightless Couriers of the Air** (mounted on the air, as on a blind horse, going in all directions), **Shall blow the horrid deed** (shall trumpet the news of my crime) **in every eye, That tears shall drown the wind** (so many tears will fall that they will drown the wind).	24 **Shall blow the horrid deed in every eye**: Note that here he names not his own conscience, but the public backlash.
25 **I have no Spur To prick the sides of my intent**: There's no circumstance forcing me to act, the way a rider's spur goads a horse forward.	25 Seeking, and failing to find, an excuse for murdering Duncan.
27-28 **o'er-leaps itself, And falls on th' other**: Picture a rider vaulting clear over its horse and landing on the other side. Ambition is the rider and being king is the horse.	27 **TURN:** He decides he can't kill Duncan now.

Enter Lady Macbeth.

29 How now? What News?

LADY MACBETH

30 He has almost supp'd: why have you left the chamber?

MACBETH

31 Hath he ask'd for me?

LADY MACBETH

32 Know you not, he has?

MACBETH

33 We will proceed no further in this Business:
34 He hath Honour'd me of late, and I have bought
35 Golden Opinions from all sorts of people,
36 Which would be worn now in their newest gloss,
37 Not cast aside so soon.

LADY MACBETH

38 Was the hope drunk,
39 Wherein you dress'd yourself? Hath it slept since?
40 And wakes it now to look so green, and pale,
41 At what it did so freely? From this time,
42 Such I account thy love. ¶ Art thou affear'd
43 To be the same in thine own Act, and Valour,
44 As thou art in desire? Wouldst thou have that
45 Which thou esteem'st the Ornament of Life,
46 And live a Coward in thine own Esteem?
47 Letting 'I dare not', wait upon 'I would',
48 Like the poor Cat i' th' Adage.

MACBETH

49 Prythee peace:
50 I dare do all that may become a man,
51 Who dares do more, is none.

LADY MACBETH

52 What Beast was 't then
53 That made you break this enterprise to me?
54 ¶ When you durst do it, then you were a man:

1.7.b Purpose: to further heighten our anticipation. In the seesaw battle in Macbeth's mind (I will; I won't; I will; I won't), this is the last stand of 'I won't'.

Drama: Can Lady Macbeth change her husband's mind? (see Endnote 6, page 192)

What	Why
30 **He has almost supp'd**: Duncan has almost finished supper.	30 Upbraiding him for fleeing his own banquet. She has tracked him down to bring him back to the party to prevent suspicion.
	31 **Hath he ask'd for me**: angling for confirmation that Duncan's suspicion has not been aroused.
	32 **Know you not, he has:** Chiding him for risking arousing Duncan's suspicion.
33 **Business**: the murder.	33 Finally blurting it out: backing out.
34 **of late** = recently. **bought** = earned.	34 Proving why he is right to cancel.
35 **Golden Opinions** = high esteem.	
36 **Which would be** (should be) **worn now in their newest gloss**: Likening his popularity to a beautiful garment, which should be worn while shiny and new.	36 Note: It hasn't occurred to Macbeth that he can kill Duncan secretly. He assumes everyone will know he did it, and only changes his mind below when his wife has the idea of blaming the chamberlains.
38-39 **Was the hope** (of royalty) **drunk** (and therefore unreliable), **Wherein you dress'd yourself** (with which you disguised yourself, as if with another's clothes)**?**	38 Motivating him by invoking him to keep his word.
40 **green, and pale** = sick with hangover (continuing the 'drunk' metaphor).	
41 **what it did so freely:** i.e. his desire to kill Duncan.	
42 **Such I account thy love** = I will assume your love of me is no more reliable than your drunken ambition.	42 **Art thou affear'd**: Adding another incentive: threatening to reduce her love to the wavering and unreliable level of his resolve.
43-44 **To be the same in thine own Act, and Valour** (in actual deed and valor), **As thou art in desire** (as in your fantasy).	
44-46 **Wouldst thou have** (would you desire to have) **that Which thou esteem'st the Ornament of Life** (the crown), **And live a Coward In thine own Esteem** (a coward by your own rules)**?**	48 The **Adage** she refers to: 'The cat would eat fish, but would not wet her feet'. Note: The word 'would' has two meanings here: 'wants to' and the modern sense. She also uses both senses: 'Wouldst have' refers to desire; 'would live' refers to what would happen. She is challenging him by calling him a 'fraidy cat'.
49 **Prythee** = I pray you. **peace** = shut up.	49 Defending his honor against the charge of cowardice.
50 **I dare do all that may become** (that is befitting) **a man.**	
51 **Who dares do more, is none** = There is no one who dares more than I.	51 **do**: Folio has 'no'.
52 **What Beast was 't then**: since no man dares more, it must have been a beast.	52 Manipulating him into going ahead with it, by questioning his manhood.
53 **break** = bring up, as in 'break the news'.	
54 **durst** = dared – when you said you would do it.	

55 And to be more than what you were, you would
56 Be so much more the man. ¶ Nor time, nor place
57 Did then adhere, and yet you would make both:
58 They have made themselves, and that their fitness now
59 Does unmake you. ¶ I have given Suck, and know
60 How tender 'tis to love the Babe that milks me,
61 I would, while it was smiling in my Face,
62 Have pluck'd my Nipple from his Boneless Gums,
63 And dash'd the Brains out, had I so sworn
64 As you have done to this.

MACBETH

65 If we should fail?

LADY MACBETH

66 We fail?
67 But screw your courage to the sticking place,
68 And we'll not fail: ¶ when *Duncan* is asleep,
69 (Whereto the rather shall his day's hard Journey
70 Soundly invite him) his two Chamberlains
71 Will I with Wine, and Wassail, so convince,
72 That Memory, the Warder of the Brain,
73 Shall be a Fume, and the Receipt of Reason
74 A Lymbeck only: when in Swinish sleep,
75 Their drenched Natures lie as in a Death,
76 What cannot you and I perform upon
77 Th' unguarded *Duncan*? what not put upon
78 His spongy Officers? Who shall bear the guilt
79 Of our great quell.

MACBETH

80 Bring forth Men-Children only:
81 For thy undaunted Mettle should compose
82 Nothing but Males. ¶ Will it not be receiv'd,
83 When we have mark'd with blood those sleepy two
84 Of his own Chamber, and us'd their very Daggers,
85 That they have done 't?

LADY MACBETH

86 Who dares receive it other,
87 As we shall make our Griefs and Clamour roar,
88 Upon his Death?

What	Why
55-56 **to be more than what you were** (to be a King), **you would Be so much more the man** (more manly than when you only planned to do it).	
56-57 **Nor time, nor place** (neither time nor place for it) **Did then adhere** (existed then), **and yet you would make both** (you said you would create an opportunity).	56 That attempt having failed, trying a new angle: chastising him for breaking promise.
58-59 **They have made themselves**: the ideal time and place to act have created themselves without your help. **their fitness now Does unmake you** = opportunity has presented itself, and it undoes (unmakes) your resolve.	
59 **given Suck** = nursed a baby.	59 That attempt having failed, escalating: shaming him for breaking promise. Note: apparently they had a child who died.
63 **had I** = if I had.	65 **If we should fail**: sharing that his faith in the Sisters' prophecy has slipped. Fearing.
	66 **We fail**: refusing to entertain the possibility.
67 **But** = only. **screw your courage**: on a crossbow, the **screw** draws the string until it catches on **the sticking place**. Tighten your courage until it clicks into place.	68 **When *Duncan* is asleep**: TURN - IDEA! Lady Macbeth has just had the inspiration that changes the whole story. Sharing and explaining her idea.
69 **Whereto** = towards which. **the rather** = most likely.	69 FORWARD: She paints a picture of the murder in vivid detail. Will we see it come true?
70 **Soundly** = firmly. **Chamberlains** = chamber-servants.	
71 **Wassail** = spiced ale. **convince** = change their minds.	
72 **Warder** = guardian.	
73 **Fume** = fog. **Receipt** = receptacle.	
74 **Lymbeck** = alembic – the top of a whiskey still, which is full of steam. Their minds will be cans of fog. **Swinish** = gross. She is blaming them in advance.	
75 **drenched Natures** = their minds, drenched in alcohol. **as in a Death** = passed out.	
76 **What** (deed) **cannot you and I perform.**	
77 **put upon** = blame on.	
78 **spongy** = wine-soaked.	
79 **quell** = act of crushing; murder.	
80 **Bring forth Men-Children only**: You should have only male children (because boys need your courage).	80 TURN! Her idea has solved their problem. Now he knows they can get away with it. Exclaiming with joy.
81 **thy undaunted Mettle** = fearless fighting spirit. **compose** = create.	
82-83 **Will it not be receiv'd** (be immediately obvious), **When we have mark'd with blood** (smeared blood all over) **those sleepy two** (sleeping chamberlains).	82 IDEA! Getting it — repeating, in his own words, her brilliant idea.
85 **That they** (the chamberlains) **have done 't** (have killed Duncan).	
86 **Who dares receive** (believe) **it other** (otherwise).	86 IDEA! Pouring more fuel on the fire.
87 **As** (since) **we shall make our Griefs and Clamour** (noise of lamentation) **roar.**	

MACBETH

89 I am settled, and bend up

90 Each corporal Agent to this terrible Feat.

91 ¶ Away, and mock the time with fairest show,

92 False Face must hide what the false Heart doth know.

Exeunt.

What	Why
89 **bend up** = make taut, like a bowstring.	
90 **Each corporal Agent** = each part of my body — arm, hand, eye.	90 Decision made, moving to the action phase.
91 (let us go) **Away, and mock the time** (delude all observers) **with fairest show** (most pleasant appearance).	
92 **False Face** (lying, smiling facade) **must hide what the false Heart** (treacherous intent) **doth know.**	

ACTUS SECUNDUS. SCENA PRIMA.

Enter Banquo, and Fleance, with a Torch before him.

BANQUO

1 How goes the Night, Boy?

FLEANCE

2 The Moon is down: I have not heard the Clock.

BANQUO

3 And she goes down at Twelve.

FLEANCE

4 I take 't, 'tis later, Sir.

BANQUO

5 Hold, take my Sword:
6 ❡ There's Husbandry in Heaven,
7 Their Candles are all out: ❡ take thee that too.
8 ❡ A heavy Summons lies like Lead upon me,
9 And yet I would not sleep:
10 Merciful Powers, restrain in me the cursed thoughts
11 That Nature gives way to in repose.

2.1.b -

Enter Macbeth, and a Servant with a Torch.

12 ❡ Give me my Sword: who's there?

MACBETH

13 A Friend.

BANQUO

14 What Sir, not yet at rest? ❡ The King's abed.
15 He hath been in unusual Pleasure,
16 And sent forth great Largesse to your Offices.
17 This Diamond he greets your Wife withal,
18 By the name of most kind Hostess,
19 And shut up in measureless content.

MACBETH

20 Being unprepar'd,

2.1.a A courtyard in Macbeth's castle at Inverness. Interior. Night.

Purpose: 1. To build foreboding: The midnight hour and Banquo's fear serve to put us on edge. 2. To show that Banquo, in contrast to Macbeth, fears dire consequences from the prophecy. 3. To show Banquo's love of Fleance.

Drama: Can Banquo quiet his mind, which is racing because part of the prophecy has come true?

What	Why
1 **How goes the Night** = what time is it?	1 Keeping his son close.
2 **The Moon is down** = the moon has set. **Clock**: Perhaps the bell is supposed to have rung at midnight?	2 Innocently trying to help figure out what time it is.
3 **she** = the moon; therefore it is at least midnight.	3 Note: Midnight is the witching hour, when it was believed the ordinary rules of nature are suspended and black magic comes forth.
4 **'tis later** = therefore it must be past midnight.	
6-7 **Husbandry** = thrift, They've put out the **Candles** (stars) to save wax.	5 **take my Sword**: perhaps unbuckling his armor to prepare for bed? There is a powerful symbolism here: the father passes his sword – his power – to his son.
7 **that too**: perhaps a dagger? armor? The torch?	
8 **Summons**: subpoena to the court of sleep. **like Lead**: When sleepy, our limbs and eyelids are heavy like lead.	
9 **would not sleep** = want to stay awake. I need to sleep but I'm afraid of what will happen while I'm asleep.	9 Worrying about the prophecy.
10-11 **Merciful Powers** (God) **restrain in me** (spare me from) **the cursed thoughts** (evil imaginings) **That Nature gives way to** (that human nature falls victim to) **in repose** (when asleep).	10 Praying for calm. This indicates he's been having nightmares stemming from the prophecy.

2.1.b Purpose: To put yet another obstacle in the way of the murder: Macbeth's best friend tries (obliquely) to talk him out of it.

Drama: 1. Can Banquo get some reassurance that Macbeth's not going to betray Duncan? 2. Can Macbeth get some sign from Banquo that he may join him?

What	Why
12 **who's there**: It's too dark for Banquo to recognize the newcomer.	12 **Give me my Sword**: hearing somebody coming; fearing the newcomer. **who's there**: Challenging the intruder.
	13 **A Friend**: identifying himself; reassuring Banquo.
14 **at rest** = in bed.	14 Recognizing Macbeth.
15 **unusual Pleasure** = He's been unusually pleased.	
16 **Largesse** = gifts. **Offices**: service areas in the castle — kitchen, stables.	
17-19 **This Diamond he greets your Wife withal** (which he presents to your wife as a greeting) **By the name of** (as a way of calling her) **most kind Hostess, and** (he is) **shut up** (enveloped) **in measureless content** (contentment).	17 Encouraging Macbeth to be happy with Duncan's showering rewards, and not seek more by treachery. Note: The subject of treason is so explosive that they must not mention it. So both Banquo and Macbeth must make their points in an oblique fashion.
20 **unprepar'd** = unprepared for guests.	20 Deflecting Banquo's drift, resorting to meaningless cliché.

Macbeth   *2.1.b*   47

21 Our will became the servant to defect,
22 Which else should free have wrought.

BANQUO
23 All's well.
24 ¶ I dreamt last Night of the three weird Sisters:
25 To you they have show'd some truth.

MACBETH
26 I think not of them:
27 ¶ Yet when we can entreat an hour to serve,
28 We would spend it in some words upon that Business,
29 If you would grant the time.

BANQUO
30 At your kind'st leisure.

MACBETH
31 If you shall cleave to my consent,
32 When 'tis, it shall make Honour for you.

BANQUO
33 So I lose none,
34 In seeking to augment it, but still keep
35 My Bosom franchis'd, and Allegiance clear,
36 I shall be counsell'd.

MACBETH
37 Good repose the while.

BANQUO
38 Thanks Sir: the like to you.
Exit Banquo [and Fleance].

MACBETH
39 Go, bid thy Mistress, when my drink is ready,
40 She strike upon the Bell. ¶ Get thee to bed.
Exit servant.

2.1.c -

41 Is this a Dagger, which I see before me,
42 The Handle toward my Hand? Come, let me clutch thee:
43 ¶ I have thee not, and yet I see thee still.
44 Art thou not, fatal Vision, sensible
45 To feeling, as to sight? or art thou but

What	Why
21-22 Our will (our desire) **became the servant to** (had to take orders from) **defect** (our lack of provisions) **Which else** (which, if we had had time to prepare) **should free have wrought** (would have feted Duncan liberally).	
23 All's well = fine.	**24 I dreamt last Night**: trying again to circle round to the heart of the matter; pressing harder.
	26 I think not of them: TURN: Macbeth has rejected Banquo's coded plea to ignore the prophecy and pledge his loyalty to Duncan. **NEW DRAMA**: Can Macbeth persuade Banquo to join the plot? Rather than pledging to keep Duncan safe, Macbeth hints at an invitation to join him in a conspiracy, but in a veiled way, to preserve deniability. Like Banquo, Macbeth is talking about the conspiracy without talking about the conspiracy.
27-29 Yet, when we can entreat an hour (beg an hour from our full days) **to serve** (to serve the purpose), **We would spend it in some words upon that Business** (we would do well to spend that hour discussing that business), **If you would grant the time** (if you could spare the time).	
30 At your kind'st leisure = when you have the leisure to spend the time, and the kindness to spend it on me.	30 Jumping at the chance to talk it out and assuage his fears.
31-32 If you shall cleave to (stick to) **my consent** (my counsel), **When 'tis** (when it's time), **It shall make Honour for you** (you will be rewarded with honors).	31 Feeling Banquo out for a possible conspiracy.
33-36 So I lose none (as long as I lose no honor) **In seeking to augment it** (in seeking to increase my honor), **but still keep My Bosom** (heart) **franchis'd** (free), **and Allegiance** (to Duncan) **clear** (unclouded by treachery), **I shall be counsell'd** (by you).	33 Politely but firmly refusing.
37 repose = rest. **the while** = meanwhile, until we talk.	37 **TURN**: Giving up the attempt. Letting him go.
39-40 Go, bid thy Mistress (tell your mistress, my wife), **when my drink is ready, She strike upon the Bell** (to ring the bell).	39 Dismissing the servant. Note: Apparently this is a prearranged signal — when all is ready to kill Duncan, Lady Macbeth is to ring the bell. (stage direction) **[and Fleance]**: not in Folio.

2.1.c Purpose: To pose one last obstacle in the way of the murder. Moral scruples have failed to deter him, strategic concerns have failed to deter him, his best friend has failed to dissuade him. Now he faces the sheer horror of plunging a knife into his friend and king.

Drama: Will he go through with it?

What	Why
42 let me clutch thee: (to the dagger) let me grasp you.	42 Reacting to the shock of seeing a dagger in mid-air. Trying to figure out if the dagger he sees is real, or a hallucination. He is in such a heightened state that he is hallucinating.
43 I have thee not = I don't hold you in my hand.	
44 fatal Vision = deadly hallucination. **sensible** = detectable. Can you not be sensed by touch as well as by sight?	

46 A Dagger of the Mind, a false Creation,
47 Proceeding from the heat-oppressed Brain?
48 ¶ I see thee yet, in form as palpable,
49 As this which now I draw.
50 Thou marshall'st me the way that I was going,
51 And such an Instrument I was to use.
52 ¶ Mine Eyes are made the fools o' th' other Senses,
53 Or else worth all the rest: ¶ I see thee still;
54 And on thy Blade, and Dudgeon, Gouts of Blood,
55 Which was not so before. ¶ There's no such thing:
56 It is the bloody Business, which informs
57 Thus to mine Eyes. ¶ Now o'er the one half World
58 Nature seems dead, and wicked Dreams abuse
59 The Curtain'd sleep: Witchcraft celebrates
60 Pale *Hecate's* Offerings: and wither'd Murder,
61 Alarum'd by his Sentinel, the Wolf,
62 Whose howl's his Watch, thus with his stealthy pace,
63 With *Tarquin's* ravishing strides, towards his design
64 Moves like a Ghost. ¶ Thou sure and firm-set Earth
65 Hear not my steps, which way they walk, for fear
66 Thy very stones prate of my where-about,
67 And take the present horror from the time,
68 Which now suits with it. ¶ Whiles I threat, he lives:
69 Words to the heat of deeds too cold breath gives.

A Bell rings.

70 ¶ I go, and it is done: the Bell invites me.
71 ¶ Hear it not, *Duncan*, for it is a Knell,
72 That summons thee to Heaven, or to Hell.

Exit.

What	Why
46 **Dagger of the Mind**: Do you exist only in my mind?	
47 **heat-oppressed** = feverishly excited.	
48-49 **I see thee yet** (I see you still), **in form as palpable** (as tangibly real), **As this** (as this other dagger) **which now I draw** (pull from its scabbard).	
50 **marshall'st** = command me to go, as a military marshal.	
51 **And such an Instrument I was to use** = And I was planning to use a dagger just like you.	
52 Here is the sentence, reordered (cf. Introduction, page xi): My **other Senses** (touch, etc.) prove that **Mine Eyes** have been **fool**ed.	52 Deciding it's not real.
53 **Or else worth all the rest** = or else the eyes report true and the rest of the senses are fooled.	53 Changing his mind: maybe it's a true message from the supernatural world.
54 **Dudgeon** = wooden handle. **Gouts** = drops.	
	55 **There's no such thing**: deciding it's a hallucination.
56-57 **It is the bloody Business** (murder) **which informs** (takes form) **Thus** (in this way) **to mine Eyes.**	
57 **the one half World**: the half where it's night.	
58 **Nature seems dead** = there's no sign of life.	58 Moving on to a new topic. Looking around and realizing that "time and place do now adhere".
59-60 **the Curtain'd sleep**: Picture a four-poster bed with curtains around it. **Witchcraft celebrates**: Witches **celebrate** their ritual **Offerings** to Pale *Hecate*, their goddess.	
60-64 **and wither'd Murder** (murder, the withered old man), **Alarum'd** (awakened to action) **by his Sentinel** (lookout), **the Wolf, Whose howl's his Watch** (whose howl is murder's signal to act), **thus** (as I now move) **with his stealthy pace, With** *Tarquin's* **ravishing** (pillaging) **strides, towards his design** (towards his intended prey) **Moves like** (as silent as) **a Ghost.**	63 **strides**: Folio has 'sides'. **Tarquin** was King of Rome, who committed such savage atrocities that they abolished the monarchy in 500 B.C.
64-68 **firm-set**: unlike everything else in this shifty night. **which way they walk** = which direction my steps go. **prate** = tattle. **the present horror** = the spell of horror of this moment. **suits with it**: is suitable for a murder. In other words, Earth, don't hear my clattering steps, for fear your stones will tattle where I am (and call somebody in) and break the spell of horror, which suits a murder.	64 Praying to not be interrupted. 65 **which way they walk**: Folio has 'which they may walk'.
68 **Whiles I threat, he lives** = while I stand here threatening murder, he lives.	68 Deciding to shut up and act.
69 **Words to the heat of deeds too cold breath gives**: While I stand here talking, the air coming from my mouth cools my heat of passion.	
71 **Knell** = funeral bell.	

SCENA SECUNDA.

Enter Lady Macbeth.

LADY MACBETH

1   That which hath made them drunk, hath made me bold:
2   What hath quench'd them, hath given me fire.
3   ❡ Hark, ❡ peace: it was the Owl that shriek'd,
4   The fatal Bell-man, which gives the stern'st good-night.
5   ❡ He is about it, the Doors are open:
6   And the surfeited Grooms do mock their charge
7   With Snores. I have drugg'd their Possets,
8   That Death and Nature do contend about them,
9   Whether they live, or die.

2.2.b -

Enter Macbeth.

MACBETH

10   Who's there? What ho?

LADY MACBETH

11   Alack, I am afraid they have awak'd,
12   And 'tis not done: th' attempt, and not the deed,
13   Confounds us: ❡ Hark: ❡ I laid their Daggers ready,
14   He could not miss 'em. ❡ Had he not resembled
15   My Father as he slept, I had done 't.
16   My Husband?

MACBETH

17   I have done the deed:
18   ❡ Didst thou not hear a noise?

LADY MACBETH

19   I heard the Owl scream, and the Crickets cry.
20   Did not you speak?

MACBETH

21   When?

LADY MACBETH

22   Now.

MACBETH

23   As I descended?

LADY MACBETH

24   Ay.

2.2.a A court in Macbeth's castle at Inverness. Interior. Night.

Purpose: To show Lady Macbeth's new state of mind. Before the murder she was resolute; now that it's done, she has already begun to waver and fear.

Drama: Will they be caught?

What	Why
1 **That**: the wine. It made them drunk, but I drank and it made me bold.	1 Congratulating herself; noting how clear-headed and brave she feels.
2 **What** (wine), **hath quench'd them** (put their fire out; put them to sleep) **hath given me fire** (courage).	
3 **Hark** = Listen. **peace** = (to herself) be quiet! The **Owl's shriek** was an omen of death.	3 Startling badly. Implied stage direction: noise offstage.
4 **fatal Bell-man**: The town crier rang the bell when someone was near death. **stern'st good-night**: sternest because it's forever.	4 Scrambling over things in her mind to make sure they have thought of everything.
5. **He** (Macbeth) **is about it** (is doing it now). **the Doors are open**: Presumably Macbeth has opened Duncan's door.	
6 **surfeited**: over-served with wine. **mock their charge** (make a mockery of their guard duty).	
7 **Possets** = bowls of hot milk curdled with a strong infusion of liquor.	
8 **contend about them** = argue over whether they are alive or dead.	

2.2.b Purpose: 1. To draw a sharp contrast between 'before' and 'after'. The man who went in was the redoubtable hero who defeated two armies and saved Scotland; the man who comes out is rudderless, terrified by a cricket. 2. To put Lady Macbeth where she must witness the dead Duncan. For her role in the rest of the play to work, she must also have blood on her hands.

Drama: Can Lady Macbeth prevent Macbeth from falling to pieces?

What	Why
	10 **Who's there**: reacting to a noise as he leaves Duncan's chamber.
11 **they have awak'd**: the chamberlains.	11 Panicking that it was the sound of Macbeth getting caught in the act.
12-15 **th' attempt and not the deed, Confounds us**: If Macbeth has attempted but not killed Duncan, we are undone. **their Daggers**: those of the chamberlains. **He** (Macbeth) **could not miss 'em**. Had he (Duncan) **not resembled My Father as he slept, I had done 't** (I would have killed him myself).	13 **Hark**: Implied stage direction: she hears Macbeth, but does not yet see him.
	16 **My Husband**: flooding with relief.
	17 **I have done the deed**: in shock. Fearing they will be caught.
	19 **Owl** and **Crickets**: assuring him the noises were not threats.
	20 **Did not you speak?**: making sure it was him she heard.
23 **Descended** = came downstairs	
24 **Ay** = yes	

MACBETH

25 Hark, who lies i' th' second Chamber?

LADY MACBETH

26 *Donalbain.*

MACBETH

27 This is a sorry sight.

LADY MACBETH

28 A foolish thought, to say a sorry sight.

MACBETH

29 There's one did laugh in's sleep,
30 And one cried 'Murder', that they did wake each other:
31 I stood, and heard them: but they did say their Prayers,
32 And address'd them again to sleep.

LADY MACBETH

33 There are two lodg'd together.

MACBETH

34 One cried 'God bless us', and 'Amen' the other,
35 As they had seen me with these Hangman's hands:
36 ¶ List'ning their fear, I could not say 'Amen',
37 When they did say 'God bless us'.

LADY MACBETH

38 Consider it not so deeply.

MACBETH

39 But wherefore could not I pronounce 'Amen'?
40 I had most need of Blessing, and 'Amen' stuck in my throat.

LADY MACBETH

41 These deeds must not be thought
42 After these ways: so, it will make us mad.

MACBETH

43 Methought I heard a voice cry, 'Sleep no more:
44 *Macbeth* does murder Sleep', the innocent Sleep,
45 Sleep that knits up the ravel'd Sleeve of Care,
46 The death of each day's Life, sore Labour's Bath,
47 Balm of hurt Minds, great Nature's second Course,
48 Chief nourisher in Life's Feast.

LADY MACBETH

49 What do you mean?

What	Why
25 **Who lies i' th' second Chamber**: Who is sleeping in the second room?	25 **Hark**: Implied stage direction: noise offstage. Worrying about an experience he just had involving the occupants of the chamber next to Duncan's. 26 *Donalbain*: settling the question. 27 **This is a sorry sight**: looking at his blood-soaked hands, realizing he's done a terrible thing. 28 **A foolish thought, to say a sorry sight**: snapping him back to focus on the plan; 'don't think about it'.
29-32 **There's one did laugh in's sleep, And one cried 'Murder'**: On his way from Duncan's room, Macbeth heard two men wake up from dreams — one dreamed of something funny, the other of murder. **address'd them again to sleep** = went back to sleep.	29-32 Fretting over the fact he was not able to say 'Amen', as he explains below.
33 **lodg'd**: put to bed. Related to the modern term, 'lodgings'.	33 **two lodg'd together**: mistakenly believing he's worried about being caught, reassuring him that what he heard was only two guests sleeping.
35 **As** = as if. **Hangman's hands**: blood-covered hands. 36 **List'ning** (to) **their fear:** hearing their fearful voices.	35 Finally getting to his point: fearing that he has severed himself from God.
38 **Consider it not so deeply** = don't think about it. 39 **wherefore** = why. 40 **'Amen' stuck in my throat**: I was not able to utter 'Amen'; not able to get the word past my throat. 41 **thought** = thought of. 42 **After these ways** = in this way. **so** = if we do so. 43 **Methought** = I thought. 45 **knits up** = repairs. **ravel'd** = tangled. **Sleeve** = skein or length of thread. **Care** = worry. Sleep, that soothes worry the way a weaver untangles thread. 46 **The death of each day's Life:** When we fall asleep, that day is gone forever. **sore Labour's Bath**: Sleep is like a soothing bath after a hard day's work. 47-48 **Balm of hurt Minds**: Sleep soothes a troubled mind the way an ointment (balm) soothes an injury. **Nature's second Course**: If **Life** is a **Feast**, being awake is the first course; dreaming is the second. 48 **Chief nourisher** = which gives the most nutrition.	38 Exhorting him to be brave and focus on getting out of the hall where they might be caught. 39 Refusing to be quieted; demanding help. 41 Again trying to end the conversation and get him out of the dangerous hall. 43 Panicking that he'll never sleep again. Begging for relief from this state. 46 **FORWARD**: will Macbeth ever be able to sleep again?
	49 **What do you mean**: Snapping him to attention.

MACBETH

50 Still it cried, 'Sleep no more' to all the House:

51 '*Glamis* hath murder'd Sleep, and therefore *Cawdor*

52 Shall sleep no more: *Macbeth* shall sleep no more'.

LADY MACBETH

53 Who was it, that thus cried? Why worthy *Thane*,

54 You do unbend your Noble strength, to think

55 So brain-sickly of things: ¶ Go get some Water,

56 And wash this filthy Witness from your Hand.

57 ¶ Why did you bring these Daggers from the place?

58 They must lie there: go carry them, and smear

59 The sleepy Grooms with blood.

MACBETH

60 I'll go no more:

61 I am afraid, to think what I have done:

62 Look on 't again, I dare not.

LADY MACBETH

63 Infirm of purpose:

64 Give me the Daggers: ¶ the sleeping, and the dead,

65 Are but as Pictures: 'tis the Eye of Childhood,

66 That fears a painted Devil. ¶ If he do bleed,

67 I'll gild the Faces of the Grooms withal,

68 For it must seem their Guilt.

Exit.

Knock within.

MACBETH

69 Whence is that knocking?

70 ¶ How is 't with me, when every noise appalls me?

71 ¶ What Hands are here? hah: they pluck out mine Eyes.

72 Will all great *Neptune's* Ocean wash this blood

73 Clean from my Hand? No: this my Hand will rather

74 The multitudinous Seas incarnadine,

75 Making the Green one, Red.

Enter Lady Macbeth.

LADY MACBETH

76 My Hands are of your colour: but I shame

77 To wear a Heart so white.

Knock.

78 I hear a knocking at the South entry:

hyperbole

What	Why
	50 **Still it cried**: escalating; begging harder for relief.
54 **unbend** = unstring, like a bow.	54 Changing tack. Bracing him didn't work, so now she's soft-talking him to soothe him.
56 **filthy Witness**: blood, which gives evidence.	56 Redirecting him to be practical.
58-59 **They** (the daggers) **must lie there** (in Duncan's room): **go carry them, and smear The sleepy Grooms with blood** (smear blood on the sleeping chamberlains).	57 **Why did you bring these Daggers**: realizing the deep danger of being caught with the murder weapons, commanding him to return and fix it. This is an implied stage direction: he has two daggers in hand, but they were hidden, and he has now carelessly revealed them.
61-62 **I am afraid, to** even **think of what I have done**: to **Look on 't again** would be even worse, so **I dare not.**	61 Caving in to fear.
63 **Infirm** = enfeebled by illness.	63 Berating him for being a failure.
65-66 **Pictures** = pictures of each other. Looking at a dead person is the same as looking at a sleeping person. **the Eye of Childhood, That fears a painted Devil**: A child fears a picture of a devil as if it were an actual devil.	65 Giving up on him and doing the job herself.
66-68 **If he** (Duncan) **do bleed, I'll gild** (cover with gold; she means with blood) **the Faces of the Grooms withal** (with it), **For it must seem their Guilt** (It must seem they are guilty of the murder).	66 Note: Lady Macbeth is still in command of herself enough to remember their plan to smear blood on the grooms.
	69 **Whence is that knocking**: startling at the noise.
	70 **every noise appalls me**: berating himself for being afraid.
71 **they pluck out mine Eyes**: The Bible enjoins, 'If thine eye offend thee, pluck it out'.	71 Beginning to see the magnitude of his crime.
72 *Neptune's* **Ocean**: all the oceans of the world. Neptune was god of the sea.	72 Trying to get the blood off his hands.
73 **rather** = instead.	
74-75 **The multitudinous Seas incarnadine** = make the many oceans blood-colored. Rather than the sea washing my hand, my hand will make all the world's green seas turn red.	
76-77 **of your colour**: My hands are red like yours. **I shame To wear a Heart so white**: I would be ashamed to be as afraid (white-hearted) as you.	76 Shaming him into action.

79 Retire we to our Chamber:

80 A little Water clears us of this deed.

81 How easy is it then? ¶ Your Constancy

82 Hath left you unattended.

Knock.

83 Hark, more knocking.

84 Get on your Night-Gown, lest occasion call us,

85 And show us to be Watchers: ¶ Be not lost

86 So poorly in your thoughts.

MACBETH

87 To know my deed,

Knock.

88 'Twere best not know myself.

89 ¶ Wake *Duncan* with thy knocking:

90 I would thou couldst.

Exeunt.

SCENA TERTIA.

Enter a Porter.
Knocking within.

PORTER

1 Here's a knocking, indeed: If a man were Porter of Hell Gate, he
2 should have old turning the Key. *[Knock.]*¶ Knock, Knock, Knock.
3 Who's there i' th' name of *Beelzebub*? ¶ Here's a Farmer, that hang'd
4 himself on th' expectation of Plenty: Come in time, have Napkins
5 enough about you, here you'll sweat for 't. *[Knock.]* ¶ Knock,
6 knock. Who's there, i' th' other Devil's Name? ¶ Faith here's an
7 Equivocator, that could swear in both the Scales against either Scale,
8 who committed Treason enough for God's sake, yet could not
9 equivocate to Heaven: oh come in, Equivocator. *[Knock.]* ¶ Knock,
10 Knock, Knock. Who's there? ¶ 'Faith here's an English Tailor come
11 hither, for stealing out of a French Hose: come in Tailor, here you
12 may roast your Goose. *[Knock.]* ¶ Knock, Knock. Never at quiet:
13 What are you? ¶ But this place is too cold for Hell. I'll Devil-Porter
14 it no further: I had thought to have let in some of all Professions,
15 that go the Primrose way to th' everlasting Bonfire. *[Knock.]* ¶
16 Anon, anon, I pray you remember the Porter.

What	Why
79 **Retire we to our Chamber** = Let's go to our room.	
81-82 **Your Constancy** (usual firmness) **Hath left you unattended** (has abandoned and left you unguarded).	Upbraiding him for not paying attention.
84-85 **lest** (for fear) **occasion call us** (we are called), **And show us to be Watchers** (ones who are awake during sleeping hours): If they find us in day clothes, they'll know we were not in bed. 86 **poorly** = dejectedly.	84 Hustling him back on track and under control.
87 **To know my deed**: Knowing that Macbeth killed Duncan, it would be better to not know that I am Macbeth. 90 **I would thou couldst**: I wish you could wake him.	87 Saying goodbye to his former self. 90 Regretting.

2.3.a Courtyard, Macbeth's castle at Inverness. Exterior. Dawn.

Purpose: 1. To provide comic relief after the unbearable tension of the murder. 2. To show the gravity of Macbeth's regicide (killing the king): The porter's imagined victims are in Hell for far lighter crimes. 3. To give the Macbeths time to wash off the blood before returning to the stage.

Drama: Will he ever open the gate?

What	Why
1-2 **he should have old**: In Shakespeare's day, more than enough. cf. the modern colloquialism, 'this is getting old'. 3 **i' th' name of** *Beelzebub*: Play on 'in the name of God'. Beelzebub was one of the princes of Hell in the Bible. 3-4 **hang'd himself on th' expectation of Plenty** = perhaps, ruined himself by borrowing money using his expected crop as collateral. **come in time** = be sure to come on time. 4-6 **have Napkins enough about you, here you'll sweat for 't**: Bring enough napkins to wipe your brow, because in Hell you'll **sweat** for what you've done. **th' other Devil** = Satan. 6 **Equivocator** = one who uses verbal tricks to play both sides. 7 **in both the Scales** = on both sides of the scales of justice at once.	1 Entertaining the audience: pretending he is the keeper of Hell's gate, welcoming different kinds of sinners. Note that of all possible humorous subjects, he chooses condemnation to Hell, which Macbeth was just discussing in very different tones.
8-9 **committed Treason enough for God's sake** (equivocated enough to get God to punish him for treason) **yet could not equivocate to Heaven** (but could not equivocate himself into Heaven). 11 **stealing out of a French Hose**: A customer brought cloth to be made into pants (**hose**), and the tailor made them too tight and stole the leftover cloth. 12 **roast your Goose**: A goose was a tailor's iron. You may heat your iron, but also you may 'cook your goose' – ruin yourself.	*[Knock]*: brackets not in Folio.
13-14 **I'll Devil-Porter it no further**: I'm cold and will give up this game of devil's porter. 14-15 **I had thought to have let in some of all Professions**: I had planned to do a joke on every profession. **Primrose way**: a well-known image for the path of temptation; the 'primrose path of dalliance'. **th' everlasting Bonfire** = Hell. **anon** = soon. 16 **remember the Porter** = remember my performance.	14 **TURN**: tiring of the game, deciding to finally open the gate.

2.3.b -

Enter Macduff, and Lenox.

MACDUFF

17   Was it so late, friend, ere you went to Bed,

18   That you do lie so late?

PORTER

19   Faith Sir, we were carousing till the second Cock: And Drink, Sir,

20   is a great provoker of three things.

MACDUFF

21   What three things does Drink especially provoke?

PORTER

22   Marry, Sir, Nose-painting, Sleep, and Urine. ¶ Lechery, Sir, it

23   provokes, and unprovokes: it provokes the desire, but it takes

24   away the performance. Therefore, much Drink may be said to be

25   an Equivocator with Lechery: it makes him, and it mars him; it

26   sets him on, and it takes him off; it persuades him, and

27   disheartens him; makes him stand to, and not stand to: in

28   conclusion, equivocates him in a sleep, and giving him the Lie,

29   leaves him.

MACDUFF

30   I believe, Drink gave thee the Lie last Night.

PORTER

31   That it did, Sir, i' the very Throat on me: but I requited him for

32   his Lie, and (I think) being too strong for him, though he took up

33   my Legs sometime, yet I made a Shift to cast him.

2.3.c -

Enter Macbeth.

MACDUFF

34   Is thy Master stirring?

35   ¶ Our knocking has awak'd him: here he comes.

LENOX

36   Good morrow, Noble Sir.

MACBETH

37   Good morrow both.

MACDUFF

38   Is the King stirring, worthy *Thane*?

MACBETH

39   Not yet.

2.3.b Purpose: To build anticipation for the revelation of the murder. There is a razor-sharp irony in their laughing expectation of a celebration day with the newly-victorious Duncan, and what we know awaits them in the next room.

Drama: 1. When will they find out Duncan is dead? 2. How will they react?

What	Why
17-18 **Was it so late, friend, ere you went to Bed** (is the fact that you went to bed so late last night) **That you do lie so late** (the reason that you stayed in bed so late this morning)?	17 Teasing him for being slow to let them in.
19 **till the second Cock** = the second time the cock crowed; near dawn.	19 Using humor to make up for his tardiness.
22-24 **Nose-painting** = figuratively, reddening the nose with drink. **provokes the desire** = inflames sexual passion. **takes away the performance** = inhibits sexual performance.	
25-26 **an Equivocator with Lechery**: like the Equivocator above, drink advocates both for and against lechery (unrestrained sexual indulgence). **makes him, and it mars him** = builds up and destroys his (lechery's) reputation. **sets him on, and it takes him off**: sets him onto his beloved like a dog, but also calls him off.	
26-27 **persuades him, and disheartens him** = gives him courage and takes it away.	
27 **stand to** = get an erection.	
28-29 **equivocates him in a sleep** = pun: tricks him (lechery) into sleep; and tricks him during sleep. **giving him the Lie** = pun: accusing him of lying; and making him lie down. **leaves him** = abandons him.	
30 **Drink gave thee the Lie** = Drink proved you false.	
31-33 **i' the very Throat on me** = pun: It poured wine down my throat; also 'in the throat' was a common way to add sharp emphasis to 'give the lie'. **requited** = paid back; got even. Wrestling image: I was **too strong for him**, but **he took up my Legs sometime** = pun: pulled my leg off the ground in wrestling; also made me lift my leg to urinate. **made a Shift** = managed. **cast him** = pun: throw the wrestler to the ground; also urinate or vomit wine to the ground.	

2.3.c Purpose: To further heighten anticipation of the revelation of Duncan's death.

Drama: 1. When will they discover Duncan's been killed? 2. Can Macbeth maintain a facade of innocence?

What	Why
34 **stirring** = awake and moving.	34 Tiring of the game, moving on to business. 35 **Our knocking has awak'd him**: noticing Macbeth's entrance.
36 **Good morrow** = good morning.	
	37 **Good morrow both**: Macbeth playing innocent.

MACDUFF

40 He did command me to call timely on him,

41 I have almost slipp'd the hour.

MACBETH

42 I'll bring you to him.

MACDUFF

43 I know this is a joyful trouble to you:

44 But yet 'tis one.

MACBETH

45 The labour we delight in, Physics pain:

46 This is the Door.

MACDUFF

47 I'll make so bold to call, for 'tis my limited service.
Exit Macduff.

2.3.d -

LENOX

48 Goes the King hence today?

MACBETH

49 He does: ¶ he did appoint so.

LENOX

50 The Night has been unruly:

51 Where we lay, our Chimneys were blown down,

52 And (as they say) lamentings heard i' th' Air;

53 Strange Screams of Death,

54 And Prophesying, with Accents terrible,

55 Of dire Combustion, and confus'd Events,

56 New hatch'd to th' woeful time.

57 The obscure Bird clamour'd the live-long Night.

58 Some say, the Earth was feverous,

59 And did shake.

MACBETH

60 'Twas a rough Night.

LENOX

61 My young remembrance cannot parallel

62 A fellow to it.

What	Why
40 **timely** = early. 41 **slipp'd the hour** = missed the deadline.	40 Apologizing for being a little late.
43 **joyful trouble:** referring to the effort and expense of hosting the King. 44 **yet 'tis one**: Although it is joyful, yet it is a trouble nonetheless. 45 **The labour we delight in** (the work we love)**, Physics pain** (cures pain). This sense of 'physic' is related to the modern 'physician'.	43 Thanking Macbeth for hosting, and congratulating him for being honored with a royal visit. 45 Saying 'It's no trouble'.
47 **I'll make so bold to call** = I will be bold and wake the King. **'tis my limited service** = it's my small job (an accolade to Macbeth, whose service is large).	47 Moving on to the next thing.

2.3.d Purpose and Drama continued from above: to heighten even further anticipation of the revelation.

What	Why
48 **Goes the King hence** = Does the King leave today? 49 **he did appoint so** = he planned to. 50 **The Night has been unruly** = The weather has misbehaved, like a child breaking the rules. 51 **where we lay**: where we lay in bed. **our Chimneys were blown down** = wind blowing down the chimneys sounded like screaming. 52 **as they say:** Perhaps 'lamentings were heard in the air' was a common saying. 54 **with Accents terrible** = in terrifying voices. 55 **dire Combustion** = deadly conflagration. **confus'd Events** = chaos. 56-57 **New hatch'd to th' woeful time** = hatched for the purpose of heralding the impending doom. **obscure Bird** = the owl, symbol of death. 57-59 **clamour'd the live-long Night** = screamed all night. **the Earth was feverous, And did shake**: the earth was like a sick patient, shaking with fever. 61 **My young remembrance** (my memory, which is short because I am young) **cannot parallel** (cannot match). 62 **A fellow to it** (one like it).	48 Getting information on which to base his own plans for the day. 49 Trying to appear nonchalant, but stumbling. 50 Sharing a lingering misgiving that something is amiss, in the hope Macbeth will assuage him. 60 **'Twas a rough Night:** equivocating. Neither refuting nor elaborating. 61 Not satisfied, pressing again for either reassurance or confirmation of his fear.

2.3.e -

Enter Macduff.

MACDUFF

63   O horror, horror, horror,

64   Tongue nor Heart cannot conceive, nor name thee.

MACBETH AND LENOX

65   What's the matter?

MACDUFF

66   Confusion now hath made his Masterpiece:

67   Most sacrilegious Murder hath broke ope

68   The Lord's anointed Temple, and stole thence

69   The Life o' th' Building.

MACBETH

70   What is 't you say? the Life?

LENOX

71   Mean you his Majesty?

MACDUFF

72   Approach the Chamber, and destroy your sight

73   With a new *Gorgon*. ¶ Do not bid me speak:

74   See, and then speak yourselves: ¶ awake, awake,

Exeunt Macbeth and Lenox.

2.3.f -

75   Ring the Alarum Bell: Murder, and Treason,

76   *Banquo,* and *Donalbain: Malcolm* awake,

77   Shake off this Downy sleep, Death's counterfeit,

78   And look on Death itself: up, up, and see

79   The great Doom's Image: *Malcolm, Banquo,*

80   As from your Graves rise up, and walk like Sprites,

81   To countenance this horror. Ring the Bell.

2.3.g -

Bell rings. Enter Lady Macbeth.

LADY MACBETH

82   What's the Business?

83   That such a hideous Trumpet calls to parley

84   The sleepers of the House? Speak, speak.

MACDUFF

85   O gentle Lady,

86   'Tis not for you to hear what I can speak:

2.3.e Purpose: 1. This is the resolution of the long build-up to the revelation that Duncan's been murdered. The old world (Scotland at peace under the benevolent Duncan) dies, the new world (chaos and paranoia under Macbeth) begins. 2. To begin the next drama. 3. To reveal Macduff's character: In contrast to the treacherous Macbeth and the strategic Malcolm, Macduff is ruled by a powerful instinctual sense of right and wrong.

Drama: 1. How will each person react to the news of Duncan's death? 2. Can the Macbeths hide their guilt and get away with murder?

What	Why
64 **Tongue nor Heart cannot conceive, nor name thee** (About the scene he just witnessed) The **Heart** cannot understand (conceive) you, nor can the **Tongue** describe (name) you.	64 Trying, but unable, to report what he's seen.
66 If **Confusion** were an artist, this would be its **Masterpiece.**	66 Lamenting.
67-69 This line turns on a pun: Duncan's body, as the saying goes, is the 'temple of his spirit', as the church is the Temple of God. Duncan is Lord of Scotland; God is Lord of all. Duncan's soul is the spirit of his body; the spirit of God is the life of the church. **Most sacrilegious** (because Duncan is King by divine right) **Murder hath broke ope** (broken open) **The Lord's anointed** (made holy by the application of sanctified ointment) **Temple** (Duncan's body), **and stole thence** (stolen from it) **The Life o' th' Building** (Duncan's soul).	70 **the Life?** playing innocent — pretending not to understand.
73 **new *Gorgon*:** in Greek mythology, Gorgons (including Medusa) were monstrous sisters. If you looked at one you would turn to stone. Duncan's room is now like a Gorgon: Look and you will be destroyed. **Do not bid me speak:** It's too awful to tell.	

2.3.f (Purpose and Drama continued from above)

What	Why
77 **Downy** = soft and gentle. **Death's counterfeit:** sleep is counterfeit death. 79 **great Doom** = final Judgment Day. Duncan's room looks like the end of the world. 80 **as from your Graves:** Harking back to 'death's counterfeit'. **Sprites** = spirits; ghosts. 81 **countenance** = face.	76 **Awake:** sounding the alarm — getting everybody to help him find the murderers.

2.3.g (Purpose continued from above)

Drama: Will Lady Macbeth succeed in masking her guilt?

What	Why
83 **hideous Trumpet** = frightening call to battle. **parley:** in war, a conference of enemies for truce or terms.	83 Playing innocent. 'defending' the house — likening the state of the house to a battlefield.

87 The repetition in a Woman's ear,
88 Would murder as it fell.

2.3.h -
Enter Banquo.
89 O *Banquo, Banquo,* Our Royal Master's murder'd.

LADY MACBETH
90 Woe, alas:
91 What, in our House?

BANQUO
92 Too cruel, anywhere.
93 ¶ Dear *Duff,* I prythee contradict thyself,
94 And say, it is not so.
Enter Macbeth, Lenox, and Rosse.

MACBETH
95 Had I but died an hour before this chance,
96 I had liv'd a blessed time: for from this instant,
97 There's nothing serious in Mortality:
98 All is but Toys: Renown and Grace is dead,
99 The Wine of Life is drawn, and the mere Lees
100 Is left this Vault, to brag of.

2.3.i -
Enter Malcolm and Donalbain.

DONALBAIN
101 What is amiss?

MACBETH
102 You are, and do not know 't:
103 The Spring, the Head, the Fountain of your Blood
104 Is stopp'd, the very Source of it is stopp'd.

MACDUFF
105 Your Royal Father's murder'd.

MALCOLM
106 Oh, by whom?

LENOX
107 Those of his Chamber, as it seem'd, had done 't:
108 Their Hands and Faces were all badg'd with blood,
109 So were their Daggers, which unwip'd, we found
110 Upon their Pillows: they star'd, and were distracted,
111 No man's Life was to be trusted with them.

What	Why
87-88 The repetition in a Woman's ear, Would murder as it fell = It would kill a woman to hear what I can speak.	87 Being gentle and considerate towards her; protecting her.

2.3.h (Purpose continued)

Drama: 1. Will Banquo suspect Macbeth? 2. Can Macbeth mask his guilt?

What	Why
	89 **O *Banquo***: reporting the news; seeking consolation. Note: He has forgotten his intention to shield Lady Macbeth. 91 **in our House**: disguising her unhideable distress as concern for the reputation of her house.
92 **Too cruel, anywhere**: what's important is not that it happened in your house, but that it happened at all.	92 gently redirecting her misguided sentiment.
95-96 **Had I but** (if I had only) **died an hour before this chance** (this mishap), **I had liv'd a blessed time** (my life would have been blessed).	94 **say, it is not so**: praying it's not true. 95 in shock, because he has just murdered the two grooms. He is using a truth – his genuine guilt – to give veracity to a lie – his feigned remorse.
97 **There's nothing serious** (nothing worth caring about) **in Mortality** (before we die). 98 **All** (everything we thought was important) **is but Toys** (child's play). 99-100 **The Wine of Life is drawn** (comparing life to a wine cellar: It's empty), **and the mere Lees** (merely the dregs) **Is left this Vault** (is all that's left in this vault, or cellar), **to brag of.**	100 **brag of**: unintentionally revealing his own worldview, in which personal worth equals bragging rights.

2.3.i Purpose: 1. To begin the chain of murders Macbeth must commit to cover his first one. 2. To show Lady Macbeth beginning to unravel. 3. To show Malcolm's character - he thinks clearly even in an overwhelming crisis.

Drama: 1. Can Macbeth get away with these additional murders? 2. Can Lady Macbeth distract the other men from her husband's crime? 3. Can Malcolm and Donalbain escape?

What	Why
101 **amiss** = gone wrong; out of place. 102 **You are** (amiss), **and do not know 't** (yet). 103 **Spring** source; where water springs from the ground. **Head** = fountainhead. **your Blood**: your bloodline; your family heritage. Conflating blood as in bloodline with literal blood: Duncan's blood has stopped coursing; the bloodline from which you sprang is stopped.	103 Struggling, but unable to clearly tell Donalbain his father is dead because it's so distressing. 105 **Your Royal Father's murder'd**: explaining in clearer terms what Macbeth has spoken perhaps too poetically to be understood.
107 **seem'd** = appeared. 108 **badg'd** = smears of blood looked like badges. 109 **unwip'd**: still bloody. 110 **star'd** = were unfocused. **distracted** = unresponsive. 111 **No man's Life**: They were not fit **to be trusted** guarding anyone, least of all the King.	107 Reporting the disgusting news. **as it seem'd**: perhaps suspecting that the chamberlains were framed.

MACBETH

112 O, yet I do repent me of my fury,

113 That I did kill them.

MACDUFF

114 Wherefore did you so?

MACBETH

115 Who can be wise, amaz'd, temp'rate, & furious,

116 Loyal, and Neutral, in a moment? No man:

117 Th' expedition of my violent Love

118 Outrun the pauser, Reason. Here lay *Duncan*,

119 His Silver skin, lac'd with his Golden Blood,

120 And his gash'd Stabs, look'd like a Breach in Nature,

121 For Ruin's wasteful entrance: there the Murderers,

122 Steep'd in the Colours of their Trade; their Daggers

123 Unmannerly breech'd with gore: who could refrain,

124 That had a heart to love; and in that heart,

125 Courage, to make's love known?

LADY MACBETH

126 Help me hence, ho.

MACDUFF

127 Look to the Lady.

MALCOLM

128 *[aside to Donalbain]* Why do we hold our tongues,

129 That most may claim this argument for ours?

DONALBAIN

130 *[aside to Malcolm]* What should be spoken here,

131 Where our Fate hid in an auger-hole,

132 May rush, and seize us? ¶ Let's away,

133 Our Tears are not yet brew'd.

MALCOLM

134 *[aside to Donalbain]* Nor our strong Sorrow

135 Upon the foot of Motion.

BANQUO

136 Look to the Lady:

137 ¶ And when we have our naked Frailties hid,

138 That suffer in exposure; let us meet,

139 And question this most bloody piece of work,

What	Why
	112 **I do repent me of my fury**: Chastising himself. **NEW DRAMA**: Can Macbeth persuade them that he was justified in killing the chamberlains — that he did it not to prevent them giving evidence, but in a vengeful rage?
114 **wherefore** = why.	114 Thrown by this revelation; asking for justification.
116 **in a moment** = all at the same time.	116 Making his case: excusing himself by pleading an excess of love for Duncan.
117 **Th' expedition** (the haste) **of my violent Love** (of my passionate love for Duncan).	
118 **pauser** = thing which gives pause.	
119 **Silver** = very valuable. **Golden** = most valuable.	
120 **Breach in Nature** = rupture in the natural order.	
121 **for Ruin's wasteful entrance** = through which ruin entered to waste Duncan's life. **there** lay **the Murderers.**	
122 **Colours of their Trade** = the blood red that is the hallmark of murderers.	
123 **Unmannerly** = indecently. **breech'd** = clothed (as in breeches). **refrain** = hold back.	
124-125 **that had a heart to love** = that loved Duncan. **and in that heart, Courage** = and also had courage in his heart. **to make's** (make his) **love known** = to show his love, by killing his murderers.	
127 **Look to** = see to.	126 **Help me hence**: presumably, Lady Macbeth faints. Or maybe uses a truth (her genuine horror) to give veracity to a lie (a pretended faint to distract them from establishing the identity of the murderer).
128-129 **Why do we hold our tongues** (why are you and I silent) **That most may claim this argument for ours** (who as Duncan's sons can most claim to be affected by this)?	128 Noticing that he and Donalbain have instinctively kept quiet; puzzling over it.
130 **What should be spoken** = what is there to say?	130 Counseling his brother to trust no one.
131-132 **Fate**: an enemy waiting to kill us. **auger-hole** = a hole in a post or beam made by an auger or hand-drill. We are right to hold our tongues when our enemy could be anywhere (perhaps spying through an auger-hole). **Let's** (run) **away.**	132 Suggesting that both of them should flee. **NEW DRAMA**: Can Malcolm and Donalbain escape?
133 **Our Tears are not yet brew'd** = We can't cry until we are safe.	
134-135 **Nor our strong Sorrow** yet **Upon the foot of Motion**: Our strong grief hasn't yet begun to emerge.	134 Agreeing to Donalbain's suggestion to flee. They can't grieve until they are safe.
136 **Look to the Lady** = Take care of the Lady.	
137-138 **when we have our naked Frailties hid, That suffer in exposure** = when we have clothed our frail bodies which suffer from exposure to cold. They just got out of bed and are still in nightgowns.	137 Note their state of undress corresponds to how vulnerable they feel in the face of the tragedy. Getting dressed is a step back towards normal.
139 **question this most bloody piece of work** = investigate this murder.	

140 To know it further. ⸿ Fears and scruples shake us:
141 In the great Hand of God I stand, and thence,
142 Against the undivulg'd pretence, I fight
143 Of Treasonous Malice.

MACDUFF
144 And so do I.

ALL
145 So all.

MACBETH
146 Let's briefly put on manly readiness,
147 And meet i' th' Hall together.

ALL
148 Well contented.
Exeunt [all but Malcolm and Donalbain].

2.3.j -

MALCOLM
149 What will you do?
150 Let's not consort with them:
151 ⸿ To show an unfelt Sorrow, is an Office
152 Which the false man does easy.
153 ⸿ I'll to England.

DONALBAIN
154 To Ireland, I:
155 ⸿ Our separated fortune shall keep us both the safer:
156 Where we are, there's daggers in men's smiles;
157 The near in blood, the nearer bloody.

MALCOLM
158 This murderous Shaft that's shot,
159 Hath not yet lighted: and our safest way,
160 Is to avoid the aim. ⸿ Therefore to Horse,
161 ⸿ And let us not be dainty of leave-taking,
162 But shift away: there's warrant in that Theft,
163 Which steals itself, when there's no mercy left.
Exeunt.

What	Why
140-143 Fears and scruples (doubts) **shake us** (make us weak of purpose). Reordered: **In the great Hand of God** (in the stronghold of God's justice) **I stand, and thence** (from that stronghold), **I fight Against the undivulg'd pretence** (the still-hidden falseness) **Of Treasonous Malice** (malice against the King).	140 Asserting his own innocence and his determination to unmask the treason.
	144 **so do I**: seconding Banquo.
	145 **So all**: everybody jumping in.
146 briefly = quickly. **put on manly readiness** = pull ourselves together; also, literally get dressed and perhaps arm ourselves.	
	(stage directions) *[all but Malcolm and Donalbain]*: not in Folio. Inferred.

2.3.j Purpose: To show Malcolm in a crisis, clear-headed, strategic and decisive. This prepares us to believe that he can capably lead an army, and that ultimately he will be a good king.

Drama: Can the princes escape?

What	Why
151-153 To show an unfelt Sorrow (to feign sorrow, **is an Office** (task) **Which the false man** (liar or traitor) **does easy** (easily). **I'll** (go) **to England.**	151 Realizing that any one – or all – of the men around them could be an enemy merely pretending to grieve for Duncan. Deciding to leave right now.
156-157 daggers in men's smiles = any one of them could be false, hiding murderous plans behind a smile. **The near in blood** (the more closely related to Duncan – us, his sons), **the nearer bloody** (the more likely to be bloodied). Whoever killed Duncan probably wants us dead, too.	156 Realizing they are in danger not merely generally, but in this very moment.
158 Shaft = arrow. 159 **lighted** = landed. The crime is not yet complete.	158 Further realizing that it's time to break the rules to save themselves, even the basic rules of civility.
161 dainty = particular in manners. **162-163 shift** = sneak. **there's warrant** (justification) **in that Theft, Which steals itself** (stealing away; sneaking away without leave), **when there's no mercy left** (when one is in danger of murder).	162 TURN: By sneaking away, Malcolm prevents Macbeth from ensnaring him and his brother.

Scena Quarta.

OLD MAN

1 Threescore and ten I can remember well,
2 Within the Volume of which Time, I have seen
3 Hours dreadful, and things strange: but this sore Night
4 Hath trifled former knowings.

ROSSE

5 Ha, good Father,
6 Thou seest the Heavens, as troubled with man's Act,
7 Threatens his bloody Stage: by th' Clock 'tis Day,
8 And yet dark Night strangles the travelling Lamp:
9 Is 't Night's predominance, or the Day's shame,
10 That Darkness does the face of Earth entomb,
11 When living Light should kiss it?

OLD MAN

12 'Tis unnatural,
13 Even like the deed that's done: ¶ On Tuesday last,
14 A Falcon tow'ring in her pride of place,
15 Was by a Mousing Owl hawk'd at, and kill'd.

ROSSE

16 And *Duncan's* Horses,
17 (A thing most strange, and certain)
18 Beauteous, and swift, the Minions of their Race,
19 Turn'd wild in nature, broke their stalls, flung out,
20 Contending 'gainst Obedience, as they would
21 Make War with Mankind.

OLD MAN

22 'Tis said, they eat each other.

ROSSE

23 They did so:
24 To th' amazement of mine eyes that look'd upon 't.

2.4.b -

Enter Macduff.

25 Here comes the good *Macduff*.
26 ¶ How goes the world Sir, now?

2.4.a Inverness. Exterior. Day.

Purpose: 1. To show that time has passed. 2. To show how Macbeth's rule has poisoned the whole country.

Drama: Can they come to grips with the unnatural and threatening omens?

What	Why
1 **Three score and ten** = seventy years (a score is twenty).	1 Sharing his suffering.
2 **Within the Volume of which Time**: Imagine Time as a multi-volume encyclopedia - within that particular book.	
3 **sore Night** = bitter night.	
4 **trifled former knowings**: made formerly known ills seem as trifles.	
6-7 **Thou seest the Heavens** (you see that God), **as troubled with man's Act** (because He is angry over the murder), **Threatens his bloody Stage** (threatens the world – man's stage – which man has made bloody). God is punishing mankind by threatening to destroy the world.	6 Puzzling out what's happening in the world.
7 **by th' Clock 'tis Day** = according to the clock it's day.	
8 **Night strangles** (suffocates) **the travelling Lamp** (the sun, which travels through the sky).	
9-11 What is the reason — **Is 't Night's predominance** (has night overwhelmed day), **or the Day's shame** (or is the day ashamed to appear), **That Darkness does the face of Earth entomb** (that darkness buries the Earth as if in a tomb), **When living Light should kiss it?** (in day-time, when the sun should kiss the Earth's face). **living Light**: in contrast to being entombed.	
12-13 'Tis (the darkness is) **unnatural, Even like** (just like) **the deed that's done** (the murder).	12 Offering a possible explanation. Elaborating with further evidence.
14-15 **tow'ring in her pride of place**: circling high in the air ('towering' is a falconry term). **Mousing Owl** = an owl whose usual prey is tiny mice. **hawk'd at** = attacked from the air.	
17 **most strange, and certain** = very strange but definitely true.	17 Amplifying with further strange evidence.
18 **Minions** = favorites.	
20 **Contending 'gainst Obedience** = fighting against their customary obedience. **as** = as if.	
22 **they** = the horses.	22 Going one further.
23 **They did so**: The horses did eat each other.	23 Confirming.

2.4.b Purpose: To inform the audience how Macbeth has gotten away with the murder (for now) and become King.

Drama: 1. What is the state of Scotland? 2. Can Macduff resolve their uncertainty?

What	Why
	25 **Here comes the good *Macduff***: welcoming him.

MACDUFF

27   Why see you not?

ROSSE

28   Is 't known who did this more than bloody deed?

MACDUFF

29   Those that *Macbeth* hath slain.

ROSSE

30   Alas the day,
31   What good could they pretend?

MACDUFF

32   They were suborned,
33   *Malcolm*, and *Donalbain* the King's two Sons
34   Are stol'n away and fled, which puts upon them
35   Suspicion of the deed.

ROSSE

36   'Gainst Nature still,
37   Thriftless Ambition, that will ravin up
38   Thine own life's means: ¶ Then 'tis most like,
39   The Sovereignty will fall upon *Macbeth*.

MACDUFF

40   He is already nam'd, and gone to Scone
41   To be invested.

ROSSE

42   Where is *Duncan's* body?

MACDUFF

43   Carried to Colmekill,
44   The Sacred Storehouse of his Predecessors,
45   And Guardian of their Bones.

ROSSE

46   Will you to Scone?

MACDUFF

47   No Cousin, I'll to Fife.

ROSSE

48   Well, I will thither.

MACDUFF

49   Well may you see things well done there: Adieu
50   Lest our old Robes sit easier than our new.

What	Why
27 **Why see you not** = Why do you ask – don't you see (that it's still dark at noon)?	27 Sharing his suffering.
28 **more than bloody** = worse than ordinary murder. Regicide was sacrilege.	28 Seeking news.
29 **Those that *Macbeth* hath slain** = Duncan's chamberlains.	29 Giving the bad news.
30 **Alas**: an expression of sorrow or pity. **Alas the day** = I am sorry that day ever happened. 31 **What good** (good result) **could they pretend** (intend to achieve)?	30 Puzzling mingled with sorrow.
32 **suborned** = paid or induced to do it.	32 Answering Rosse's question with more bad news.
34-35 **Are stol'n away** = have sneaked off. **which puts upon them Suspicion** = which makes them suspects.	
36 **still** = more; parricide (killing one's father) on top of regicide (killing one's king). 37-38 **Thriftless** (wasteful) **Ambition, that will ravin up** (greedily devour) **Thine own life's means** (means of support). **ravin** or ravish = plunder or rape. 38 **most like** = most likely. 39 **The Sovereignty** = the crown. 40 **Scone** = the ancient royal site where Scottish Kings were crowned. Edward the Confessor stole the Stone of Scone in 1296 and took it to Westminster Abbey in London, where all English monarchs have been crowned since.	36 Pronouncing judgment on the princes. 38 Now that's settled, moving on to the consequence. 40 Reporting more facts. Note: It would have been important to Shakespeare's audience to know that Duncan was properly interred. Also: Macbeth is being crowned instead of attending the funeral because the country is in danger without a King.
43 **Colmekill:** the island of Iona on Scotland's west coast. Like St. Colme's Inch, it was named after St. Columba who established a monastery there in A.D. 563. 44 **The Sacred Storehouse of his Predecessors**: Iona was the traditional burial ground for Scottish Kings.	
47 **I'll** (I'll go) **to Fife**: Macduff is the Thane of Fife.	47 Note: By choosing to skip the coronation and go home, Macduff seems to already have doubts about Macbeth. And the next time Macbeth mentions Macduff, it is with mistrust.
48 **thither** = to there; to Scone.	
49 **may you see things well done there** = I hope you will see the coronation done well there. **Adieu** = French for goodbye. 50 **Lest** =I hope not. **Robes** = metaphor for government: I hope we can wear our new rule under Macbeth as well as the old under Duncan.	49 Saying goodbye and wishing them all better days.

Rosse

51   Farewell, Father.

Old Man

52   God's benison go with you, and with those

53   That would make good of bad, and Friends of Foes.

Exeunt omnes.

What	Why
51 **Father**: a term of affection.	
52-53 **benison** = blessing. **and** (may God's blessing also go) **with those That would make good of bad** (make the best of a bad situation)**, and Friends of Foes** (and reconcile enemies).	52 Agreeing, and also wishing for better days.
	omnes = all

ACTUS TERTIUS. SCENA PRIMA.

Enter Banquo.

BANQUO

1 Thou hast it now, King, Cawdor, Glamis, all,
2 As the weird Women promis'd, and I fear
3 Thou play'dst most foully for 't: yet it was said
4 It should not stand in thy Posterity,
5 But that myself should be the Root, and Father
6 Of many Kings. If there come truth from them,
7 As upon thee *Macbeth*, their Speeches shine,
8 Why by the verities on thee made good,
9 May they not be my Oracles as well,
10 And set me up in hope. ¶ But hush, no more.

3.1.b -

Sennet sounded. Enter Macbeth as King, Lady Macbeth, Lenox, Rosse, Lords and Attendants.

MACBETH

11 Here's our chief Guest.

LADY MACBETH

12 If he had been forgotten,
13 It had been as a gap in our great Feast,
14 And all-thing unbecoming.

MACBETH

15 Tonight we hold a solemn Supper sir,
16 And I'll request your presence.

BANQUO

17 Let your Highness
18 Command upon me, to the which my duties
19 Are with a most indissoluble tie
20 Forever knit.

MACBETH

21 Ride you this afternoon?

BANQUO

22 Ay, my good Lord.

MACBETH

23 We should have else desir'd your good advice

3.1.a Forres castle — the royal seat (Macbeth, now king, has moved to Forres). Interior. Day.

Purpose: To set up the murder of Banquo. He should realize he's in danger, and either persuade Macbeth of his loyalty, or flee to England like Malcolm. Instead, he decides to remain silent, which neither assuages Macbeth's suspicion nor puts him safely out of Macbeth's reach.

Drama: How will Banquo decide to act on the prophecy?

What	Why
2-3 **I fear Thou play'dst most foully** = I fear you cheated. 4 **It** (the succession of the crown) **should not stand** (remain) **in thy Posterity** (in your bloodline). 6 **If there come truth from them** = if they speak truth. 7 **their Speeches shine** = their sayings shine truly. 8-9 **verities** = truths. **Oracles** = mouthpieces of fate. Why shouldn't I believe that they foretell my future as well?	1 Trying to figure out what to do: Macbeth has acted on the prophecy and become king. But I too had a part in the prophecy. Should I act to bring about the coronation of my offspring? 8 **TURN**: He decides to trust the prophecy, which is his undoing. Note: The Witches tricked him exactly as he foretold: They 'won him with an honest trifle, to betray him in deepest consequence'. **FORWARD**: reemphasize the question, will Banquo's offspring be kings? 10 **hush, no more**: implied stage direction. He hears them coming. We'll never know what he was going to say.

3.1.b Purpose: To further prepare for the murder of Banquo. We see Macbeth distancing himself from his comrade, and also gleaning certain information, which we later learn are details Macbeth needs to plan the murder. This is our first view of the new Macbeth, whose only concern is to eliminate potential threats by any means necessary.

Drama: 1. Can Banquo assuage Macbeth's fear of him? 2. Can Macbeth assuage Banquo's fear of him?

What	Why
(stage directions) **Sennet**: signal call on a trumpet	11 **Here's our chief Guest**: buttering up Banquo so that he won't get suspicious. Note: Macbeth uses the royal 'we' nine times in this interview, underlining his royal status.
12 **If he had been forgotten** = if we had forgotten to invite him. 13 **It had been** = it would have been. **gap** = omission. 14 **all-thing** = in all ways. 15 **solemn Supper** = formal banquet (to mark his ascension to the throne).	12 Following her husband's lead, exalting Banquo by saying he's the most important guest.
17-20 **Let your Highness Command upon me** (give me any command), **to the which my duties** (my loyalties) **Are with a most indissoluble tie** (unbreakable bond) **Forever knit** (forever bound). Give me any command and I will do it, because of my unbreakable loyalty to you.	16 All but commanding Banquo to attend. 17 Jumping to obey even more than asked, to assure Macbeth that, although he is a witness to Macbeth's secret (the prophecy), he is not a danger.
21 **Ride you** = will you go horseback riding?	21 Perhaps seeing that Banquo is equipped for riding? **FORWARD**: Why does Macbeth want to know if Banquo is going riding?
23 **We should have** (I would have) **else** (if you weren't going) **desir'd** (sought) **your good advice**.	23 Downplaying his displeasure at Banquo's planned absence, to lure him into a false sense of security.

24 (Which still hath been both grave, and prosperous)
25 In this day's Council: but we'll take tomorrow.
26 ¶ Is 't far you ride?

BANQUO

27 As far, my Lord, as will fill up the time
28 'Twixt this, and Supper. Go not my Horse the better,
29 I must become a borrower of the Night,
30 For a dark hour, or twain.

MACBETH

31 Fail not our Feast.

BANQUO

32 My Lord, I will not.

MACBETH

33 We hear our bloody Cousins are bestow'd
34 In England, and in Ireland, not confessing
35 Their cruel Parricide, filling their hearers
36 With strange invention. ¶ But of that tomorrow,
37 When therewithal, we shall have cause of State,
38 Craving us jointly. ¶ Hie you to Horse:
39 Adieu, till you return at Night.
40 ¶ Goes *Fleance* with you?

BANQUO

41 Ay, my good Lord: our time does call upon's.

MACBETH

42 I wish your Horses swift, and sure of foot:
43 And so I do commend you to their backs.
44 Farewell.

Exit Banquo.

45 ¶ Let every man be master of his time,
46 Till seven at Night, to make society
47 The sweeter welcome:
48 We will keep ourself till Supper time alone:
49 While then, God be with you.

Exeunt Lords [all except Macbeth and a Servant].

50 Sirrah, a word with you: Attend those men
51 Our pleasure?

SERVANT

52 They are, my Lord, without the Palace Gate.

What	Why
24 **still** = always. **grave** = serious. **prosperous** = profitable. 25 **we'll take** (settle for) receiving your advice **tomorrow.**	
	26 **Is 't far you ride**: getting information to plan Banquo's murder. 27 Demonstrating his loyalty by reporting his plans as faithfully as he can.
27-28 **As far, my Lord, as will fill up the time 'Twixt this and Supper:** as far as I can go before supper time. 28 **Go not my Horse the better** = if my horse doesn't go faster. 29-30 **twain** = two. **I must become a borrower of the Night, For a dark hour, or twain** = My day's ride must borrow an hour or two from the night. I won't be back until past sunset. 31 **Fail not our Feast** = Don't fail to be on time at my feast.	31 Adding a slight threat, to make sure he does as planned. 32 **I will not**: acknowledging the threat.
33 **bloody Cousins**: Malcolm and Donalbain. **bestow'd** = hidden. 35-36 **Parricide** = father murder. **filling their hearers** = filling their hearers' ears. **strange invention** = lies. 36 **But** we will talk **of that tomorrow.** 37 **therewithal** = upon that topic. **cause of State**: official State business. 38-39 **Craving us jointly** = requiring both our participation. **Hie you** = go. **Adieu** = goodbye (in French).	33 Inciting the Lords' anger against the princes (and directing it away from himself).
	40 **Goes *Fleance* with you**: offhandedly ascertaining Fleance's whereabouts. **FORWARD**: Does Macbeth have designs on Fleance as well? Taking his leave.
41 **our time does call upon's** = it's time to go.	
43 **to their backs** = to your horses' backs. 'Good riding'.	43 Giving him an elaborate farewell.
45 **Let every man be master of his time** = All of you are free to do as you will.	45 Releasing them from his audience.
46-47 **to make society The sweeter welcome** = In order to be a better host to society. 48 **We will keep ourself till Supper time alone** = I will remain alone until supper time. 49 **While** = until. 50-51 **Attend those men** (are those men waiting) **Our pleasure** (to see what I want)? 52 **without** = outside.	46 Making excuse for why he wants them to leave (he can't tell them he has an appointment with assassins). 48 Note that he has now also excluded his wife. (stage directions) *[all except Macbeth and a Servant]*: not in Folio. Inferred.

MACBETH

53   Bring them before us.
Exit Servant.

3.1.c -

54   To be thus, is nothing, but to be safely thus:
55   Our fears in *Banquo* stick deep,
56   And in his Royalty of Nature reigns that
57   Which would be fear'd. 'Tis much he dares,
58   And to that dauntless temper of his Mind,
59   He hath a Wisdom, that doth guide his Valour,
60   To act in safety. ¶ There is none but he,
61   Whose being I do fear: and under him,
62   My *Genius* is rebuk'd, as it is said
63   *Mark Anthony's* was by *Caesar*. He chid the Sisters,
64   When first they put the Name of King upon me,
65   And bade them speak to him. Then Prophet-like,
66   They hail'd him Father to a Line of Kings.
67   Upon my Head they plac'd a fruitless Crown,
68   And put a barren Sceptre in my Gripe,
69   Thence to be wrench'd with an unlineal Hand,
70   No Son of mine succeeding: ¶ if 't be so,
71   For *Banquo's* Issue have I fil'd my Mind,
72   For them, the gracious *Duncan* have I murder'd,
73   Put Rancours in the Vessel of my Peace
74   Only for them, and mine eternal Jewel
75   Given to the common Enemy of Man,
76   To make them Kings, the Seeds of *Banquo* Kings.
77   ¶ Rather than so, come Fate into the List,
78   And champion me to th' utterance.
79   ¶ Who's there?
Enter Servant, and two Murderers.
80   Now go to the Door, and stay there till we call.
Exit Servant.

3.1.c Purpose: 1. To advance the plot towards the murder of Banquo. 2. To show Macbeth's new mindset: Now he sees only threats, and he no longer confides in Lady Macbeth.

Drama: Can he persuade himself — and us — that he has no choice but to kill Banquo?

What	Why
54 **To be thus** (to be temporarily king) **is worth nothing, but to be safely thus** would fulfill finally give me what I need.	54 Building his case for why he must kill Banquo.
55 **in** = of. **stick** = stab.	
56 **his Royalty of Nature** = his moral self, which is worthy of a king.	55 The first argument: I can't use my power as King to cow Banquo into submission. His royalty of nature — his integrity — won't be subdued.
56-57 **that Which would be fear'd**: he is man enough that he wouldn't be afraid to expose me. **'Tis much he dares**: he is very brave.	
58 **And** = in addition to. **dauntless** = fearless.	
59 **He hath a Wisdom, that doth guide his Valour**: If he does expose me, he will have the wisdom to keep himself safe from me.	
60 **none but he** = no one but Banquo.	
61-63 **under him** (compared to Banquo), **My Genius is rebuk'd** (my genius appears less), as **Mark Anthony** was eclipsed by **Caesar.** Mark Anthony was a great Roman leader in the 1st century B.C., but lived in the shadow of the much-greater emperor Julius Caesar.	61 The second argument: Banquo is better than me. People won't look up to me as long as Banquo is there, 'rebuking my genius'.
63 **chid** = chided; chastised.	
65 **Prophet-like** = in the manner of prophecy.	
67 **fruitless Crown**: i.e. I would be King without heirs.	67 The third argument: I can't bear to have sacrificed myself only for the sake of Banquo's heirs.
68 **barren Sceptre** = same as fruitless crown. **Gripe** = grip.	
69 **Thence** (from my grip) **to be wrench'd with** (by) **an unlineal Hand** (the hand of someone not of my descent; another's son).	
70 **succeeding** = succeeding to the throne.	
71 **Issue** = progeny. **fil'd** = defiled.	
72 **them**: Banquo's sons.	
73-74 Reordered: **Only for them** I have **put Rancours** (bitter ill-feelings) **in the Vessel** (cup) **of my** (from which I should drink) **Peace. eternal Jewel** = soul.	
75 **Enemy of Man** = Satan. For Banquo's sons I have condemned myself to Hell.	
76 **Seeds** = progeny.	
77-78 **Rather than so** (rather than let that happen), **come Fate into the List** (jousting arena), **And champion me** (be my champion) **to th' utterance** (to the utter end). A champion in jousting fought on someone else's behalf.	77 Praying to Fate to be on his side.

81 Was it not yesterday we spoke together?

FIRST MURDERER

82 It was, so please your Highness.

MACBETH

83 Well then,

84 Now have you consider'd of my speeches:

85 Know, that it was he, in the times past,

86 Which held you so under fortune,

87 Which you thought had been our innocent self.

88 ¶ This I made good to you, in our last conference,

89 Pass'd in probation with you:

90 How you were borne in hand, how cross'd:

91 The Instruments: who wrought with them:

92 And all things else, that might

93 To half a Soul, and to a Notion craz'd,

94 Say, 'Thus did *Banquo*'.

FIRST MURDERER

95 You made it known to us.

MACBETH

96 I did so:

97 And went further, which is now

98 Our point of second meeting.

99 ¶ Do you find your patience so predominant,

100 In your nature, that you can let this go?

101 Are you so Gospel'd, to pray for this good man,

102 And for his Issue, whose heavy hand

103 Hath bow'd you to the Grave, and beggar'd

104 Yours forever?

FIRST MURDERER

105 We are men, my Liege.

MACBETH

106 Ay, in the Catalogue ye go for men,

107 As Hounds, and Greyhounds, Mongrels, Spaniels, Curs,

108 Shoughs, Water-Rugs, and Demi-Wolves are clept

109 All by the Name of Dogs: ¶ the valued file

110 Distinguishes the swift, the slow, the subtle,

111 The Housekeeper, the Hunter, every one

3.1.d Purpose: 1. To advance the plot further towards the murder of Banquo. 2. To prepare for later in the play, so that we will believe Macbeth has the persuasive power to consolidate control and that defeating him will require an army.

Drama: Can he persuade them to murder Banquo?

What	Why
	81 Note: Macbeth knows that when the time comes to actually stab Banquo, deep resolve will be needed. They have to hate Banquo in order for this plan to succeed.
84 **have you consider'd of** (thought over) **my speeches** (the things I said).	84 Making certain they are completely persuaded that Banquo was their persecutor.
85 **he** = Banquo.	
86 **held you so under fortune** = held you back. Perhaps they were passed over for promotion?	
87 **our** = my. You must know that it was Banquo, not me, who kept you down.	
88 **made good** = proved.	
89 **Pass'd in probation** = passed the test of proof.	
90 **borne in hand** = deceived. **cross'd** = betrayed.	
91 **Instruments** = tools or agents whereby he secretly betrayed you. **who he wrought** (whom he turned against you) **with them** (with these means).	
93-94 The facts are so obvious that they would say **To half a Soul, and to a Notion craz'd** (even to a half-wit or a crazy person), **Thus did _Banquo_** (Banquo did this).	
97 **further**: from the problem to the solution.	
99-100 **Do you find your patience so predominant, In your nature**: in your nature, does patience so outweigh honor and justice.	99 Daring them: 'Are you man enough?'
101 **Gospel'd** = influenced by the Bible.	
102 **Issue** = children.	
102-104 Banquo, **whose heavy hand** (powerful secret dealings) **Hath bow'd you to the Grave** (crushed you almost to death), **and beggar'd Yours** (made your families beggars) **forever.**	
105 **We are men**: In other words, no, we are not ruled by patience, but by self-preservation.	105 Proving his manhood.
106 **in the Catalogue**: Your names are on the list of men.	106 Again, asking if they are man enough to do it. Rather than simply saying 'are you man enough', he expertly draws an elaborate image of the men of the world, sorted into ranks according to their relative bravery, then asks which rank they are in.
107-109 **Cur** = mongrel or aggressive dog. **Shough** = rough-haired lapdog. **Water-Rug** = water-spaniel (a now extinct breed). **Demi-Wolf** = half-breed wolf-dog. **clept** = named. **All by the Name of Dogs**: all dogs, from the best to the worst, are called 'dogs', and all men, from the best to the worst, are called 'men'. **the valued file** = the file in which men are sorted by their value.	
110 **subtle** = clever.	
111 **Housekeeper** = watch dog.	

Murderers are so desperate for money → will kill
Macbeth only wants to kill to get to place
of higher power

112 According to the gift, which bounteous Nature
113 Hath in him clos'd: whereby he does receive
114 Particular addition, from the Bill,
115 That writes them all alike: and so of men.
116 ¶ Now, if you have a station in the file,
117 Not i' th' worst rank of Manhood, say 't,
118 And I will put that Business in your Bosoms,
119 Whose execution takes your Enemy off,
120 Grapples you to the heart; and love of us,
121 Who wear our Health but sickly in his Life,
122 Which in his Death were perfect.

SECOND MURDERER
123 I am one, my Liege,
124 Whom the vile Blows and Buffets of the World
125 Hath so incens'd, that I am reckless what I do,
126 To spite the World.

FIRST MURDERER
127 And I another,
128 So weary with Disasters, tugg'd with Fortune,
129 That I would set my Life on any Chance,
130 To mend it, or be rid on 't.

MACBETH
131 Both of you know *Banquo* was your Enemy.

SECOND MURDERER
132 True, my Lord.

MACBETH
133 So is he mine: and in such bloody distance,
134 That every minute of his being, thrusts
135 Against my near'st of Life: ¶ and though I could
136 With bare-fac'd power sweep him from my sight,
137 And bid my will avouch it; ¶ yet I must not,
138 For certain friends that are both his, and mine,
139 Whose loves I may not drop, but wail his fall,
140 Who I myself struck down: ¶ and thence it is,
141 That I to your assistance do make love,
142 Masking the Business from the common Eye,
143 For sundry weighty Reasons.

What	Why
112-113 According to the gift (to his natural gifts)**, which bounteous** (generous) **Nature Hath in him clos'd** (has bestowed within him, like a gift enclosed in a box).	112 Note: The length to which Macbeth bolsters them shows that he well understands how much easier it is to promise than to actually stab a man to death.
114-115 Particular addition = particular adjective added to his name; swift, slow, subtle. **the Bill, That writes them all alike** = the sheet upon which all are listed as merely men. Imagine two lists: The first is just a list of names; the second – 'the valued file' – sorts them into categories, from best to worst.	
116-117 if you have a station in the file, Not i' th' worst rank of Manhood: Imagine a stack of file folders, sorted from best to worst, each containing men's names. If your names are filed not under 'worst'.	
117 **say 't =** then speak up for yourselves.	
118 **I will put that Business in your Bosoms** = I will entrust your hearts with that business.	
119 **whose execution takes your Enemy off** = (that business) whose completion gets rid of your enemy.	
120 **Grapples you** = binds you. **us** = me, your King.	
121-122 Who wear our Health but sickly in his Life = I, whose health is sickly so long as he lives. **Which in his Death were perfect** = but which would be perfect if he were dead.	
123-126 I am one (I am a man), **my Liege** (my King), **Whom the vile Blows and Buffets of the World** (the hard knocks of life) **Hath so incens'd** (have so enraged)**, that I am reckless** (careless of the consequences) **what I do, To spite the World** (to get even with the world).	123 Guaranteeing his capacity for violence, regardless of the consequences.
127-130 And I am another like him, **So weary with** (because of) **Disasters,** and **tugg'd with** (dragged down by bad) **Fortune, That I would set** (gamble) **my Life on any Chance, To** either **mend it** (mend my life)**, or be rid on 't** (be rid of my life, i.e. be dead).	127 Also guaranteeing violence and complete recklessness.
	131 *Banquo* was your Enemy: making extra certain.
133-135 mine = my enemy. **bloody distance**: a fencing image: Banquo is at the right distance for stabbing Macbeth. **That every minute of his being** (every minute he remains alive)**, thrusts Against my near'st of Life** (stabs at my vital organs; threatens my life).	133 Providing an excuse for keeping his own role secret.
135-136 I could With bare-fac'd power (without hiding my power behind this secrecy) **sweep him from my sight** (kill him as easily as sweeping a roach from the kitchen floor).	
137 **bid my will avouch it** = justify it as the King's prerogative.	
138 **friends that are both his, and mine** = mutual friends.	
139 **I may not drop** = I may not alienate. **but wail his fall** = but I must bewail the fall of Banquo.	
140 **Who I myself** (will secretly have) **struck down.**	
141 **I to your assistance do make love** = I court your assistance.	
142 **Masking** (keeping hidden) **the Business from the common Eye** (from public view).	
143 **For sundry weighty Reasons** = for various important reasons.	

Second Murderer

144   We shall, my Lord,

145   Perform what you command us.

First Murderer

146   Though our Lives—

Macbeth

147   Your Spirits shine through you.

148   ❡ Within this hour, at most,

149   I will advise you where to plant yourselves,

150   Acquaint you with the perfect Spy o' th' time,

151   The moment on 't, for 't must be done Tonight,

152   ❡ And something from the Palace: always thought,

153   That I require a clearness; ❡ and with him,

154   To leave no Rubs nor Botches in the Work:

155   *Fleance,* his Son, that keeps him company,

156   Whose absence is no less material to me,

157   Than is his Father's, must embrace the fate

158   Of that dark hour: ❡ resolve yourselves apart,

159   I'll come to you anon.

Second Murderer

160   We are resolv'd, my Lord.

Macbeth

161   I'll call upon you straight: abide within,

162   ❡ It is concluded: *Banquo,* thy Soul's flight,

163   If it find Heaven, must find it out Tonight.

Exeunt.

Scena Secunda.

Enter Lady Macbeth, and a Servant.

Lady Macbeth

1   Is *Banquo* gone from Court?

Servant

2   Ay, Madam, but returns again Tonight.

Lady Macbeth

3   Say to the King, I would attend his leisure,

4   For a few words.

What	Why
	144 **We shall**: **TURN**: Success. The murderers are committed.
147 **Your Spirits shine through you**: I see in your faces that I can trust you.	147 Politely cutting him off with a compliment. Ending the conversation.
149 **where to plant yourselves** = where to hide. 150 **Acquaint you with the perfect Spy o' th' time** = tell you the perfect time to look out for him. 151 **The moment on 't** = the exact moment. 152-153 **something** (some distance) **from the Palace: always thought** (always keep the thought in mind), **That I require a clearness** (clearness from blame). 154 **Rubs nor Botches** = rough spots or bungling.	
156 **absence**: absence from life. **material** = important.	
157-158 **must embrace the fate Of that dark hour**: must die. 158 **resolve yourselves apart** = make up your minds in private. 159 **anon** = soon.	
161 **straight** = straightaway. **abide within** = wait inside (presumably: I will return to give you further instructions). 162-163 **thy Soul's flight, If it find Heaven, must find it out Tonight** = If your soul is ever to find Heaven, it must find it tonight.	

3.2.a A room at Forres. Interior. Dusk.

Purpose: 1. To show the distance that has opened between Lady Macbeth and her husband. 2. To show how far she has disintegrated: She now envies the dead.

Drama: Can she get her husband to relieve her anguish of remorse?

What	Why
	1 **Is** *Banquo* **gone**: 1. Trying to find out what's happening. 2. Trying to hide her anxiety from the servant. Note: Why is she asking about Banquo? Macbeth has never told her (at least not on stage) about Banquo's role in the prophecy. But his behavior toward Banquo has been so fearful that, even if he hasn't told her, she knows something is very wrong.
3 **I would attend his leisure**: probably to ask for information and assurance regarding Banquo.	3 Note how the relationship between Macbeth and his wife has changed. In Act 1 she was his 'dearest partner of greatness'. Now she must '**attend his leisure**', like a common courtier.

SERVANT

5   Madam, I will.

Exit.

LADY MACBETH

6   Nought's had, all's spent,

7   Where our desire is got without content:

8   'Tis safer, to be that which we destroy,

9   Than by destruction dwell in doubtful joy.

3.2.b -

Enter Macbeth.

10   How now, my Lord, why do you keep alone?

11   Of sorriest Fancies your Companions making,

12   Using those Thoughts, which should indeed have died

13   With them they think on: things without all remedy

14   Should be without regard: what's done, is done.

MACBETH

15   We have scorch'd the Snake, not kill'd it:

16   She'll close, and be herself, whilst our poor Malice

17   Remains in danger of her former Tooth.

18   ❡ But let the frame of things disjoint,

19   Both the Worlds suffer,

20   Ere we will eat our Meal in fear, and sleep

21   In the affliction of these terrible Dreams,

22   That shake us Nightly: Better be with the dead,

23   Whom we, to gain our peace, have sent to peace,

24   Than on the torture of the Mind to lie

25   In restless ecstasy.

26   ❡ *Duncan* is in his Grave:

27   After Life's fitful Fever, he sleeps well,

28   Treason has done his worst: nor Steel, nor Poison,

29   Malice domestic, foreign Levy, nothing,

Banquo is still alive

What	Why
6 **Nought's had** (nothing's gained)**, all's spent**: We've spent all — sold our souls to the Devil — but in exchange, can't enjoy the crown. 7 **Where our desire is got** (We got what we wanted; the crown) **without content** (but we can't enjoy it). 8-9 **'Tis safer, to be that which we destroy** (Duncan, whom we destroyed, who is safe from further harm), **Than by destruction dwell** (than by having destroyed him gained a life) **in doubtful** (uncertain, because of the great danger of being found out) **joy.**	8 Regretting her folly. Her envy of the dead Duncan is a measure of the depth of her regret.

3.2.b Purpose: This is a major plot step in their downward trajectory. Macbeth is now driving ahead with his program of murders, without consulting his wife; she has lost her fire and lapsed into a paralysis of regret.

Drama: 1. Can she regain her place as his dearest partner of greatness? 2. Can he get relief from the 'scorpions' in his mind?

What	Why
10 **why do you keep alone**: Why do you keep away from me? 11 **Of sorriest Fancies your Companions making** = keeping company with your worst fantasies of failure. 12-13 **Using** = dwelling on. **Thoughts** (thoughts of the murdered Duncan), **which should indeed have died With them they think on** (with Duncan and the grooms). You should have forgotten the murders as soon as they were done.	10 Seeking to comfort him, and get comfort from him.
13-14 **things without all remedy** (problems with no solution) **Should be without regard** (should not be dwelled upon). **what's done, is done**: it's impossible to change what we've done, so there's nothing to be gained from dwelling on it.	13 Trying to persuade him — and herself — not to dwell on it.
15 **scorch'd** = slashed; or perhaps burned on the surface only, without damaging it internally. 16 **close** = heal. **be herself** = return to her healthy state. **poor Malice** — weak desire to harm her. 17 **former Tooth** = capacity for harm she had before we wounded her.	15 Rejecting her call for calm; sounding the alarm. Angrily demanding that she see it his way.
18-19 **let the frame of things disjoint** = Let the framework that holds the world together come apart at the joints. **Both the Worlds** = Earth and Heaven. I would rather destroy Heaven and Earth than continue to suffer these nightmares. 22-23 **Better be** = it would be better to be. **to gain our peace** = to get relief from the sting of ambition. **sent to peace** = sent to the peace of Heaven.	18 In other words, it's time not for calm but for killing. Remember, he has just contracted the murder of Banquo and Fleance.
24-25 **on the torture of the Mind to lie** = to be stretched on the torture rack of my paranoid dreams and imaginings. **ecstasy** = chaos of the mind. In Shakespeare's day, 'ecstasy' did not have the modern meaning of euphoria. 28 **Treason has done his worst**: Duncan has been killed by treason. It cannot harm him further. **Steel**: sword or knife. 29 **Malice domestic** = rebellion. **foreign Levy** = a demand for money or troops from a foreign power, at threat of invasion.	27 **after Life's fitful Fever**: Note: Macbeth now sees life as no more than a fitful fever.

30 Can touch him further.

LADY MACBETH

31 Come on:
32 Gentle my Lord, sleek o'er your rugged Looks,
33 Be bright and Jovial among your Guests Tonight.

MACBETH

34 So shall I Love, ¶ and so I pray be you:
35 Let your remembrance apply to *Banquo,*
36 Present him Eminence, both with Eye and Tongue:
37 ¶ Unsafe the while, that we must lave
38 Our Honours in these flattering streams,
39 And make our Faces Vizards to our Hearts,
40 Disguising what they are.

LADY MACBETH

41 You must leave this.

MACBETH

Psychic Pain →

42 O, full of Scorpions is my Mind, dear Wife:
43 Thou know'st, that *Banquo* and his *Fleance* lives.

LADY MACBETH

44 But in them, Nature's Copy's not eterne.

MACBETH

45 There's comfort yet, they are assailable,
46 ¶ Then be thou jocund: ere the Bat hath flown
47 His Cloister'd flight, ere to black *Hecate's* summons
48 The shard-born Beetle, with his drowsy hums,
49 Hath rung Night's yawning Peal,
50 There shall be done a deed of dreadful note.

LADY MACBETH

51 What's to be done?

MACBETH

52 Be innocent of the knowledge, dearest Chuck,
53 Till thou applaud the deed: ¶ Come, seeling Night,
54 Scarf up the tender Eye of pitiful Day,
55 And with thy bloody and invisible Hand
56 Cancel and tear to pieces that great Bond,

What	Why
30 (None of these) **Can touch him further**: Duncan is now safe from all these threats.	
32 **sleek o'er your rugged Looks** = smooth over your worried face.	32 **TURN**: She gives up cheering him up. **NEW DRAMA**: Can she at least get him to keep up appearances?
34 **So shall I** = I will be so. **so I pray be you** = I pray that you be so as well.	34 Promising to be good.
35 **Let your remembrance apply to** *Banquo* = especially remember Banquo.	35 Ensuring that, if Banquo makes it to the feast, she will not give Banquo any cause for suspicion. Note: If Banquo arrives, it means the murder attempt has failed. **FORWARD**: What will happen with Banquo at the feast?
36 **Present him Eminence** = honor him above others. **Eye and Tongue** = looks and words.	
37 **Unsafe the while** = while we are unsafe in our position; new to the crown.	
37-38 **lave Our Honours in these flattering streams** = wash our reputations by pouring streams of flattery. **lave** = wash, as in 'lavatory'.	
39 **Vizards** = masks. Until we are secure in the throne, we must flatter the nobles to hide what we are.	37 **Unsafe the while**: inventing a false justification for why he has asked her to butter up Banquo. So far, he plans to keep the Banquo murder secret from even her.
41 **this** = this irrational obsession.	41 Tugging him back toward rational balance. Note: The fact that she says this indicates that Macbeth is very distressed.
	42 **Scorpions**: desperately trying to get her to see how bad it is.
44 **Nature's Copy**: their existence; they are copies of Human Nature. Or perhaps 'copy' as in 'copyhold' or lease: Their lease on life will expire. They will die.	44 Soothing him with the idea that they won't last forever; all he has to do is wait them out.
45 **assailable** = attackable.	45 **TURN**: Taking comfort, but not in the sense she means: taking comfort in their imminent death.
46 **jocund** = jolly.	
46-47 **ere** = before. **Cloister'd flight** = hidden, as a monk in a cloister is hidden from the world. (It's hard to see bats fly at night.) **Hecate** = queen of the Witches.	
48 **shard-born** = dung-bred. **drowsy hums**: beetles emerge at twilight, so the hum of their wings heralds night.	50 **There shall be done a deed of dreadful note**: violating his own resolve to keep it secret from her in his desire to share their reason to celebrate. 'As soon as Banquo and Fleance are dead, we can relax'.
49 **Night's yawning Peal** = the bell that makes us yawn by reminding us to go to bed. Before the beetle, responding to Hecate's summons, summons us to bed with his humming.	
	51 **What's to be done**: demanding to know exactly what 'the deed of dreadful note' will be.
52 **Chuck**: a term of endearment; chicken.	52 **Be innocent**: protecting her from having to share in the guilt.
53 **seeling** = to sew a cover over a falcon's eyes to tame it. Macbeth wants Night to sew a scarf over Day's eyes, so it can't see his deed.	
54 **Scarf up** = blindfold. **pitiful** = full of compassion.	
55 **thy bloody and invisible Hand:** anthropomorphizing Night, as a murderer. (Anthropomorphizing = speaking as if it were a person.)	
56 **Cancel and tear to pieces that great Bond**: cancel the contract. Perhaps referring to Banquo's lease on life as above? Or the prophecy that torments Macbeth? Or the moral law preventing him from killing Banquo and his issue?	

57 Which keeps me pale. Light thickens,
58 And the Crow makes Wing to th' Rooky Wood:
59 Good things of Day begin to droop, and drowse,
60 Whiles Night's black Agents to their Preys do rouse.
61 ¶ Thou marvell'st at my words: but hold thee still,
62 Things bad begun, make strong themselves by ill:
63 So prythee go with me.

Exeunt.

SCENA TERTIA.

Enter three Murderers.

FIRST MURDERER
1 But who did bid thee join with us?

THIRD MURDERER
2 *Macbeth.*

SECOND MURDERER
3 He needs not our mistrust, since he delivers
4 Our Offices, and what we have to do,
5 To the direction just.

FIRST MURDERER
6 Then stand with us:
7 ¶ The West yet glimmers with some streaks of Day.
8 Now spurs the lated Traveler apace,
9 To gain the timely Inn, and near approaches
10 The subject of our Watch.

THIRD MURDERER
11 Hark, I hear Horses.

BANQUO
12 *[within]* Give us a Light there, ho.

SECOND MURDERER
13 Then 'tis he:
14 The rest, that are within the note of expectation,
15 Already are i' th' Court.

FIRST MURDERER
16 His horses go about.

What	Why
57-58 **pale** = sick with worry. **thickens** = darkens. **Crow makes Wing to th' Rooky Wood**: Crows roost at sunset. A **rook** is a kind of crow. 59 **Good things of Day begin to droop, and drowse**: Innocent creatures of the day are getting sleepy. 60 **Night's black Agents** = nocturnal predators. **to their Preys do rouse** = wake up to go seek their prey. 61 **marvell'st** = look astonished. 62 **Things bad begun, make strong themselves by ill** = The fruits of a crime are secured by more crime.	61 Note: This is an implied stage direction. She has frozen with fear upon learning he is murdering again. **TURN**: now it is Macbeth who is eager to kill, and Lady Macbeth who hesitates.

3.3.a On the road, a mile from Forres. Exterior. Night.

Purpose: To sharpen our anxiety for Banquo's impending danger.

Drama: Will the murderers be able to properly execute their plan?

What	Why
	1 **who did bid thee join with us**: They enter in the middle of a conversation. Apparently Macbeth, to ensure success, has sent a Third Murderer to join the ambush. First Murderer was suspicious of the new arrival. Second now soothes his worry.
3 **He needs not our mistrust** = We don't need to mistrust him. 3-4 **delivers Our Offices** = relays our instructions. 5 **To the direction just** = exactly the same; as in 'to a man' or 'to the letter'. **Just**: as in 'just the same'.	3 Mini-drama: Will 1 and 2 accept 3 as accomplice? This perhaps shows us that Macbeth's mistrust now extends to his own assassins. 5 In other words, since his instructions are identical to ours, he must have heard them from Macbeth, which proves he's trustworthy.
6 **Then stand with us**: Then you can stay. 7 **yet** = still. There is still some light in the western sky. 8-9 **Now spurs** (now is the hour that hastens) **the lated Traveler** (the traveler who has been made late) **apace** (to hurry) **To gain the timely Inn** (to reach the inn in time, before dark).	6 **TURN**: He is persuaded. 8 Banquo and son are returning. He cautions that they will be hurrying.
9-10 **near approaches The subject of our Watch** = Here comes the person we are watching for.	9 Alerting them the time has come.
	11 **I hear horses**: Agreeing the horses are coming. 12 **Give us a Light**: Speaking to a groom, to whom he and Fleance are giving their horses.
13 **Then 'tis he**: then it's Banquo.	13 Making sure they are about to kill the right people.
14 **note of expectation** = list of expected guests. The rest of the invited guests are already inside the castle. 16 **His horses go about**: The groom is taking his horses around (presumably to the stable in back).	16 Worrying that this will interrupt their plan.

THIRD MURDERER

17 Almost a mile: but he does usually,
18 So all men do, from hence to th' Palace Gate
19 Make it their walk.

3.3.b -
Enter Banquo and Fleance, with a Torch.

SECOND MURDERER

20 A Light, a Light.

THIRD MURDERER

21 'Tis he.

FIRST MURDERER

22 Stand to 't.

BANQUO

23 It will be Rain Tonight.

FIRST MURDERER

24 Let it come down. *[Strikes out Banquo's light]*

BANQUO

25 O, Treachery!
26 Fly good *Fleance*, fly, fly, fly,
27 Thou may'st revenge. ¶ O Slave! *[Dies.]*
Fleance escapes.

THIRD MURDERER

28 Who did strike out the Light?

FIRST MURDERER

29 Was 't not the way?

THIRD MURDERER

30 There's but one down: the Son is fled.

SECOND MURDERER

31 We have lost
32 Best half of our Affair.

FIRST MURDERER

33 Well, let's away, and say how much is done.
Exeunt.

What	Why
18 **So all men do**: Banquo, like everyone, usually dismounts here and walks almost a mile to the palace gate.	18 Reassuring First Murderer that this will not disrupt the plan. Note: Shakespeare may have inserted this to solve the problem of horses on stage.

3.3.b Purpose: To resolve the long-building drama of Macbeth's mistrust of Banquo, and launch a new set of dramas.

Drama: Will the murderers kill Banquo and Fleance?

What	Why
20 **A Light:** I see a light coming. In other words, 'Here they come!'	20 Readying himself to jump out.
	21 **'Tis he:** Also readying himself.
22 **Stand to 't:** Don't fall back from it (from the job of murdering); don't flinch; don't fail.	22 Also readying himself.
	23 Dramatic contrast between Banquo's relaxed observing and the tense murderers.
	24 *Strikes out Banquo's light*: This is not in the Folio, but is inferred from the remark on line 28.
26 **Fly** = flee. 27 **Thou may'st revenge:** You may live to revenge my murder. **Slave** = worthless person.	26 Seeing they can't both get away, Banquo fights the murderers to protect his son's escape.
	Fleance escapes: inferred. Not in Folio.
	28 **Who did strike out the Light:** Angrily demanding to know whom to blame.
29 **Was 't not the way:** Wasn't that the plan?	
30 **but** = only. 31-32 **We have lost** (we have failed) **Best half of our Affair** (half of our job) 'best' maybe for emphasis, as in 'fully half'.	30 **the Son is fled: TURN:** they've succeeded in killing Banquo, but failed to kill Fleance. **FORWARD:** Will Fleance become king?
33 **let's away** = let's get away. **and say** (tell Macbeth) **how much** (of the job) **is done.**	

SCENA QUARTA.

Banquet prepared. Enter Macbeth, Lady Macbeth, Rosse, Lenox, Lords, and Attendants.

MACBETH

1 You know your own degrees, sit down:
2 At first and last, the hearty welcome.

LORDS

3 Thanks to your Majesty.

MACBETH

4 Ourself will mingle with Society,
5 And play the humble Host:
6 ¶ Our Hostess keeps her State, but in best time
7 We will require her welcome.

LADY MACBETH

8 Pronounce it for me Sir, to all our Friends,
9 For my heart speaks, they are welcome.

3.4.b -

Enter First Murderer.

MACBETH

10 See they encounter thee with their hearts' thanks.
11 Both sides are even: here I'll sit i' th' midst,
12 ¶ Be large in mirth, anon we'll drink a Measure
13 The Table round. *[Goes to door.]* ¶ There's blood upon thy face.

FIRST MURDERER

14 'Tis *Banquo's* then.

MACBETH

15 'Tis better thee without, than he within.
16 Is he dispatch'd?

FIRST MURDERER

17 My Lord his throat is cut, that I did for him.

MACBETH

18 Thou art the best o' th' Cut-throats,
19 ¶ Yet he's good that did the like for *Fleance:*
20 If thou didst it, thou art the Nonpareil.

FIRST MURDERER

21 Most Royal Sir

3.4.a A state room at Forres. Interior. Night.

Purpose: To give the Macbeths — and the audience — a fleeting glimpse of the life they dreamed of (and for which they killed Duncan) before it is wrenched away.

Drama: Can they succeed at being a gracious King and Queen?

What	Why
1-2 **degrees** = ranks. Presumably, the highest-ranking sits closest to the King. **first and last** = highest to lowest.	1 Playing the magnanimous and lighthearted King.
4 **Ourself** (royal 'we') **will mingle with Society** (will rise from my throne and mix with the guests).	4 Unlike Duncan, who actually was a humble king, Macbeth is attempting to elicit approval by calling himself a humble king.
6 **keeps her State** = stays in her throne. 6-7 **in best time** (when the time is most appropriate), **We will require her welcome** (I will ask her to welcome you).	6 Following protocol: The king welcomes them first, then the queen.
8 **Pronounce it for me**: She prefers to stay in her throne, and let him do the personal greeting. 9 **my heart speaks, they are welcome**: although I'm not getting up to go embrace them, my heart is full of welcome for them.	8 Note that both Lady Macbeth and her husband make excuses for her not getting up from her throne. Why doesn't she? Perhaps the thrill of sitting in state as queen for the first time? Perhaps protocol?

3.4.b Purpose: 1. To witness Macbeth's anguish of failure. We can almost hear the Witches laughing: They tricked him into murdering his best friend for nothing. 2. To establish that what he had hoped was a one-time necessity is now a pattern: Each murder requires further murders.

Drama: 1. Will the Murderer confess that Fleance got away? 2. How will Macbeth react to this news?

What	Why
10 **encounter** = respond to. 11 **Both sides are even** (There are equal numbers seated at both sides of the table): **here I'll sit i' th'midst** (so I'll sit in the middle).	10 Pointing out that the Lords have acknowledged her, e.g. by applauding or bowing.
12-13 **Be large in mirth**: Enjoy yourselves fully. **anon we'll drink a Measure The Table round** = Soon all of us around the table will have a drink together.	12 Excusing himself from the table for a moment. Encouraging them to enjoy themselves meanwhile. *Goes to door*: Inferred. Not in Folio.
13 **There's blood upon thy face**: To the murderer.	13 Chastising him for potentially giving away the secret.
14 '**Tis** *Banquo's* **then** = If so, then it is Banquo's blood.	14 Defending himself; and bragging that he has succeeded in killing Banquo.
15 **better thee without, than he within** = That blood is better on your outside than Banquo's inside.	15 Praising him.
16 **dispatch'd** = killed.	
	18 **Thou art the best**: Praising him. Worrying they didn't finish the job.
19 **he's** also **good that did the like** (the same thing) **for** *Fleance*. 20 **Nonpareil** = one without equal.	

₂₂ *Fleance* is scap'd.

MACBETH
₂₃ Then comes my Fit again:
₂₄ I had else been perfect;
₂₅ Whole as the Marble, founded as the Rock,
₂₆ As broad, and general, as the casing Air:
₂₇ ¶ But now I am cabin'd, cribb'd, confin'd, bound in
₂₈ To saucy doubts, and fears. ¶ But *Banquo's* safe?

FIRST MURDERER
₂₉ Ay, my good Lord: safe in a ditch he bides,
₃₀ With twenty trenched gashes on his head;
₃₁ The least a Death to Nature.

MACBETH
₃₂ Thanks for that:
₃₃ ¶ There the grown Serpent lies, the worm that's fled
₃₄ Hath Nature that in time will Venom breed,
₃₅ No teeth for th' present. ¶ Get thee gone, tomorrow
₃₆ We'll hear ourselves again.
Exit Murderer.

3.4.c -

LADY MACBETH
₃₇ My Royal Lord,
₃₈ You do not give the Cheer, the Feast is sold
₃₉ That is not often vouch'd, while 'tis a-making:
₄₀ 'Tis given, with welcome: to feed were best at home:
₄₁ From thence, the sauce to meat is Ceremony,
₄₂ Meeting were bare without it.

3.4.d -
Enter the Ghost of Banquo, and sits in Macbeth's place.
MACBETH
₄₃ Sweet Remembrancer:

What	Why
22 **scap'd** = escaped.	22 Mustering his courage and confessing.
23 **Then comes my Fit again**: I can feel another panic attack rising.	
24 **else** = if not for this.	24 Struggling to control his panic at the news. The escape of Fleance causes the Witches' prophecy – that Banquo's issue will be kings – to loom huge in his imagination. It's so extreme that he gives four consecutive images of his fear closing in around him.
25 **Whole as the Marble** = as imperturbable as a marble statue. **founded** = rooted in the ground. cf. 'foundation'	
26 **casing Air** = the air around us. In other words, as expansive as the atmosphere.	
27 **cabin'd, cribb'd** = locked in a cabin or corncrib.	
28 **saucy** = insolent; pushing themselves in where they are not wanted. **safe** = safely dead.	28 **But *Banquo's* safe**: Grasping at the shred of good news in an effort to regain control.
29 **safe** = dead. Macbeth is safe from Banquo. **bides** = waits.	
30 **trenched gashes** = cuts in his head that lay open like trenches in the earth.	30 Reassuring him.
31 **The least a Death to Nature** = the smallest of the gashes would alone be enough to kill him.	32 **Thanks for that:** Taking some comfort.
33 **grown Serpent** = Banquo. **worm** = Fleance.	
34-35 **Hath Nature that in time will Venom breed** (although in time it will grow poisonous), **No teeth for th' present** (so far it has no teeth to harm us).	34 Telling himself he may still be safe: He has time to deal with Fleance later.
36 **We'll hear ourselves again:** We will speak again.	36 **FORWARD:** what murder is he going to plan tomorrow?

3.4.c Purpose: To remind us of the easy grace Lady Macbeth had hoped to project, to sharpen by contrast the image of what actually follows.

Drama: 1. Can Lady Macbeth get the dinner back on track? 2. More generally, can she keep alive the picture of them as honored royals?

What	Why
38-42 **You do not give the Cheer** (You do not cheer the guests with your talk), **the Feast is sold** (It may as well be just a meal bought in an inn), **That is not often vouch'd, while 'tis a-making: 'Tis given, with welcome** (if you don't often assure them, during the meal, that it is freely given): **to feed were best at home** (mere eating is best done at home): **From thence** (when away from home), **the sauce to meat** (the relish that makes it tasty) **is Ceremony** (is the feasting rituals, e.g. toasts and welcome), **Meeting were bare** (feasting would be meaningless) **without it.**	38 Pulling him back to his duties as host. Note: At the top of the play, Macbeth and his wife were in complete unison. Now he is doing things without including her.

3.4.d Purpose: 1. To irrevocably shatter the Macbeths' dream of graced royalty, in front of everyone. 2. To destroy the old Macbeth and usher in the new one, governed not by strategy but by terrifying supernatural visions.

Drama: 1. Can Lady Macbeth maintain a veneer of normalcy? 2. Will Macbeth unwittingly reveal to the Lords that he ordered Banquo's murder?

What	Why
43 **Remembrancer**: officer whose job is to remind the King of his appointments.	43 Thanking her for bringing him back to the task at hand.

44 ¶ Now good digestion wait on Appetite,
45 And health on both.

LENOX

46 May 't please your Highness sit.

MACBETH

47 Here had we now our Country's Honour, roof'd,
48 Were the grac'd person of our *Banquo* present:
49 Who, may I rather challenge for unkindness,
50 Than pity for Mischance.

ROSSE

51 His absence (Sir)
52 Lays blame upon his promise. ¶ Please 't your Highness
53 To grace us with your Royal Company?

MACBETH

54 The Table's full.

LENOX

55 Here is a place reserv'd Sir.

MACBETH

56 Where?

LENOX

57 Here my good Lord.
58 ¶ What is 't that moves your Highness?

MACBETH

59 Which of you have done this?

LORDS

60 What, my good Lord?

MACBETH

61 Thou canst not say I did it: never shake
62 Thy gory locks at me.

ROSSE

63 Gentlemen rise, his Highness is not well.

LADY MACBETH

64 Sit worthy Friends: my Lord is often thus,
65 And hath been from his youth. Pray you, keep Seat,
66 The fit is momentary, upon a thought
67 He will again be well. If much you note him
68 You shall offend him, and extend his Passion,

What	Why
44-45 **good digestion wait on Appetite:** (to the guests) let good digestion follow appetite. **And health on both** = and good health follow both.	44 Blessing the meal.
47-48 **Here had we now our Country's Honour, roof'd** (We would have all the nobility of the country under our roof), **Were the grac'd person of our *Banquo* present** (if the gracious Banquo were present).	48 Providing himself with an alibi — pretending he doesn't know Banquo is already dead.
49-50 **Who, may I rather challenge for unkindness, Than pity for Mischance**: I hope he is merely truant, in which case I will challenge him for being unkind, rather than absent due to an accident, in which case I will pity him.	
52 **Lays blame upon his promise** = Banquo's absence makes him blameworthy, in light of his promise to attend.	52 Rosse is taking the King's side against Banquo.
52-53 **Please't your Highness To grace us with your Royal Company?** = Will you please sit with us?	52 Reminding the king as tactfully as he can that it's time to sit.
55 **Here is a place reserv'd** = A place is saved for you here.	55 Indicating where Macbeth is supposed to sit.
58 **moves** = causes you distress.	58 Implied stage direction: Macbeth has seen the ghost and reacted strongly.
	59 **Which of you have done this**: Accusing. He mistakenly assumes they all see the ghost too; shifting the blame.
	61 **Thou canst not say I did it**: Denying blame. (This is to Banquo: if he were speaking to the nobles he would have used 'you' instead of 'thou'.)
62 **gory locks** = bloody hair.	
63 **rise:** stand up out of respect for the King.	63 Trying to figure out how to help the King.
64 **my Lord is often thus:** Macbeth is often in this state.	64 Covering for Macbeth's crazy behavior.
66 **upon a thought** = in a moment. 67 **If much you note him** = If you stare at him. **note** = notice 68 **extend his Passion** = make his fit last longer.	

69   Feed, and regard him not. *[To Macbeth privately]* Are you a man?

MACBETH

70   Ay, and a bold one, that dare look on that
71   Which might appall the Devil.

LADY MACBETH

72   O proper stuff:
73   This is the very painting of your fear:
74   This is the Air-drawn-Dagger which you said
75   Led you to *Duncan*. ¶ O, these flaws and starts
76   (Impostors to true fear) would well become
77   A woman's story, at a Winter's fire
78   Authoriz'd by her Grandam: ¶ shame itself,
79   Why do you make such faces? When all's done
80   You look but on a stool.

MACBETH

81   Prythee see there:
82   Behold, look, lo, how say you:
83   ¶ *[To Ghost]* Why what care I, if thou canst nod, speak too.
84   If Charnel houses, and our Graves must send
85   Those that we bury, back; our Monuments
86   Shall be the Maws of Kites.

Ghost disappears.

LADY MACBETH

87   What? Quite unmann'd in folly.

MACBETH

88   If I stand here, I saw him.

LADY MACBETH

89   Fie for shame.

MACBETH

90   Blood hath been shed ere now, i' th' olden time
91   Ere humane Statute purg'd the gentle Weal:
92   Ay, and since too, Murders have been perform'd
93   Too terrible for the ear. The time has been,
94   That when the Brains were out, the man would die,
95   And there an end: but now they rise again
96   With twenty mortal murders on their crowns,
97   And push us from our stools. This is more strange
98   Than such a murder is.

What	Why
69 **Feed, and regard him not** = Eat and don't pay attention to him.	69 *[To Macbeth privately]*: inferred. Not in Folio.
	70 **a bold one**: defending his bravery.
71 **appall** = terrify.	
72 **proper stuff** = (sarcastically) nonsense! 73 **This is the very painting of your fear** = You see a picture painted by your fear.	72 Shaming him into mastering himself. Note: the flame of her ambition is still burning.
74 **Air-drawn** = drawn in the air. 75 **flaws** = sudden bursts of wind, i.e. bursts of passion. **starts** as in startle. 76 **Impostors to true fear**: the ghost and the **Air-drawn-Dagger** (line 74) are impostors, not truly to be feared. **become** = befit. 78 **Authoriz'd by her Grandam** = believed by her grandmother.	
	79 **Why do you make such faces**: implied stage direction. Macbeth is grimacing.
81 **Prythee** = I pray thee = please.	83 **If thou canst nod**: refusing to be cowed by the ghost. (Stage direction *[To Ghost]* is inferred; not in Folio)
84 **Charnel houses** = crypts for bones. 85 **Monuments** = mausoleums; burial chambers. 86 **Maws of Kites** = stomachs of hawks. Our final resting places will be inside hawks (because our corpses will be eaten by them).	
	(Stage direction): *Ghost disappears*: not in Folio, but inferred from the dialogue.
87 **unmann'd** = your manhood undone. **folly** = not foolishness, but mental failure.	87 Again, challenging his manhood to get him to straighten up.
88 **If I stand here, I saw him** = I saw him as surely as I stand here.	88 Defending himself.
89 **Fie** = an exclamation of contempt.	
90 **Blood hath been shed ere now**: Murders have been committed before this. 91 **humane Statute** = humane laws. **purg'd** = got rid of violence. **Weal** = commonwealth. In the olden time, before humane laws purged the commonwealth of violence and made it gentle. 92 **Ay, and since too**: not only before, but also since. 93-94 **The time has been** (It used to be), **That when the Brains were** knocked **out, the man would die.** 96 **twenty mortal murders on their crowns** = twenty lethal gashes on their heads. 97 **push us from our stools**: Macbeth can't sit because the ghost is in his stool. 97-98 **more strange Than such a murder**: The ghost is more strange than the murder.	91 Grappling with the impossibility of the situation: He killed Banquo and Banquo is still not gone.

LADY MACBETH

99 My worthy Lord

100 Your Noble Friends do lack you.

MACBETH

101 I do forget:

102 ¶ Do not muse at me my most worthy Friends,

103 I have a strange infirmity, which is nothing

104 To those that know me. ¶ Come, love and health to all,

105 Then I'll sit down: Give me some Wine, fill full:

Enter Ghost.

106 I drink to th' general joy o' th' whole Table,

107 And to our dear Friend *Banquo*, whom we miss:

108 Would he were here: to all, and him we thirst,

109 And all to all.

LORDS

110 Our duties, and the pledge.

MACBETH

111 Avaunt, & quit my sight, let the earth hide thee:

112 Thy bones are marrowless, thy blood is cold:

113 Thou hast no speculation in those eyes

114 Which thou dost glare with.

LADY MACBETH

115 Think of this good Peers

116 But as a thing of Custom: 'Tis no other,

117 Only it spoils the pleasure of the time.

MACBETH

118 What man dare, I dare:

119 Approach thou like the rugged Russian Bear,

120 The arm'd Rhinoceros, or th' Hyrcan Tiger,

121 Take any shape but that, and my firm Nerves

122 Shall never tremble. ¶ Or be alive again,

123 And dare me to the Desert with thy Sword:

124 If trembling I inhabit then, protest me

125 The Baby of a Girl. ¶ Hence horrible shadow,

126 Unreal mock'ry hence. *[Ghost disappears.]* ¶ Why so, being gone

127 I am a man again: ¶ pray you sit still.

LADY MACBETH

128 You have displac'd the mirth,

129 Broke the good meeting, with most admir'd disorder.

What	Why
100 **lack** = miss you at table.	100 Bringing him back to the present.
101 **I do forget**: I forgot where I am.	101 Remembering where he is and what he's supposed to be doing.
102 **muse** = wonder.	102 Excusing himself.
103-104 **I have a strange infirmity** (illness), **which is nothing** (completely unimportant) **To those that know me.**	
	104 **love and health to all**: toasting the room.
	105 **Then I'll sit**: stalling the moment when he has to face the stool with Banquo's ghost in it.
106 **general joy**: He drinks to everyone at the table generally, and to Banquo particularly.	106 Emphasizing that he's not thinking about Banquo's ghost.
108 **to all** (to all here)**, and him we thirst** (and to Banquo, whom we thirst for).	
109 **all to all**: Everyone drink to everyone else.	
110 **pledge** = drinking a toast to someone.	
111 **Avaunt** = begone (with the implication of contempt or abhorrence). **quit** = leave. **let the earth hide thee** = go be buried.	111 Finally seeing the ghost has reentered. Trying to scare away the ghost. Saying 'I'm not scared of you'.
112 **marrowless** = lifeless.	
113 **speculation** = power of sight.	
116 **a thing of Custom** = just a habit.	116 Excusing Macbeth's outburst.
118 **What man dare, I dare** = I dare as much as any man.	118 Challenging the ghost to fight fair by appearing in any other form but the murdered Banquo.
119-122 **Approach thou like** (Come at me in the shape of) **the rugged Russian Bear, The arm'd Rhinoceros, or th' Hyrcan Tiger, Take any shape but that** (any shape but the murdered Banquo)**, and my firm Nerves Shall never tremble** (My nerves will be firm and I will not tremble). **Hyrcan**: from Hyrcania on the Caspian Sea, known in Virgil as a place with tigers.	
122-123 **Or be alive again** (or be the living Banquo again)**, And dare me to the Desert with thy Sword** (and challenge me to go with you to the desert to fight with swords).	
124-125 **inhabit** = take the habit of. **protest** = proclaim. **Baby of** = baby form of. If I tremble then, proclaim me a baby girl.	
126 **Unreal mock'ry** = False illusion. **hence** = get out of here.	126 *[Ghost disappears]*: inferred. Not in Folio.
126-127 **being gone I am a man again** = now that the ghost is gone, I am myself again.	127 **pray you sit still**: remembering he is among company, asking the Lords to return to their seats and go back to normal.
128 **displac'd the mirth** = driven out the festive atmosphere.	128 Castigating him for ruining the party.
129 **admir'd** = wondered at. **disorder** = loss of control.	

MACBETH

130 Can such things be,
131 And overcome us like a Summer's Cloud,
132 Without our special wonder? You make me strange
133 Even to the disposition that I owe,
134 When now I think you can behold such sights,
135 And keep the natural Ruby of your Cheeks,
136 When mine is blanch'd with fear.

ROSSE

137 What sights, my Lord?

LADY MACBETH

138 I pray you speak not: he grows worse & worse.
139 Question enrages him: at once, good night.
140 Stand not upon the order of your going,
141 But go at once.

LENOX

142 Good night, and better health
143 Attend his Majesty.

LADY MACBETH

144 A kind good night to all.
Exit Lords.

3.4. e -

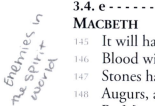

MACBETH

145 It will have blood they say:
146 Blood will have Blood:
147 Stones have been known to move, & Trees to speak:
148 Augurs, and understood Relations, have
149 By Magot-Pies, & Choughs, & Rooks brought forth
150 The secret'st man of Blood. ¶ What is the night?

LADY MACBETH

151 Almost at odds with morning, which is which.

MACBETH

152 How say'st thou that *Macduff* denies his person
153 At our great bidding.

LADY MACBETH

154 Did you send to him Sir?

MACBETH

155 I heard it by the way: But I will send:

What	Why
130 **Can such things** (ghosts) **be** (exist).	
131 **like a Summer's Cloud**: like an unexpected burst of summer rain.	
132 **Without our special wonder** = without us especially wondering at them.	132 To guests: asking how they can be calm at the sight of the terrifying ghost (we know he's talking to the room because Rosse answers).
132-133 **owe** = own. **You make me strange Even to the disposition that I owe**: I thought I possessed a dauntless disposition, but your calm in the face of this terror makes me seem a stranger to it.	
	138 **speak not**: jumping in to prevent them eliciting an incriminating answer from Macbeth. (period after '**worse & worse**' inferred; not in Folio)
140 **Stand not upon the order of your going** = Never mind the protocol of going out in order of rank.	

3.4.e Purpose: 1. To set in motion Macbeth's next horrible crime. 2. To introduce the next interview with the Witches. 3. To show Lady Macbeth accepting defeat: she no longer tries to influence his thinking. 4. To give us a glimpse into his regime (spies in every house).

Drama: 1. Can Macbeth get relief from the torment of fear? 2. Can he get Lady Macbeth to engage with him in finding a way?

What	Why
146 **Blood will have Blood** = The murdered will have their revenge.	146 Realizing the new state of things: The spirits he murdered are his enemies now. Racking his brain for any scrap he may have heard about the behavior of murdered ghosts, in the hope of finding something that helps
147-149 This is a list of known ill omens and divinations. **Augurs** = divinations. **understood Relations** = secret connections understood by witchcraft, **Magot-Pies** = magpies. **Choughs** = crows. **Rooks** = another kind of crow. It was believed that moving trees and talking crows sometimes revealed secret murders.	
150 **The secret'st man of Blood** = the man who kept a murder most secret. **What is the night** = what time of night is it?	
151 **Almost at odds with morning, which is which** = (The night is) almost arguing with morning, whether it's night or dawn.	
152-153 **How say'st thou** (what do you think about this), **that _Macduff_ denies his person** (denies to present himself in person) **At our great bidding** (at the bidding of the king).	152 Accepting his fate. Moving on to settle his next fear. _Macduff_ **denies his person**: **FORWARD**: What is his intention towards Macduff?
154 **Did you send** (an invitation) **to him Sir?**	154 Note: She calls him 'sir', indicating their new distance.
155 **I heard it by the way** = I overheard it (that Macduff isn't coming). Note: He probably actually heard it from his spies.	155 Moving on: taking action to protect himself against the next threat — Macduff — regardless of the cost.

156 ¶ There's not a one of them but in his house
157 I keep a Servant Fee'd. ¶ I will tomorrow
158 (And betimes I will) to the weird Sisters.
159 More shall they speak: for now I am bent to know
160 By the worst means, the worst, for mine own good,
161 All causes shall give way. ¶ I am in blood
162 Stepp'd in so far, that should I wade no more,
163 Returning were as tedious as go o'er:
164 ¶ Strange things I have in head, that will to hand,
165 Which must be acted, ere they may be scann'd.

LADY MACBETH
166 You lack the season of all Natures, sleep.

MACBETH
167 Come, we'll to sleep: ¶ My strange & self-abuse
168 Is the initiate fear, that wants hard use:
169 We are yet but young in deed.
Exeunt.

SCENA QUINTA.

Thunder. Enter the three Witches, meeting Hecate.

FIRST WITCH   Head witch
1 Why how now *Hecate*, you look angerly?

HECATE
2 Have I not reason (Beldams) as you are?
3 Saucy, and overbold, how did you dare
4 To Trade, and Traffic with *Macbeth*,
5 In Riddles, and Affairs of death;
6 And I the Mistress of your Charms,
7 The close contriver of all harms,
8 Was never call'd to bear my part,
9 Or show the glory of our Art?
10 ¶ And which is worse, all you have done
11 Hath been but for a wayward Son,
12 Spiteful, and wrathful, who (as others do)
13 Loves for his own ends, not for you.
14 ¶ But make amends now: Get you gone,
15 And at the pit of Acheron
16 Meet me i' th' Morning: thither he

What	Why
157 **I keep a Servant Fee'd** = I pay a servant to act as my spy. **I will** (go) **tomorrow.**	
158 **betimes** = soon – before it's too late.	158 **FORWARD**: What will the Weird Sisters say tomorrow?
159 **bent to know** = bent on knowing.	
160-161 **the worst means**: relying on witchcraft was a sin. **for mine own good** (for my own preservation), **All causes shall give way** (all other concerns will be set aside) I will stop at nothing to protect myself.	
161-163 **I am in blood Stepp'd in so far** (I have committed so many murders)**, that should I wade no more** (that if I stop now)**, Returning were as tedious as go o'er** (to go back would be as difficult as to plunge ahead). Imagine he's waded so far into a river of blood that it will be easier to cross over than go back.	
164 **Strange things** (dark plans) **I have in head** (in mind)**, that will to hand** (will be enacted by my hand).	164 **FORWARD**: What are the strange things he has in head?
165 **scann'd** = carefully considered.	
166 **season** = seasoning, as in food. You lack sleep, which keeps all natures fresh and flavorful.	166 **sleep**: Redirecting his energy to a more constructive direction. Counseling him to stop and rest.
167-168 **strange & self-abuse** = my strange self-delusion – Banquo's ghost. **the initiate fear** = novice's fear. **wants hard use** = requires hard practice. With practice, I'll be able to murder without seeing ghosts.	167 **TURN**: accepting her guidance. Allowing himself to be led to bed for now.
169 **We are yet but young in deed** = we are still just starting out on this new life of (evil) deeds.	

3.5 Heath near Forres. Exterior. Day.

Purpose: To build anticipation for Macbeth's next meeting with the Witches. Specifically, to paint the picture of exactly how Hecate intends to bring about his ruin.

Drama: 1. Will Hecate put the other Witches in their place? 2. Can Hecate induce Macbeth to spurn fate, scorn death and bear his hopes above wisdom, grace and fear?

What	Why
2 **Beldams**: a term of contempt for an old woman.	2 Chastising her minions for operating without her.
3 **Saucy** = impudent.	
6 **Mistress** = boss.	Note: Many scholars believe that Shakespeare did not write either this or the other Witches' poems (1. 3 and 4.5).
7 **contriver** = schemer.	
8 **bear my part** = play my role.	
11 **wayward** = capricious, obstinate.	
15 **Acheron**: a river or burning lake in Hades, the Greek underworld.	
16 **thither** = to there (to the pit of Acheron).	

17 Will come, to know his Destiny.
18 Your Vessels, and your Spells provide,
19 Your Charms, and everything beside;
20 ¶ I am for th' Air: this night I'll spend
21 Unto a dismal, and a Fatal end.
22 Great business must be wrought ere Noon.
23 Upon the Corner of the Moon
24 There hangs a vap'rous drop, profound,
25 I'll catch it ere it come to ground;
26 And that distill'd by Magic sleights,
27 Shall raise such Artificial Sprites,
28 As by the strength of their illusion,
29 Shall draw him on to his Confusion.
30 He shall spurn Fate, scorn Death, and bear
31 His hopes 'bove Wisdom, Grace, and Fear:
32 And you all know, Security
33 Is Mortals' chiefest Enemy.

Music, and a Song.

34 Hark, I am call'd: my little Spirit see
35 Sits in a Foggy cloud, and stays for me.

Sing within. Come away, come away, &c.

FIRST WITCH

36 Come, let's make haste: she'll soon be
37 Back again.

Exeunt.

SCENA SEXTA.

Enter Lenox, and another Lord.

LENOX

1 My former Speeches,
2 Have but hit your Thoughts
3 Which can interpret farther: Only I say
4 Things have been strangely borne. The gracious *Duncan*
5 Was pitied of *Macbeth*: marry he was dead:
6 And the right valiant *Banquo* walk'd too late,
7 Whom you may say (if 't please you) *Fleance* kill'd,
8 For *Fleance* fled: Men must not walk too late.
9 Who cannot want the thought, how monstrous
10 It was for *Malcolm*, and for *Donalbain*
11 To kill their gracious Father? Damned Fact,

What	Why
17 **to know his Destiny** = to learn his destiny.	
18 **Vessels**: potion cauldrons.	
20 **I am for th' Air** = I am flying away.	
21 **Unto a dismal, and a Fatal end** = working to effect a dismal conclusion; to ruin somebody.	
23 **the Corner of the Moon** = the point of the crescent moon.	
24 **a vap'rous drop**: a drop of magic potion.	
26 **Magic sleights** = tricks, as in sleights of hand.	
27 **Artificial Sprites**: deceiving spirits; skilled in artifice.	27 Note: Here Hecate explains how she will create the illusions that will delude Macbeth in 4.1.
29 **Confusion** = ruin.	
30-31 **He shall spurn Fate** (he will ignore his own fate)**, scorn Death** (laugh derisively at death)**, and bear His hopes 'bove Wisdom, Grace, and Fear** (and make his ambition a higher priority than wisdom, grace or fear). By making him believe he is invulnerable, we will trick him into contempt of danger, causing his own downfall.	30 **FORWARD**: Will we see Macbeth spurn Fate, scorn Death, and bear his hopes above Wisdom, Grace and Fear?
32-33 A false sense of **Security Is Mortals' chiefest Enemy.**	
35 **stays** = waits.	
	36 **make haste:** Let's hurry and prepare our vessels, spells, and charms so we can ensnare Macbeth tomorrow morning, as she commands.

3.6 A road somewhere in Scotland. Exterior. Day.

Purpose: To bring us up to date on all the story threads so far, and to paint a picture of the hoped-for outcome. This picture becomes the basis of the overarching question of the rest of the play (see Drama below).

Drama: 1. Will the Lord join with Lenox against Macbeth? 2. (for the rest of the play) Will Macduff and Malcolm succeed in recruiting English help, dethroning Macbeth, and restoring peace and happiness in Scotland?

What	Why
1-2 **My former Speeches** (what I said earlier) **Have but hit your Thoughts** (agree with your thinking).	1 Seeking to make the Lord an accomplice in his desire to depose Macbeth. Lenox is implying as strongly as he can (without saying it outright and thus risking execution for treason) that Macbeth killed Duncan and Banquo and blamed the sons.
3 **Which can interpret farther** = You can infer the rest. **Only I say** = I can only permit myself to say.	
4 **Things have been strangely borne** = Macbeth has responded to events strangely.	
5 **pitied of** (by) *Macbeth*. Macbeth says he was sorry for Duncan, which cost him nothing since Duncan was dead. **marry:** a mild oath to indicate indignant surprise, derived from the name of the holy virgin. A modern equivalent might be 'Holy Mary!'	
6 *Banquo* **walk'd too late** = Banquo was at fault for being out after dark.	
7 **you may say (if 't please you)** *Fleance* **kill'd:** In other words, nobody could actually believe it was true.	
9 **Who cannot want the thought** = who could fail to think.	
11 **Damned Fact** = evil deed.	

12 How it did grieve *Macbeth?* Did he not straight
13 In pious rage, the two delinquents tear,
14 That were the Slaves of drink, and thralls of sleep?
15 Was not that Nobly done? Ay, and wisely too:
16 For 'twould have anger'd any heart alive
17 To hear the men deny 't. So that I say,
18 He has borne all things well, and I do think,
19 That had he *Duncan's* Sons under his Key,
20 (As, and 't please Heaven he shall not) they should find
21 What 'twere to kill a Father: So should *Fleance.*
22 But peace; for from broad words, and 'cause he fail'd
23 His presence at the Tyrant's Feast, I hear
24 *Macduff* lives in disgrace. ❡ Sir, can you tell
25 Where he bestows himself?

LORD
26 The Sons of *Duncan*
27 (From whom this Tyrant holds the due of Birth)
28 Lives in the English Court, and is receiv'd
29 Of the most Pious *Edward,* with such grace,
30 That the malevolence of Fortune, nothing
31 Takes from his high respect. ❡ Thither *Macduff*
32 Is gone, to pray the Holy King, upon his aid
33 To wake Northumberland, and warlike *Seyward,*
34 That by the help of these (with him above
35 To ratify the Work) we may again
36 Give to our Tables meat, sleep to our Nights:
37 Free from our Feasts, and Banquets bloody knives;
38 Do faithful Homage, and receive free Honours,
39 All which we pine for now. ❡ And this report
40 Hath so exasperate their King, that he
41 Prepares for some attempt of War.

LENOX
42 Sent he to *Macduff?*

What	Why
12-14 **Did he not straight** (straightway; immediately), **In pious** (indignant) **rage, the two delinquents tear** (stab the two delinquent chamberlains), **That were the Slaves of drink** (who were controlled by drunkenness), **and thralls of sleep** (and passed out, ruled by sleep)?	12 Employing sarcasm so that he can condemn Macbeth without openly doing so and thus risking execution for treason.
15 **and wisely too**: It was wise for Macbeth to kill them before they had a chance to deny the blame.	
16-17 '**twould have anger'd any heart alive To hear the men deny 't**: It's a good thing Macbeth killed the chamberlains, because it would have made us angry to hear them deny guilt.	
18 **borne** = past tense of 'bear', i.e. he has conducted himself well.	
19 **had he** *Duncan's* **Sons under his Key** = if he had Duncan's sons locked up.	
20-21 **and 't please Heaven** = if it please God. i.e. I pray Macbeth shall not capture them. **they should find What 'twere to kill a Father**: i.e. he would execute them.	
22-23 **peace** = silence (because I have more to tell). **broad words** = gossip heard abroad. '**cause he fail'd His presence** = because Macduff failed to attend.	
24 **in disgrace** = out of favor with the king.	24 Asking where to find Macduff, a natural ally against Macbeth.
25 **bestows** = hides.	25 Sharing good news supporting Lenox' cause.
26 **Sons of** *Duncan*: Malcolm and Donalbain.	
27 **From whom this Tyrant holds the due of Birth** = who is kept from his birthright (the crown) by the tyrant (Macbeth).	
29 **Of** = by. **Pious** *Edward* = Edward the Confessor, King of England.	
30-31 **malevolence of Fortune** = curse of fate. **nothing Takes from his high respect** = does not detract from Edward's respect. Edward receives Malcolm as graciously as if Malcolm were King.	Folio has ')' after '**him above**'. We think that was a typo.
31 **Thither** *Macduff* = Macduff goes there.	
32 **pray** = petition. **Holy King** = Edward. **upon his aid** = in aid of Malcolm.	
33 **wake** = stir to action.	33 Note: He refers to Seyward, Earl of Northumberland and his son, also named Seyward. Northumberland is in northern England, bordering on Scotland. Edward could induce (but not compel) them to attack Macbeth.
34-35 **with him above To ratify the Work** = with God's blessing.	
36 **Give to our Tables meat**: Apparently Macbeth's reign has disrupted farming so much that they can't get food, and they can't sleep for fear.	
37 **Free from our Feasts, and Banquets bloody knives**: Perhaps he refers to the blood-spattered murderer at the door at Macbeth's feast (in 3.4)?	
38 **Do faithful Homage, and receive free Honours** = give homage to the King and receive honors freely given by him.	
40 **Hath so exasperate their King** = has so enraged Macbeth.	
42 **Sent he to** *Macduff?* = Did Macbeth send a summons to Macduff?	

LORD

43 He did: and with an absolute 'Sir, not I'
44 The cloudy Messenger turns me his back,
45 And hums; as who should say, 'you'll rue the time
46 That clogs me with this Answer'.

LENOX

47 And that well might
48 Advise him to a Caution, t' hold what distance
49 His wisdom can provide. ⁊ Some holy Angel
50 Fly to the Court of England, and unfold
51 His Message ere he come, that a swift blessing
52 May soon return to this our suffering Country,
53 Under a hand accurs'd.

LORD

54 I'll send my Prayers with him.
Exeunt.

What	Why
43-46 He did (Yes, Macbeth did send for Macduff)**: and with an absolute 'Sir, not I'** (and Macduff told the messenger to tell Macbeth, 'Sir, I absolutely will not come') **The cloudy** (grim-faced, in reaction to this wrong answer) **Messenger turns me his back** (turns his back on Macduff)**, And hums** (and makes a guttural noise to indicate his disapproval)**; as who should say** (as if to say), **'you'll rue** (you'll regret) **the time That clogs me with this Answer'** (the time you burdened me with this answer).	43 Sharing his admiration for Macduff. In other words, the messenger was forbidden by protocol from saying it out loud, but hummed to indicate, 'Macbeth is going to kill you for this'. **FORWARD**: Will Macduff rue the time?
47-49 And that (and having given that answer) **well might Advise him to a Caution** (might well give him reason to take caution), **t' hold what distance** (to keep as far from Macbeth) **His wisdom can provide** (as he is able to devise).	47 Hoping aloud that, having openly defied Macbeth, Macduff will have the sense to stay as far from him as he can. Lenox is afraid Macbeth will have Macduff killed if he gets the chance.
	48 the apostrophe in 't' hold' is inferred. Folio just has 't hold'.
49-53 Some holy Angel Fly to the Court of England (I pray some angel may fly to England)**, and unfold His Message ere he come** (and tell them Macduff's story, before Macduff arrives)**, that a swift blessing May soon return to this our suffering Country, Under a hand accurs'd** (so that our country, suffering under Macbeth's cursed hand, may swiftly be blessed).	49 Praying that an angel will induce Edward to save Scotland from the accursed hand of Macbeth. **FORWARD**: Will Edward bring his strength to Malcolm's aid?

ACTUS QUARTUS. SCENA PRIMA.

Thunder. Enter the three Witches.

FIRST WITCH

1   Thrice the brinded Cat hath mew'd.

SECOND WITCH

2   Thrice, and once the Hedge-Pig whin'd.

THIRD WITCH

3   Harpier cries, 'Tis time, 'tis time.

FIRST WITCH

4   Round about the Cauldron go:

5   In the poison'd Entrails throw

6   Toad, that under cold stone,

7   Days and Nights, has thirty one:

8   Sweltered Venom sleeping got,

9   Boil thou first i' th' charmed pot.

ALL

10   Double, double, toil and trouble;

11   Fire burn, and Cauldron bubble.

SECOND WITCH

12   Fillet of a Fenny Snake,

13   In the Cauldron boil and bake:

14   Eye of Newt, and Toe of Frog,

15   Wool of Bat, and Tongue of Dog:

16   Adder's Fork, and Blind-worm's Sting,

17   Lizard's leg, and Owlet's wing:

18   For a Charm of powerful trouble,

19   Like a Hell-broth, boil and bubble.

ALL

20   Double, double, toil and trouble,

21   Fire burn, and Cauldron bubble.

THIRD WITCH

22   Scale of Dragon, Tooth of Wolf,

23   Witches' Mummy, Maw, and Gulf

24   Of the ravin'd salt Sea shark:

25   Root of Hemlock, digg'd i' th' dark:

26   Liver of Blaspheming Jew,

27   Gall of Goat, and Slips of Yew,

4.1.a A cave or house near Forres. Interior. Day.

Purpose: To sharpen our anticipation of the key scene to follow, in which Macbeth will learn the prophecies that undo him.

Drama: 1. Can the three Witches win back the approval of Hecate? 2. Can they brew a potion sufficiently powerful to ensnare Macbeth?

What	Why
1 **brinded** = striped or spotted.	1 Brewing a magic potion and conjuring evil spirits.
2 **Hedge-Pig** = hedgehog. Can denote misfortune	Implied stage direction: We hear a cat, a hedgehog and a sound to represent Harpier.
3 **Harpier** = name of another demon.	
5 **Entrails** = intestines.	
6-8 **Sweltered** = sweated. **Toad, that under cold stone, Days and Nights, has thirty one: Sweltered Venom sleeping got** = venom that was sweat (sweltered) by a toad who's been sleeping under a cold stone for thirty one days.	6 Casting a spell, and putting in the ingredients as she lists them.
10 **Double, double**: This is the magic incantation.	10 Conjuring with all their might.
12 **Fillet**: a cut of meat. **Fenny Snake**: a snake from a fen, or bog.	12 Putting these items into the brew as they name them. Note that these are not random strange ingredients. Each has a symbolic significance that contributes to their cause: The **Toad** (named above at line 6) was a well-known "familiar" of witches. The **Snake**, the way it sneaks up on its prey, represents deception, as in the saying "a snake in the grass". The **Newt** symbolized spiritual immaturity. The **Frog** represented impaired physical or spiritual condition. The **Bat**, the erratic night-flyer, is a favorite symbol of Halloween to this day. The Black **Dog** was a standard companion of Witches. The **Adder** and the **Blind-worm** were thought to be misfits of creation. The **Lizard** symbolized lack of scruples. The **Owlet** is another nocturnal animal, whose cry was a symbol of death. The **Dragon** is a mythical destroyer and a symbol of evil in the Christian tradition. The **Wolf**, with its method of pretending to be lame before an attack, symbolized deceit. The flesh of the **Mummy** was used to create medicine. The shark was a noted killer. **Hemlock** is poison. **Jews**, being unbaptised, were associated with the anti-Christ. The **Goat** symbolized the Devil, and lust. The poisonous **Yew** was associated with Hecate.
16 **Adder's Fork**: the forked tongue of an adder (poisonous snake). **Blind-worm** = a legless lizard whose shiny scales were said to be blindingly bright. Its tongue was thought to contain venom. 17 **Owlet** = a small owl.	
23-24 **Witches' Mummy** = mummified corpse belonging to witches. **Maw, and Gulf Of the ravin'd salt Sea shark** = the engulfing stomach (**maw**) of the ravenous shark. 25 **Hemlock** = a poisonous plant. 26 **Blaspheming Jew**: Blasphemy is denying Christian doctrine, so all Jews were considered blasphemers. 27 **Gall** = bile; contents of the gall bladder. **Yew** = a tree planted in church graveyards.	

28 Sliver'd in the Moon's Eclipse:
29 Nose of Turk, and Tartar's lips:
30 Finger of Birth-strangled Babe,
31 Ditch-deliver'd by a Drab,
32 Make the Gruel thick, and slab.
33 Add thereto a Tiger's Chaudron,
34 For th' Ingredience of our Cauldron.

ALL

35 Double, double, toil and trouble,
36 Fire burn, and Cauldron bubble.

SECOND WITCH

37 Cool it with a Baboon's blood,
38 Then the Charm is firm and good.
Enter Hecate, and the other three Witches.

HECATE

39 O well done: I commend your pains,
40 And every one shall share i' th' gains:
41 And now about the Cauldron sing
42 Like Elves and Fairies in a Ring,
43 Enchanting all that you put in.
Music and a Song, 'Black Spirits', &c.

SECOND WITCH

44 By the pricking of my Thumbs,
45 Something wicked this way comes:
Knocking
46 Open Locks, whoever knocks.

4.1.b -
Enter Macbeth.

MACBETH

47 How now you secret, black, & midnight Hags?
48 What is 't you do?

ALL

49 A deed without a name.

MACBETH

50 I conjure you, by that which you Profess,
51 (Howe'er you come to know it) answer me:

What	Why
28 **Sliver'd** = sliced off. 29 **Turks** and **Tartars** were abhorred non-Christians. 31 **Ditch-deliver'd by a Drab**: born in a ditch to a prostitute. 32 **Gruel** = oatmeal (or similar, made from another grain). **slab** = thick; glutinous. 33 **thereto** = to it. **Chaudron** = intestines.	28 More symbols: An **Eclipse** was a time when nature was out of joint. In Shakespeare's England, **Turks** and **Tartars**, like Jews mentioned above, were considered cursed since they were unbaptized. More than that, there were rumors that they committed cannibalism and other inhuman crimes. Another belief about witches was that they kidnapped unbaptized **Babies** to sacrifice to the Devil. The **Tiger**, like the shark, was a well-known killer.
	37 **Baboon's blood**: another symbol of death. *the other three Witches:* this is the only mention of them.
39 **I commend your pains**: I commend you for the results of your efforts. 40 **share i' th' gains** = share in the profit. 41 **about the Cauldron** = around the cauldron.	
	(stage direction) *'Black Spirits'* was the title of a song that also appears in Thomas Middleton's 1615 play, *The Witch*.
44 **By the pricking of my Thumbs** = I can tell by the intuitive prickling sensation in my thumbs. 46 **Open Locks**: casting a spell to make the door unlock.	

4.1.b Purpose: To lay four foundations of Macbeth's downfall: 1. To make Macbeth believe he's invincible, which makes him freer to commit violence and thereby increase his list of enemies. 2. To lull him into leaving himself vulnerable to attack. 3. To make him miserable with the vision of the kings descended from Banquo. 4. To establish specific details — 'none of woman born' (line 88) and 'Byrnam Wood to Dunsinane' (line 102) that will come back to haunt him later.

Drama: Can the Witches trick Macbeth into causing his own downfall?

What	Why
47 **How now**: a customary greeting. Sometimes it means, 'Please explain what is happening', other times it's a simple 'hello'. **Hag** = an ugly and wicked woman. 50 **conjure**: urgently appeal; also, summon by magic. **by that which you Profess**: by the spirits of darkness. 51 **Howe'er** = by whatever means necessary.	47 Suspiciously checking to make sure their brew is not intended against him. 49 **A deed without a name**: Tantalizing him. 50 **I conjure you**: Throwing all caution to the wind and saying everything he can to get them to tell him the whole truth, hiding nothing.

52 Though you untie the Winds, and let them fight
53 Against the Churches: Though the yesty waves
54 Confound and swallow Navigation up:
55 Though bladed Corn be lodg'd, & Trees blown down,
56 Though Castles topple on their Warders' heads:
57 Though Palaces, and Pyramids do slope
58 Their heads to their Foundations: Though the treasure
59 Of Natures Germaine, tumble all together,
60 Even till destruction sicken: answer me
61 To what I ask you.

FIRST WITCH

62 Speak.

SECOND WITCH

63 Demand.

THIRD WITCH

64 We'll answer.

FIRST WITCH

65 Say, if th' hadst rather hear it from our mouths,
66 Or from our Masters.

MACBETH

67 Call 'em: let me see 'em.

FIRST WITCH

68 Pour in Sow's blood, that hath eaten
69 Her nine Farrow: Grease that's sweaten
70 From the Murderer's Gibbet, throw
71 Into the Flame.

ALL

72 Come high or low:
73 Thyself and Office deftly show.
Thunder.
First Apparition, an Armed Head.

MACBETH

74 Tell me, thou unknown power.

FIRST WITCH

75 He knows thy thought:
76 Hear his speech, but say thou nought.

What	Why
52-60 Though = Even though. **untie the Winds**: untie the legendary sack that contains the winds; let them blow wildly. **fight Against the Churches**: blow down the Churches. **yesty** = yeasty; frothy. **Confound** = confuse. **swallow Navigation** = sink ships. **bladed Corn** = unripe wheat. **lodg'd** = flattened. **Warders** = guards. **slope Their heads to their Foundations** = let their tops fall to the ground. **Natures Germaine** = seeds. **till destruction sicken** = until destruction grows sick at the sight of its own doing.	52 Note: Macbeth is saying he doesn't care what terrible things happen to the whole world, so long as he gets what he wants. This is another big step in his descent from good man to monster.
	66 Implying that to hear directly from the masters is more authoritative, but also more dangerous. Apparently the Weird Sisters are ruled by Hecate, who is in turn ruled by a higher demon.
68 Sow = mother pig. The pig could connote taking more than you need. **69 Farrow** = piglet. **sweaten** = sweated. **70 Gibbet** = gallows.	68 Brewing the potion that summons the masters.
73 Reordered: **deftly** (quickly) **show yourself and** your **Office** (function).	
74 thou unknown power: you mysterious force.	
76 nought = nothing.	

FIRST APPARITION

77 *Macbeth, Macbeth, Macbeth*:

78 Beware *Macduff*,

79 Beware the Thane of Fife: ¶ dismiss me. Enough.

He Descends.

MACBETH

80 Whate'er thou art, for thy good caution, thanks

81 Thou hast harp'd my fear aright. ¶ But one word more.

FIRST WITCH

82 He will not be commanded: ¶ here's another

83 More potent than the first.

Thunder.

Second Apparition, a Bloody Child.

SECOND APPARITION

84 *Macbeth, Macbeth, Macbeth.*

MACBETH

85 Had I three ears, I'd hear thee.

SECOND APPARITION

86 Be bloody, bold, & resolute:

87 Laugh to scorn

88 The power of man: For none of woman born

89 Shall harm *Macbeth.*

Descends.

MACBETH

90 Then live *Macduff*: what need I fear of thee?

91 ¶ But yet I'll make assurance: double sure,

92 And take a Bond of Fate: thou shalt not live,

93 That I may tell pale-hearted Fear, it lies;

94 And sleep in spite of Thunder.

Thunder.

Third Apparition, a Child Crowned, with a Tree in his hand.

95 What is this, that rises like the issue of a King,

96 And wears upon his Baby-brow, the round

97 And top of Sovereignty?

ALL

98 Listen, but speak not to 't.

What	Why
	78 **Beware *Macduff*** Announcing. Note: Macduff is the Thane of Fife. **FORWARD:** What will Macduff do to Macbeth?
79 **dismiss me**: Let me go back to the netherworld.	
	(stage direction) ***He Descends***: presumably into a trapdoor in the stage.
80 **for thy good caution, thanks** = Thanks for the good warning.	
81 **harp'd** = hit on, as in touching the right harpstring.	
85 **Had I three ears, I'd hear thee:** If I had three ears, I could have heard each 'Macbeth' with one of them.	85 In his impatience, slipping into impertinence. Note: His personal hell has gotten so bad that he can make a joke about the apparition of a bloody child ghost.
86-88 **resolute** = decisive. **Laugh to scorn The power of man** = scornfully laugh at any man's attempt to block you.	86 Announcing.
88 **none of woman born** = no one born from a woman's womb.	88 **FORWARD**: Will someone who was not of woman born harm Macbeth? Who? How?
92 **take a Bond of Fate** = make a contract with Fate to guarantee me.	92 **thou shalt not live: FORWARD:** Will Macbeth kill Macduff?
93 **That I may tell pale-hearted Fear, it lies:** so that I can tell my fear of Macduff it is a liar (since Macduff will be dead). **pale-hearted:** It was believed that fearful people had insufficient blood in their hearts.	
94 **sleep in spite of Thunder**: sleep so well that even thunder won't wake him.	94 Note: Macbeth is so desperate for sleep he is willing to murder Macduff in the hope it will gain him enough security to sleep again.
95 **issue** = child.	
96-97 **round And top of Sovereignty** = crown.	

THIRD APPARITION

99 Be Lion mettled, proud, and take no care:
100 Who chafes, who frets, or where Conspirers are:
101 *Macbeth* shall never vanquish'd be, until
102 Great Byrnam Wood, to high Dunsinane Hill
103 Shall come against him.

Descends.

MACBETH

104 That will never be:
105 Who can impress the Forest, bid the Tree
106 Unfix his earth-bound Root? Sweet bodements, good:
107 Rebellious dead, rise never till the Wood
108 Of Byrnam rise, and our high plac'd *Macbeth*
109 Shall live the Lease of Nature, pay his breath
110 To time, and mortal Custom. ¶ Yet my Heart
111 Throbs to know one thing: Tell me, if your Art
112 Can tell so much: Shall *Banquo's* issue ever
113 Reign in this Kingdom?

ALL

114 Seek to know no more.

MACBETH

115 I will be satisfied. Deny me this,
116 And an eternal Curse fall on you: Let me know!
117 ¶ Why sinks that Cauldron? & what noise is this?

Hautboys.

FIRST WITCH

118 Show.

SECOND WITCH

119 Show.

THIRD WITCH

120 Show.

ALL

121 Show his Eyes, and grieve his Heart,
122 Come like shadows, so depart.

A show of eight Kings, and Banquo last, with a glass in his hand.

MACBETH

mirror

123 Thou art too like the spirit of *Banquo*: Down:
124 Thy Crown does sear mine Eye-balls. ¶ And thy hair

What	Why
99 **mettle** = fortitude. This may be borrowed from weapon-making. Copper is relatively soft. To make it into good stiff bronze that will hold an edge, it must be alloyed with tin, which in those days was a rather uncertain science. Hence the measure of a sword's fitness for fighting was its 'metal' or 'mettle'.	99 Advising Macbeth to throw caution to the wind.
99-100 **take no care** (don't worry about): **Who chafes** (who resists your rule, like an ox chafing at the yoke), **who frets** (who worries), **or where Conspirers** (people conspiring to rise against you) **are.**	
101 **vanquish'd** = defeated.	
101-103 **until Great Byrnam Wood, to high Dunsinane Hill Shall come against him**: until Byrnam Wood climbs the hill and attacks him at Dunsinane Castle.	101 **FORWARD**: Will Byrnam Wood come to Dunsinane?
	104 **That will never be**: Crowing with triumph.
105 **impress** = press into service. The king's officers had the right to force men into the army.	
106 **bodements** = omens.	
107 **Rebellious dead**: referring to Banquo's ghost.	107 Note: He has been living in dread of the ghost's return.
109 **Lease**: the full term; live out his natural life.	
109-110 **pay his breath To time** = pay to Time the required number of breaths. **mortal Custom** = customary death.	
111 **Art** = magic.	
	112 **Shall *Banquo's* issue ever Reign in this Kingdom?** This is the question haunting Macbeth, that drove him to summon the Witches.
115 **I will be** = I demand to be. If you **Deny me this.**	117 **Why sinks that Cauldron**: This is an implied stage direction indicating the removal of the cauldron. **what noise is this**: referring to the hautboys.
	118 **Show**: Conjuring more spirits forward.
121 **grieve his Heart** = make his heart grieve.	
122 **so depart** = depart the same way. stage direction: *glass* = mirror.	
123 **Thou art too like the spirit of *Banquo*: Down**: (to the first spirit) You resemble Banquo too much. Go back down where you came from.	123 Speaking to each in turn as they come. Registering mounting shock as he sees his worst fear realized more and more.
124 **Thy Crown does sear mine Eye-balls** = The sight of your crown burns my eyes.	

125 Thou other Gold-bound-brow, is like the first:
126 ¶ A third, is like the former. Filthy Hags,
127 Why do you show me this? — ¶ A fourth? Start eyes!
128 What will the Line stretch out to th' crack of Doom?
129 ¶ Another yet? ¶ A seventh? I'll see no more:
130 ¶ And yet the eighth appears, who bears a glass,
131 Which shows me many more: and some I see,
132 That two-fold Balls and treble Sceptres carry.
133 Horrible sight: ¶ Now I see 'tis true,
134 For the Blood-bolter'd *Banquo* smiles upon me,
135 And points at them for his. ¶ What? Is this so?

FIRST WITCH

136 Ay Sir, all this is so. ¶ But why
137 Stands *Macbeth* thus amazedly?
138 ¶ Come Sisters, cheer we up his sprites,
139 And show the best of our delights.
140 I'll Charm the Air to give a sound,
141 While you perform your Antic round:
142 That this great King may kindly say,
143 Our duties, did his welcome pay.

Music.

The Witches Dance, and vanish.

MACBETH

144 Where are they? ¶ Gone?
145 ¶ Let this pernicious hour,
146 Stand aye accursed in the calendar.
147 ¶ Come in, without there.

4.1.c -

Enter Lenox.

LENOX

148 What's your Grace's will.

MACBETH

149 Saw you the Weird Sisters?

LENOX

150 No my Lord.

MACBETH

151 Came they not by you?

What	Why
125 **Gold-bound brow**: wearing a crown (spoken to the second spirit). 127 **Start eyes** = Eyes, pop from my sockets. 128 **crack of Doom** = thunder-clap of Judgment Day.	128 Folio has **'out to' th'crack of Doom'**. We think the Folio's apostrophe after **'to'** is an error.

130 **bears a glass** = holds a mirror.
132 **two-fold** = double. **treble** = triple. **Balls** and **Sceptres** = symbols of rule. They will rule two or three kingdoms.
134 **Blood-bolter'd *Banquo*** = Banquo, with his hair matted with coagulated blood.
	The order of spirits:
	  1. (line 123) Thou art too like the spirit of Banquo
	  2. (124) And thy hair
	  3. (126) A third
	  4. (127) A fourth?
	  5. (128) What, will the line
	  6. (129) Another yet?
	  7. (129) A seventh?
	  8. (130) And yet the eighth

	136 **Ay Sir:** Needling him.
138 **sprites** = spirits. 140 **I'll Charm the Air to give a sound** = I'll cast a spell on the air to play music. 141 **your Antic round**: your circle dance.	
143 We repaid his hospitality (**welcome**) by doing our **duties**.	143 They depart, laughing at Macbeth.
145 **pernicious** = insidiously evil. 146 **Stand aye** = remain always. 147 **without there** = you who are outside.	145 He is so angry at what the Witches said that he wants to declare this date a national day of mourning.

4.1.c Purpose: To show the immediate effect of the Witches' manipulation: Macbeth is now ready to kill on the least whim.

Drama: How will Macbeth react to the news of Macduff's flight?

What	Why
148 **What's your Grace's will**: What is it that your Majesty wants?	148 Answering the King's summons.
151 **Came they not by you**: Didn't they just pass right by you on their way out?	150 **No my Lord:** he has no idea what Macbeth is talking about, but since Macbeth is king, Lenox must speak respectfully. 151 Macbeth asks Lenox twice if he saw the Witches. If the Witches were real people, Lenox would have seen them come out; if Lenox didn't see them, that would indicate that they are spirits. Perhaps Macbeth is hoping for proof that they were spirits, and therefore their terrible predictions could be discounted as malicious, rather than living soothsayers who must be believed?

LENOX

152 No indeed my Lord.

MACBETH

153 Infected be the Air whereon they ride,
154 And damn'd all those that trust them. ¶ I did hear
155 The galloping of Horse. Who was 't came by?

LENOX

156 'Tis two or three my Lord, that bring you word:
157 *Macduff* is fled to England.

MACBETH

158 Fled to England?

LENOX

159 Ay, my good Lord.

MACBETH

160 *[aside]* Time, thou anticipat'st my dread exploits:
161 The flighty purpose never is o'ertook
162 Unless the deed go with it. ¶ From this moment,
163 The very firstlings of my heart shall be
164 The firstlings of my hand. And even now
165 To Crown my thoughts with Acts: be it thought & done:
166 The Castle of *Macduff,* I will surprise,
167 Seize upon Fife; give to th' edge o' th' Sword
168 His Wife, his Babes, and all unfortunate Souls
169 That trace him in his Line. No boasting like a Fool,
170 This deed I'll do, before this purpose cool,
171 ¶ But no more sights. ¶ Where are these Gentlemen?
172 Come bring me where they are.
Exeunt.

SCENA SECUNDA.

Enter Lady Macduff, her Son, and Rosse.

LADY MACDUFF

1 What had he done, to make him fly the Land?

ROSSE

2 You must have patience Madam.

LADY MACDUFF

3 He had none:

What	Why
153 Let the **Air** they ride upon be **Infected.**	153 Deciding they are unearthly and can't be trusted. Cursing the Witches.
154 **And damn'd all those that trust them** = and to hell with anybody who believes their prophecies.	154 Disavowing his faith in the Witches.
156 '**Tis two or three** = It is two or three riders.	
	157 *Macduff* **is fled**: **TURN**: the murder plot is foiled.
160 **Time,** you anticipated and prevented **my dread exploits** (killing Macduff).	160 Gathering his resolve to murder not only Macduff, but his whole family. Making sure he doesn't repeat his mistake, allowing Macduff's children to escape and potentially threaten him, as he did with Fleance.
161 **flighty purpose** = goal that is flying away out of reach. **o'ertook** = caught up with.	
162 **go with it** = accompanies it. The elusive object is never caught unless acted upon at once.	Note: His response to the Witches is contradictory. On one hand he takes their assurance that 'none of woman born shall harm Macbeth' as license to do whatever he wants with impunity. On the other hand, he is so afraid of Macduff that he's going to murder the entire Macduff clan. **FOR-WARD**: Will he murder everyone at Fife?
163 **firstlings** = firstborn. The first thing I think will be the first thing I do.	
164 **even now**: at this moment.	
165 **To Crown** (legitimize) **my thoughts with Acts: be it thought & done** (let it be thought and immediately done).	
167 **Seize upon** = capture	
169 **trace him in his Line** = are his relatives; belong to his bloodline. **No boasting like a Fool**: rather than boasting like a fool.	
170 **before this purpose cool** = before the heat of this intention cools.	
171 **sights** — hallucinations. Let's have no more gory ghosts and spirits.	171 Note. He disavows the Witches, but does exactly what they wanted.

4.2.a A room in Macduff's castle at Fife. Interior. Day.

Purpose: To build our sense of the danger Macduff's family is in.

Drama: Can Rosse comfort Lady Macduff by convincing her that her husband did the right thing?

What	Why
1. **What had he done** (what crime did my husband Macduff commit), **to make him fly the Land** (flee Scotland)?	1 Demanding that Rosse explain her husband's behavior. Accusing him of a misdeed. We can assume Rosse has just informed her that Macduff has fled to England.
3 **none** = no patience.	3 Demanding that Rosse agree that Macduff has abandoned his family.

4 His flight was madness: when our Actions do not,

5 Our fears do make us Traitors.

ROSSE

6 You know not

7 Whether it was his wisdom, or his fear.

LADY MACDUFF

8 Wisdom? To leave his wife, to leave his Babes,

9 His Mansion, and his Titles, in a place

10 From whence himself does fly? He loves us not,

11 He wants the natural touch. ¶ For the poor Wren

12 (The most diminutive of Birds) will fight,

13 Her young ones in her Nest, against the Owl:

14 ¶ All is the Fear, and nothing is the Love;

15 As little is the Wisdom, where the flight

16 So runs against all reason.

ROSSE

17 My dearest Coz,

18 I pray you school yourself. But for your Husband,

19 He is Noble, Wise, Judicious, and best knows

20 The fits o' th' Season. ¶ I dare not speak much further,

21 But cruel are the times, when we are Traitors

22 And do not know ourselves: when we hold Rumour

23 From what we fear, yet know not what we fear,

24 But float upon a wild and violent Sea

25 Each way, and move. ¶ I take my leave of you:

26 Shall not be long but I'll be here again:

27 ¶ Things at the worst will cease, or else climb upward,

28 To what they were before. ¶ My pretty Cousin,

29 Blessing upon you.

LADY MACDUFF

30 Father'd he is, and yet he's Fatherless.

ROSSE

31 I am so much a Fool, should I stay longer

32 It would be my disgrace, and your discomfort.

33 I take my leave at once.

Exit Rosse.

4.2.b -

What	Why
4-5 when our Actions do not (even when our actions do not deserve to be called traitorous), **Our fears** (our fears of violence from Macbeth) **do make us Traitors** (make us flee, which makes us appear to be traitors).	
6-7 You know not Whether it was his wisdom, or his fear: It may have been not fear but wisdom; he may have had good reason, which he did not have a chance to explain.	6 Defending Macduff.
9-10 in a place (Fife) **From whence himself does fly** (from which he runs away).	9 Angrily contradicting Rosse and accusing her husband.
11 wants =lacks. **the natural touch** = human nature's normal protective instinct.	
12 diminutive = small.	
12-13 will fight if **Her young ones are in her Nest.**	
14 He has put **All** his emphasis on his **Fear,** and **nothing** on his **Love.**	
15 that's how **little the Wisdom** is.	
15-16 where the flight (the decision to fly) **So runs against all reason** (is so unreasonable).	
17 coz = cousin.	17 Comforting her. Patiently reemphasizing that Macduff fled for reasons that Rosse can't divulge, but if she knew them, she would approve.
18 school yourself = correct your thinking.	
19 Judicious = has good judgment.	
20 fits o' th' Season = convulsions of the times.	20 **I dare not speak much further**: If Rosse were to tell her what he knows, he would be guilty of treason.
21-22 when we are accused of being **Traitors And do not know ourselves** (do not know why we are accused).	
22-23 when we hold (hold to be true) **Rumour From what we fear** (rumor based on our fear), **yet know not what we fear** (know not whom we should be afraid of).	
25 Each way = every which way. **and move** = and get moved about.	25 **I take my leave**: breaking off so he can rush away.
27 Things at the worst will cease, or else climb upward: This is the worst, things can only get better.	
30 Father'd he is (he has a biological father), **and yet he's Fatherless** (but not a male parent at home).	
31-32 should I (if I were to) **stay longer It would be my disgrace, and your discomfort**. If I were to stay, I would cry like the fool I am, disgrace myself and embarrass you.	31 Taking his leave.

4.2.b Purpose: 1. To further heighten our sense of danger by showing that this is a household of women and children, completely defenseless. 2. To sharpen even more our anxiety for the Macduffs by showing how lovable they are. 3. To illustrate by contrast how poisoned the Macbeths are.

Drama: Can Lady Macduff's son ease his mother's mind by making her laugh?

LADY MACDUFF

34 Sirrah, your Father's dead,
35 And what will you do now? How will you live?

SON

36 As Birds do Mother.

LADY MACDUFF

37 What with Worms, and Flies?

SON

38 With what I get I mean, and so do they.

LADY MACDUFF

39 Poor Bird,
40 Thou'dst never Fear the Net, nor Lime,
41 The Pitfall, nor the Gin.

SON

42 Why should I Mother?
43 Poor Birds they are not set for:
44 ¶ My Father is not dead for all your saying.

LADY MACDUFF

45 Yes, he is dead:
46 ¶ How wilt thou do for a Father?

SON

47 Nay how will you do for a Husband?

LADY MACDUFF

48 Why I can buy me twenty at any Market.

SON

49 Then you'll buy 'em to sell again.

LADY MACDUFF

50 Thou speak'st with all thy wit,
51 And yet i' faith with wit enough for thee.

SON

52 Was my Father a Traitor, Mother?

LADY MACDUFF

53 Ay, that he was.

SON

54 What is a Traitor?

What	Why
34 **Sirrah**: a word used to address an inferior.	34 Seeking comfort from him for her own loss.
	36 **As Birds do:** Cheering her up with a joke.
37 **with Worms, and Flies**: by eating worms and flies.	37 Trying to set her terror aside by engaging him in a little game.
38 **With what I** am able to **get.**	38 Accepting her invitation to the game.
40-41 You would be caught because **Thou'dst never Fear the Net** (bird net)**, nor Lime** (birdlime, a sticky substance to catch birds with)**, The Pitfall** (pit trap)**, nor the Gin** (another kind of trap).	
43 **Poor Birds they are not set for**: The traps are not set to catch scrawny birds like me that would make poor eating.	44 **My Father is not dead:** justifying his lack of fear — calling her bluff.
	45 **Yes, he is dead**: saying what she believes, but masking it as merely a playful game.
47 **How will you do for a Husband**: How will you get a husband?	
49 **Then you'll buy 'em to sell again**: If you were so faithless to my father that you would buy twenty more, you would be equally faithless to them.	49 Teasingly accusing.
50-51 **Thou speak'st with all thy wit** (you are using all the sense you have and still make no sense) **And yet i' faith with wit enough for thee** (and yet truly with wit enough to make me laugh, which was your intent).	50 Conceding defeat in the match of wits.
	52 **was my Father a Traitor**: changing to seriousness. Seeking to learn his father's case, and how much danger he's in.

LADY MACDUFF

55 Why one that swears, and lies.

SON

56 And be all Traitors, that do so.

LADY MACDUFF

57 Every one that does so, is a Traitor,
58 And must be hang'd.

SON

59 And must they all be hang'd, that swear and lie?

LADY MACDUFF

60 Every one.

SON

61 Who must hang them?

LADY MACDUFF

62 Why, the honest men.

SON

63 Then the Liars and Swearers are Fools: for there are Liars and
64 Swearers enough, to beat the honest men, and hang up them.

LADY MACDUFF

65 Now God help thee, poor Monkey:
66 ¶ But how wilt thou do for a Father?

SON

67 If he were dead, you'd weep for him: if you would not, it were a
68 good sign, that I should quickly have a new Father.

LADY MACDUFF

69 Poor prattler, how thou talk'st?

4.2.c -

Enter a Messenger.

MESSENGER

70 Bless you fair Dame: I am not to you known,
71 Though in your state of Honour I am perfect;
72 ¶ I doubt some danger does approach you nearly.
73 If you will take a homely man's advice,
74 Be not found here: Hence with your little ones.
75 ¶ To fright you thus, Methinks I am too savage:
76 To do worse to you, were fell Cruelty,
77 Which is too nigh your person. ¶ Heaven preserve you,
78 I dare abide no longer.

Exit Messenger.

What	Why
55 **swears, and lies**: specifically, swears an oath of loyalty and breaks it.	55 Deciding to honor his request for adult information.
56 **be all Traitors, that do so** = are all who do so traitors?	
59 **swear and lie**: He thinks she means any kind of cursing and fibbing.	59 He knows it can't be true that these daily little sins will earn a sentence of death, so he concludes she's pulling his leg and it's still a game.
	62 **the honest men**: trying to give her son correct information. Triumphing in the game of wits.
63-64 He reasons that the few **honest men** who don't curse or lie must be vastly outnumbered by the **Liars and Swearers**.	
	65 **poor Monkey:** Teasingly praising him for this excellent witticism. Monkey is a term of endearment.
66 **But how wilt thou do for a Father**: She can't stop worrying about Macduff.	
67-68 **if you would not, it were a good sign, that I should quickly have a new Father** = if he died and you didn't weep, it would mean you didn't love him and would soon marry another.	67 Again, triumphing in the game of wits.
69 **prattler**: one who runs on with empty talk.	69 Again, teasingly conceding defeat.

4.2.c Purpose: To ratchet up our anxiety for the imminent murder to the highest pitch.

Drama: Can the Messenger persuade her to flee in time?

What	Why
71 **in your state of Honour I am perfect** = I am perfectly acquainted with your honored person.	71 Warning her.
72 **doubt** = fear. **nearly** = soon.	
73 **homely** = plain.	
74 **Hence** = get away from here.	
75-77 **To fright you thus, Methinks I am too savage** (it seems too cruel to frighten you thus)**: To do worse to you, were fell Cruelty** (but otherwise would be to leave you to worse cruelty)**, Which is too nigh your person** (the murderers are almost here).	74 Note: We added the period after "**little ones**", and changed the Folio's period after '**thus**' to a comma. Based on the meaning, we believe those were typos.
78 **abide** = stay.	

LADY MACDUFF

79 Whither should I fly?
80 I have done no harm. ¶ But I remember now
81 I am in this earthly world: where to do harm
82 Is often laudable, to do good sometime
83 Accounted dangerous folly. Why then (alas)
84 Do I put up that womanly defense,
85 To say I have done no harm?
86 ¶ What are these faces?

4.2.d -
Enter Murderers.

FIRST MURDERER

87 Where is your Husband?

LADY MACDUFF

88 I hope in no place so unsanctified,
89 Where such as thou may'st find him.

FIRST MURDERER

90 He's a Traitor.

SON

91 Thou lie'st thou shag-ear'd Villain.

FIRST MURDERER

92 What you Egg?
93 *[Stabbing him]* ¶ Young fry of Treachery?

SON

94 He has kill'd me Mother,
95 Run away I pray you.
Exit [Lady Macduff] crying 'Murder'.

SCENA TERTIA.

Enter Malcolm and Macduff.

MALCOLM

1 Let us seek out some desolate shade, & there
2 Weep our sad bosoms empty.

MACDUFF

3 Let us rather

What	Why
79 **Whither should I fly** = Where should I flee to?	79 Vacillating in her panic.
81 **earthly** = on earth, where what is can be very different from what should be. 82 **laudable** = praiseworthy. 83 **folly** = foolishness. 84 **womanly**: implying that men would be more pragmatic when confronted with reality.	
	86 **What are these faces**: seeing the murderers enter.

4.2.d Purpose: To make us want to see Macduff get revenge on Macbeth. Shakespeare wants us to crave that outcome as strongly as possible.

Drama: Will the Murderers kill Lady Macduff and Son?

What	Why
88 **so unsanctified**: Any place with you in it is unholy, so he wouldn't be found there.	88 Bravely challenging him.
91 **shag-ear'd**: calling him a dog or a donkey.	91 Joining his mother's challenge.
92 **Egg:** so young he's not yet hatched. In Shakespeare's day, a standard insult for a rude child. 93 **fry** = baby fish; spawn of a traitor.	93 *[Stabbing him]*: inferred. Not in Folio.

4.3.a King Edward's palace, England. Exterior. Day.

Purpose: 1. To begin the process of defeating Macbeth's reign of terror. As a first step, Malcolm must find a way to trust Macduff. 2. To demonstrate that Malcolm will be a wise and just ruler. 3. To build anticipation for the revelation to Macduff of his family's fate.

Drama: 1. Will Macduff pass Malcolm's test? 2. Will Malcolm agree to return to Scotland and challenge Macbeth? 3. When will Macduff find out his family's dead? 4. How will he react?

What	Why
1 **desolate shade** = dark, lonely place under a tree.	1 Inviting Macduff to grieve with him for Scotland.
2 **Weep our sad bosoms empty** = cry until we have no more tears left.	

4 Hold fast the mortal Sword: and like good men,
5 Bestride our downfall Birthdom: each new Morn,
6 New Widows howl, new Orphans cry, new sorrows
7 Strike heaven on the face, that it resounds
8 As if it felt with Scotland, and yell'd out
9 Like Syllable of Dolour.

MALCOLM
10 What I believe, I'll wail;
11 What know, believe; and what I can redress,
12 As I shall find the time to friend: I will.
13 ⸿ What you have spoke, it may be so perchance.
14 This Tyrant, whose sole name blisters our tongues,
15 Was once thought honest: you have lov'd him well,
16 He hath not touch'd you yet. I am young, but something
17 You may deserve of him through me, and wisdom
18 To offer up a weak, poor innocent Lamb
19 T' appease an angry God.

MACDUFF
20 I am not treacherous.

MALCOLM
21 But *Macbeth* is.
22 A good and virtuous Nature may recoil
23 In an Imperial charge. ⸿ But I shall crave your pardon:
24 That which you are, my thoughts cannot transpose;
25 Angels are bright still, though the brightest fell.
26 Though all things foul, would wear the brows of grace
27 Yet Grace must still look so.

MACDUFF
28 I have lost my Hopes.

MALCOLM
29 Perchance even there
30 Where I did find my doubts.
31 ⸿ Why in that rawness left you Wife, and Child?
32 Those precious Motives, those strong knots of Love,
33 Without leave-taking. ⸿ I pray you,
34 Let not my Jealousies, be your Dishonours,
35 But mine own Safeties: you may be rightly just,
36 Whatever I shall think.

What	Why
4 **mortal** = deadly. 5 **Bestride**: like a warrior standing over a fallen friend in battle, defending. **downfall Birthdom** = the fallen kingdom of our birth. 6-8 **new sorrows** (the cries of the new victims) **Strike heaven on the face** (are so loud they reach the sky), **that it resounds** (and echo) **As if it felt** (as if Heaven felt sympathy) **with Scotland.** 9 **like Syllable of Dolour** = similar notes of great sorrow.	4 Urging Malcolm to not go weep, but return to Scotland and fight against Macbeth. 6 **New Widows howl**: reminding him how bad it is, in hope of stirring him to act.
10 **What** (of the tales of woe, the ones) **I believe, I'll wail** (mourn for). 11 **What** (I) **know,** (I will) **believe. redress** = correct. 12 **As I shall find the time to friend** = when opportunity is friendly. 13 **What you have spoke, it may be so perchance** = What you say may perhaps be true. 14 **whose sole name** (merely speaking his name) **blisters our tongues.** 16 **touch'd** = hurt. 16-17 **something You may deserve of him through me** = You may earn some favor from him by sacrificing me. 17 **wisdom** = you may consider it wisdom. 19 **T' appease an angry God:** offer me to Macbeth like an Old Testament sacrifice.	10 Withholding from jumping in with Macduff. Malcolm is saying, 'I can't assume you are my friend. You may perhaps be here in service of Macbeth to my harm, but I must withhold judgment'. 17 **deserve**: Folio has 'discern'.
22-23 An otherwise **virtuous Nature may recoil** (may buckle) **In an Imperial charge** (under a king's command). **crave** = beg.	20 **I am not treacherous:** Vigorously defending his honor. 22 Apologetically explaining why he can't simply join with Macduff, even though he wants to.
24 **That which you are, my thoughts cannot transpose** = I cannot transfer your thoughts into my mind, to tell what you really are. 25 **brightest**: Satan, who fell from Grace. 26-27 **Though all things foul, would wear the brows of grace** (though evildoers mask themselves as gracious) **Yet Grace must still look so** (true grace also looks like grace). You can't tell false grace from true grace just by looking. 28 **I have lost my Hopes**: Then I have lost my hope that you will lead a rebellion against Macbeth (because you don't trust me). 29-30 **Perchance** you lost your hopes when you did the thing that caused me to **doubt** you. 31 **rawness** = danger.	29 Challenging Macduff to explain his suspicious behavior: Why would he go foment rebellion but leave his wife and children where Macbeth could kill them or hold them hostage?
32 **precious Motives** = motivations to protect what's precious. **knots of Love**: love binds them to you. 33 **leave-taking** = saying goodbye. 34-35 **Let not** (Please do not interpret) **my Jealousies** (my suspicions), **be your Dishonours** (as aspersions on your honor), **But mine own Safeties** (but as motivated by my own safety). 35-36 **you may be rightly just** (It may be that you are true), **Whatever I shall think** (regardless of my doubts).	32 Apologizing that he is compelled to be circumspect.

MACDUFF

37 Bleed, bleed poor Country,
38 Great Tyranny, lay thou thy basis sure,
39 For goodness dare not check thee: wear you thy wrongs;
40 The Title, is affear'd. ¶ Fare thee well Lord,
41 I would not be the Villain that thou think'st,
42 For the whole Space that's in the Tyrant's Grasp,
43 And the rich East to boot.

MALCOLM

44 Be not offended:
45 I speak not as in absolute fear of you:
46 I think our Country sinks beneath the yoke,
47 It weeps, it bleeds, and each new day a gash
48 Is added to her wounds. ¶ I think withal,
49 There would be hands uplifted in my right:
50 And here from gracious England have I offer
51 Of goodly thousands. ¶ But for all this,
52 When I shall tread upon the Tyrant's head,
53 Or wear it on my Sword; yet my poor Country
54 Shall have more vices than it had before,
55 More suffer, and more sundry ways than ever,
56 By him that shall succeed.

MACDUFF

57 What should he be?

MALCOLM

58 It is myself I mean: in whom I know
59 All the particulars of Vice so grafted,
60 That when they shall be open'd, black *Macbeth*
61 Will seem as pure as Snow, and the poor State
62 Esteem him as a Lamb, being compar'd
63 With my confineless harms.

MACDUFF

64 Not in the Legions
65 Of horrid Hell, can come a Devil more damn'd
66 In evils, to top *Macbeth*.

MALCOLM

67 I grant him Bloody,
68 Luxurious, Avaricious, False, Deceitful,
69 Sudden, Malicious, smacking of every sin

What	Why
38 **Great Tyranny** (i.e. Macbeth)**, lay thou thy basis sure** (build a solid foundation, or power base).	38 Accusing Malcolm of quitting: Macbeth is free to parade his crimes, since the rightful heir doesn't dare confront him.
39 **goodness** (virtue) **dare not check thee** (stop you). **wear you thy wrongs** = go ahead and display your crimes openly.	
40 **The Title, is affear'd** = Malcolm, who has rightful title to the throne, is afraid. **Fare thee well Lord** = Goodbye, Lord Malcolm.	40 Threatening to give up and go home.
42 **the whole Space that's in the Tyrant's Grasp**: all the land Macbeth controls.	
43 **the rich East** = India, China, etc., where silks and spices came from. **to boot** = in addition.	
45 **absolute fear** = unchangeable mistrust. I hadn't decided you were definitely a spy, but was only testing you.	44 **Be not offended - TURN**: Malcolm is persuaded that Macduff is not a spy for Macbeth.
46 **sinks beneath the yoke**: Picture an overburdened ox falling to its knees.	
48 **withal** = in addition.	
49 **hands uplifted in my right** = People would support my right to the throne.	
50 **gracious England** = the gracious King of England.	
51 **goodly thousands**, i.e. of well-trained soldiers.	51 **NEW DRAMA**: Now that Macduff has passed the first test and proven he's not a spy, Malcolm begins another test, to gauge whether Macduff's interest is for the good of Scotland or for personal greed.
52-53 **tread upon the Tyrant's head, Or wear it on my Sword**: He means this literally.	
55 **More suffer** = My country will suffer more. **sundry** = diverse and numerous.	**FORWARD**: Will we see goodly thousands of English soldiers follow Malcolm?
56 **By him** (Malcolm) **that shall succeed** (succeed to the throne).	
57 **What should he be?** = Who would that be?	
59-60 **grafted**: Imagine branches from the vice tree grafted onto the Malcolm tree, so that when they have bloomed (**opened**), black Macbeth will seem pure by comparison.	59 Pretending to confess himself unworthy to rule.
63 **confineless** = boundless.	
64-65 **Legions Of horrid Hell** = army of devils in Hell.	64 Disbelieving: You can't possibly be worse than Macbeth.
66 **top** = surpass.	
67 **Bloody** = bloodthirsty.	
68 **Luxurious** = lustful. **Avaricious** = greedy.	
69 **Sudden** = impetuous.	

70 That has a name. ¶ But there's no bottom, none
71 In my Voluptuousness: Your Wives, your Daughters,
72 Your Matrons, and your Maids, could not fill up
73 The Cistern of my Lust, and my Desire
74 All continent Impediments would o'erbear
75 That did oppose my will. ¶ Better *Macbeth*,
76 Than such an one to reign.

MACDUFF

77 Boundless intemperance
78 In Nature is a Tyranny: it hath been
79 Th' untimely emptying of the happy Throne,
80 And fall of many Kings. ¶ But fear not yet
81 To take upon you what is yours: you may
82 Convey your pleasures in a spacious plenty,
83 And yet seem cold. The time you may so hoodwink:
84 We have willing Dames enough: there cannot be
85 That Vulture in you, to devour so many
86 As will to Greatness dedicate themselves,
87 Finding it so inclin'd.

MALCOLM

88 With this, there grows
89 In my most ill-compos'd Affection, such
90 A stanchless Avarice, that were I King,
91 I should cut off the Nobles for their Lands,
92 Desire his Jewels, and this other's House,
93 And my more-having, would be as a Sauce
94 To make me hunger more, that I should forge
95 Quarrels unjust against the Good and Loyal,
96 Destroying them for wealth.

MACDUFF

97 This Avarice
98 Sticks deeper: grows with more pernicious root
99 Than Summer-seeming Lust: and it hath been
100 The Sword of our slain Kings: ¶ yet do not fear,
101 Scotland hath Foisons, to fill up your will
102 Of your mere Own. All these are portable,
103 With other Graces weigh'd.

What	**Why**
71 **Voluptuousness** = lust. 72 **Matrons and Maids** = married women and virgins. 73 **Cistern** = well. 73-75 Reordered: **my Desire would o'erbear** (would overrun) **All continent Impediments** (all the restraints of chastity) **that did oppose my will** (that got in my way). 75-76. It would be **Better** that *Macbeth* reign **than such an one.** 77-78 **Boundless intemperance** (lack of moderation) **In Nature** (character) **is a Tyranny.** 79 **untimely emptying of the happy Throne**: Good kings have fallen prematurely. 80 **yet** = nevertheless. 81 **what is yours**: your birthright, the crown. 82-83 **Convey** (manage) **your pleasures** (your appetites) **in a spacious** (ample) **plenty, And yet seem** (appear) **cold** (chaste). You may indulge your lust secretly and still appear virtuous. 83 **The time** = the world. **hoodwink** = deceive. 84-87 **there cannot be That Vulture in you** (you can't be such a vulture)**, to devour so many** (as to use so many women) **As will to Greatness dedicate themselves** (as will offer themselves to a great man) **Finding it so inclin'd** (if they find he wants them). 88 **With this** = in addition to this. 89 **ill-compos'd Affection** = badly made disposition. 90 **stanchless Avarice** = unstoppable greed. **were** = if I were. 91 **cut off** = kill. 92 **Desire his** (one man's) **Jewels.** 93 **more-having**: the more I had the more I would want. 94-95 **forge Quarrels** = invent false disputes. 98 **Sticks** = stabs. **pernicious** = subtly evil. 99 **Summer-seeming** = transient, like the summer of youth. 100 **Sword of our slain Kings** = the thing that got some of our kings killed. 101 **Foisons** = abundance. 102 **your mere Own**: merely from what you would own, i.e. the revenues of the royal estates would amply supply your greed. **portable** = supportable. 103 **With other Graces weigh'd** = if weighed against your other, more gracious, characteristics.	77 Persuading Malcolm that, even with his boundless lust, he would still be a much fitter king than Macbeth. 88 Having failed to put off Macduff with the first test, putting him to a further test. 98 The same again: still pushing Malcolm to come back to Scotland and take his rightful place as King. 101 Note: The nobles each had their own lands to support their households and armies. The King also had royal lands to support his household and army. In an emergency, the King could sometimes tax the nobles for additional support.

MALCOLM

104 But I have none: the King-becoming Graces,
105 As Justice, Verity, Temp'rance, Stableness,
106 Bounty, Perseverance, Mercy, Lowliness,
107 Devotion, Patience, Courage, Fortitude,
108 I have no relish of them, but abound
109 In the division of each several Crime,
110 Acting it many ways. Nay, had I power, I should
111 Pour the sweet Milk of Concord, into Hell,
112 Uproar the universal peace, confound
113 All unity on earth.

MACDUFF

114 O Scotland, Scotland.

MALCOLM

115 If such a one be fit to govern, speak:
116 I am as I have spoken.

MACDUFF

117 Fit to govern? No not to live. ¶ O Nation miserable!
118 With an untitled Tyrant, bloody Scepter'd,
119 When shalt thou see thy wholesome days again?
120 Since that the truest Issue of thy Throne
121 By his own Interdiction stands accus'd,
122 And does blaspheme his breed? ¶ Thy Royal Father
123 Was a most Sainted-King: the Queen that bore thee,
124 Oft'ner upon her knees, than on her feet,
125 Died every day she liv'd. ¶ Fare thee well,
126 These Evils thou repeat'st upon thyself,
127 Hath banish'd me from Scotland. ¶ O my Breast,
128 Thy hope ends here.

MALCOLM

129 *Macduff,* this Noble passion
130 Child of integrity, hath from my soul
131 Wip'd the black Scruples, reconcil'd my thoughts
132 To thy good Truth, and Honour. ¶ Devilish *Macbeth,*
133 By many of these trains, hath sought to win me
134 Into his power: and modest Wisdom plucks me
135 From over-credulous haste: ¶ but God above
136 Deal between thee and me; For even now
137 I put myself to thy Direction, and

What	Why
104 **none**: no other graces.	104 Another test. Macduff has passed the first test – Malcolm is satisfied that Macduff is not here to lure Malcolm back to be caught by Macbeth. Next he must answer the question, Is Macduff's motive selfish (to be near the king, regardless of the king's fitness), or is he genuinely interested in the health of Scotland?
105 **Verity** = truth. **Temp'rance** = moderation.	
106 **Bounty** = generosity. **Lowliness** = humility.	
107 **Fortitude** = moral strength.	
108 **relish** = taste for. **abound In** = am full of.	
109-110 **division** = variation. **several** = distinct. I am full of every kind of **Crime**, and act it out **in many ways.**	
110 **had I** = if I had.	
111 **the sweet Milk of Concord** = the delicious nourishment of peaceful coexistence.	
112 **Uproar the universal peace** = turn the universal peace into universal uproar. **confound** = prevent.	
	114 **O Scotland**: **TURN**: giving up. Grieving.
	116 **I am as I have spoken**: Making sure Macduff has changed his mind.
	117 **Fit to govern?** Lamenting that his hope is lost.
118 **untitled** = illegitimate. **bloody Scepter'd**: figuratively, Macbeth's scepter of rule is covered with the blood of his victims.	
120 **truest Issue of thy Throne** = most rightful heir, i.e. Malcolm.	
121 **Interdiction** = speaking against himself.	
122 **blaspheme his breed** = commit sacrilege against his entire lineage.	
123 **Sainted** = Godly.	
124 **upon her knees**: praying.	
125 **Died**: Denied herself pleasures of this world in contemplation of the next.	
126 **repeat'st** = the evils of which you accuse yourself.	
127 **Breast** = heart.	
130 **Child of** = born of; produced by.	129 **BIG TURN:** revealing that he was testing Macduff, and Macduff has passed the test. Apologizing for having tricked him by explaining the reason.
129-132 **this Noble passion** (Your noble passionate outburst) **Child of integrity** (born from your integrity), **hath from my soul Wip'd the black Scruples** (the dark suspicions), **reconcil'd my thoughts To** (restored my faith in) **thy good Truth, and Honour.**	
133 **trains** = stratagems. **win** = capture.	133 Note: Apparently Macbeth has already sent many false emissaries to lure Malcolm back to Scotland to be captured.
134 **modest Wisdom** = wise prudence.	
135-136 **over-credulous** = too trusting. **God above Deal between thee and me**: swearing by God to deal truthfully. cf. the current usage, 'as God is my witness'.	
136 **even now** = at this moment.	
137 **I put myself to thy Direction**: I will let you direct me.	

138 Unspeak mine own detraction. Here abjure
139 The taints, and blames I laid upon myself,
140 For strangers to my Nature. I am yet
141 Unknown to Woman, never was forsworn,
142 Scarcely have coveted what was mine own.
143 At no time broke my Faith, would not betray
144 The Devil to his Fellow, and delight
145 No less in truth than life. My first false speaking
146 Was this upon myself. What I am truly
147 Is thine, and my poor Country's to command:
148 Whither indeed, before thy here approach
149 Old Seyward with ten thousand warlike men
150 Already at a point, was setting forth:
151 ¶ Now we'll together, and the chance of goodness
152 Be like our warranted Quarrel. ¶ Why are you silent?

MACDUFF

153 Such welcome, and unwelcome things at once
154 'Tis hard to reconcile.

4.3.b -
Enter a Doctor.

MALCOLM

155 Well, more anon. ¶ Comes the King forth
156 I pray you?

DOCTOR

157 Aye Sir: there are a crew of wretched Souls
158 That stay his Cure: their malady convinces
159 The great assay of Art. But at his touch,
160 Such sanctity hath Heaven given his hand,
161 They presently amend.

Exit Doctor.

MALCOLM

162 I thank you Doctor.

MACDUFF

163 What's the Disease he means?

MALCOLM

164 'Tis call'd the Evil.
165 A most miraculous work in this good King,
166 Which often since my here remain in England,
167 I have seen him do: How he solicits heaven

What	Why
138 **Unspeak** = take back. **abjure** = solemnly renounce. I disavow the faults I accused myself of, as alien to me.	
140 **strangers to my Nature**: alien to my character.	
141 **Unknown to Woman** = a virgin. **forsworn** = swore falsely.	
143-144 **would not betray The Devil to his Fellow**: I am so loyal I would not even betray the Devil.	
144-145 **delight No less in truth than life**: truth is as dear to me as life.	
145 **false speaking:** My first lie was this, against myself.	
146-147 **What I am truly** (my real self, as opposed to the false picture I first painted) **Is thine, and my poor Country's to command**: I will be governed by you and the needs of Scotland.	
148-150: **Whither** (toward which, i.e. toward Scotland), **indeed, before thy here approach** (before your arrival), **Old Seyward with ten thousand warlike men** (soldiers), **Already at a point** (armed with pointed spears), **was setting forth.**	148 Moving on to the next topic: agreeing to go fight. **FORWARD**: again, will the vast English army go with Malcolm and depose Macbeth? **thy**: Folio has 'they'
151 **we'll together** = we'll go together.	
152 **warranted Quarrel** = our just cause. Let our chance of success be as strong as the justness of our cause.	
153 **welcome**: Malcolm's disavowal of his vices and announcement that he has 10,000 soldiers ready for attack. **unwelcome**: Malcolm's feigned catalogue of vices, from which Macduff is still reeling.	153 Reeling with the wonderful news.

4.3.b Purpose: 1. To insert a pause before Macduff learns of the death of his family. 2. To illustrate by contrast the kind of king Macbeth is.

Drama: This is an interlude to separate the two big dramas before and after.

What	Why
155 **more anon**: We'll speak more soon.	155 Turning his attention to the Doctor. Note: We think this is what in modern times would be called product placement: Edward was a forebear of King James, sponsor of Shakespeare's company.
158-159 **stay** = wait for. **convinces The great assay of Art** = defeats the best efforts (**assay**) of the physician's **Art**.	158 Worshipping the King.
159-161 **But at his touch** (when he touches them), **Such sanctity hath Heaven given his hand** (God has given him such holy powers), **They presently amend** (they are soon cured).	159 Reverencing King Edward, who is so holy that he is able to cure the sick merely by touching them, like Jesus.
164 **'Tis called the Evil**: the illness is called 'the Evil'.	164 'The King's Evil' was the contemporary name for what we now call Scrofula, a bacterial infection related to tuberculosis, which creates open sores on the skin.
165 **a most miraculous work in this good King**: a miracle this good King is able to perform.	
166 **my here remain** = my stay here.	
167 **How he solicits heaven**: how he gets God to do as he requests.	

168 Himself best knows: but strangely visited people
169 All swoll'n and Ulcerous, pitiful to the eye,
170 The mere despair of Surgery, he cures,
171 Hanging a golden stamp about their necks,
172 Put on with holy Prayers, and 'tis spoken
173 To the succeeding Royalty he leaves
174 The healing Benediction. ¶ With this strange virtue,
175 He hath a heavenly gift of Prophecy,
176 And sundry Blessings hang about his Throne,
177 That speak him full of Grace.

4.3.c -
Enter Rosse.

MACDUFF
178 See who comes here.

MALCOLM
179 My Countryman: but yet I know him not.

MACDUFF
180 My ever gentle Cousin, welcome hither.

MALCOLM
181 I know him now. ¶ Good God betimes remove
182 The means that makes us Strangers.

ROSSE
183 Sir, Amen.

MACDUFF
184 Stands Scotland where it did?

ROSSE
185 Alas poor Country,
186 Almost afraid to know itself. It cannot
187 Be call'd our Mother, but our Grave; where nothing
188 But who knows nothing, is once seen to smile:
189 Where sighs, and groans, and shrieks that rent the air
190 Are made, not mark'd: where violent sorrow seems
191 A Modern ecstasy: the Dead Man's knell,
192 Is there scarce ask'd for who, and good men's lives
193 Expire before the Flowers in their Caps,
194 Dying, or ere they sicken.

MACDUFF
195 O Relation; too nice, and yet too true.

What	Why
168 **Himself best knows**: only he knows. **strangely visited** = with strange symptoms.	
170 **The mere despair of Surgery**: surgeons utterly despair of helping them.	
171 **golden stamp**: gold medallion stamped with a special emblem.	
172 **Put on with holy Prayers**: he prays when hanging the medallion from their necks.	
173-174 **To the succeeding Royalty** (to his successor kings) **he leaves** (he bequeaths) **The healing Benediction** (the ability to heal by blessing).	
174 **With this strange virtue**: in addition to this unusual power.	
175 **He hath a heavenly gift of Prophecy**: He has a God-given power to foretell the future.	
176 **sundry** = various.	
177 **speak him** = tell that he is.	

4.3.c Purpose: 1. To make Macduff (and us) hate Macbeth, and sharpen our desire for his revenge. 2. To start the wheels of retribution turning.

Drama: 1. Can Rosse bring himself to utter his news? 2. How will Macduff react? 3. Can Malcolm persuade Macduff to convert his grief into rage?

What	Why
179 **My Countryman** (I can see from his clothes he is a fellow Scot)**: but yet I know him not** (but I still don't recognize him).	179 Note: This shows how much has happened since Macbeth became king. Either so much time has passed, or living under Macbeth's rule has so changed Rosse's appearance, that Malcolm doesn't recognize him.
181-182 **know** = recognize. **betimes** = soon. **Good God betimes remove The means that makes us Strangers**: May God soon remove Macbeth, who has separated us so long we don't recognize each other.	
183 **amen**: agreeing.	
184 **where**: in the same terrible condition.	184 Asking for the news.
	185 Reporting the heavy news – devastation, slaughter, starvation.
186-187 **afraid to know itself** = afraid to acknowledge what it's become. **Mother**: 'motherland'.	
187-188 **nothing** (nobody) **But** (except) **who knows nothing** (who knows nothing of what's happening) **is once** (ever) **seen to smile.**	
189-190 **shrieks that rent the air**: screams so pitiful they seem to tear the air. **mark'd**: heeded. We are so used to screams that we don't even notice them anymore.	
191 **A Modern ecstasy** = an emotion that's in fashion.	
191-193 **knell**: funeral bell. We no longer bother to ask who died. **Flowers in their Caps**: Imagine a youth with a flower in his cap; the flower lasts longer than the youth.	
194 **or ere** = before.	
195 **Relation** = report, as in 'relate the news'. **nice** = strange. 'Nice' had many meanings in Shakespeare's day. This one seems to make the most sense in the context. In our day we might say, 'bizarre but true'.	195 Grieving.

MALCOLM

196   What's the newest grief?

ROSSE

197   That of an hour's age, doth hiss the speaker,
198   Each minute teems a new one.

MACDUFF

199   How does my Wife?

ROSSE

200   Why well.

MACDUFF

201   And all my Children?

ROSSE

202   Well too.

MACDUFF

203   The Tyrant has not batter'd at their peace?

ROSSE

204   No, they were well at peace, when I did leave 'em.

MACDUFF

205   Be not a niggard of your speech: How goes 't?

ROSSE

206   When I came hither to transport the Tidings
207   Which I have heavily borne, there ran a Rumour
208   Of many worthy Fellows, that were out,
209   Which was to my belief witness'd the rather,
210   For that I saw the Tyrant's Power afoot.
211   ⸿ Now is the time of help: your eye in Scotland
212   Would create Soldiers, make our women fight,
213   To doff their dire distresses.

MALCOLM

214   Be 't their comfort
215   We are coming thither: Gracious England hath
216   Lent us good *Seyward*, and ten thousand men,
217   An older, and a better Soldier, none
218   That Christendom gives out.

ROSSE

219   Would I could answer
220   This comfort with the like. But I have words

What	Why
197 **hiss**: to tell a grief an hour old gets the speaker hissed at (as old news).	
198 **teems** = breeds.	
	200 **Why well**: Putting off the moment of truth.
203 **batter'd**: imagine a battering ram.	203 Note: This shows Macduff has been worrying about having left his family unprotected. Perhaps he thought he would be home before Macbeth could threaten them, but now sees that was a mistake?
204 **they were well at peace:** what Rosse leaves out is where they are at peace: in Heaven.	204 Postponing; unable to bring himself to deliver the news he came to tell.
205 **niggard** = miser.	205 Prodding for more. Implied stage direction: he can tell from Rosse's demeanor that there is more to tell.
206 **transport the Tidings** = deliver the news.	
207 **heavily borne** = which were a heavy burden.	207 Rousing Malcolm to return to Scotland and challenge Macbeth.
208 **worthy Fellows** = nobles. **out** = out of Macbeth's army.	
209 **to my belief witness'd the rather** = I witnessed rather than merely believed. In other words, I know that many worthy fellows are out of Macbeth's army, because I saw how small his army is.	
210 **Power** = army.	
211 **time of help** = time to come help. **your eye** = your presence; also, if people 'eye' you.	
212 **create Soldiers**: previously peaceful people would join the army — even women.	
213 **doff** = be rid of, as in taking off clothes.	
214 **Be 't their comfort** = Let it be their comfort.	
215 **thither** = to there. **England** = the King of England.	215 Vowing to comply.
217-218 **older** = more experienced. **Christendom** = the Christian world. **gives out** = proclaims. There is not a more experienced or better soldier in Christendom.	217 Sharing that he already has powerful resources for the fight.
219 **Would** = I wish.	219 Getting his courage up to say something very difficult.
220 **with the like** = with one as good.	

221 That would be howl'd out in the desert air,
222 Where hearing should not latch them.

MACDUFF
223 What concern they?
224 The general cause? or is it a Fee-grief
225 Due to some single breast?

ROSSE
226 No mind that's honest
227 But in it shares some woe, though the main part
228 Pertains to you alone.

MACDUFF
229 If it be mine
230 Keep it not from me, quickly let me have it.

ROSSE
231 Let not your ears despise my tongue for ever,
232 Which shall possess them with the heaviest sound
233 That ever yet they heard.

MACDUFF
234 Humh: I guess at it.

ROSSE
235 Your Castle is surpris'd: your Wife, and Babes
236 Savagely slaughter'd: To relate the manner
237 Were on the Quarry of these murder'd Deer
238 To add the death of you.

MALCOLM
239 Merciful Heaven:
240 What man, ne'er pull your hat upon your brows:
241 Give sorrow words; the grief that does not speak,
242 Whispers the o'er-fraught heart, and bids it break.

MACDUFF
243 My Children too?

ROSSE
244 Wife, Children, Servants, all that could be found.

MACDUFF
245 And I must be from thence? ¶ My wife kill'd too?

ROSSE
246 I have said.

What	Why
221 **would** = would be better. 222 **latch** = catch. I have words that should not be heard.	
224 **Fee-grief**: a grief with one particular owner, as 'fee-simple' land has a single owner. 225 **Due to some single breast** = belonging to some single person.	224 Dreading that it's about his own family.
226-227 (there is) **No mind that's honest But in it shares some woe** There's no honest person who doesn't feel the woe of it.	226 Preparing Macduff for the bad news.
	230 **Keep it not from me:** He knows it's about him. Getting it over with.
232 **possess them** = put them in possession of. Don't hate me forever for relating this worst news that you ever heard.	232 Stalling, because it's so hard to say.
234 **Humh**: inarticulate sound of distress.	234 Already registering the shock.
235 **surpris'd** = taken by surprise.	235 Finally blurting it all out as quickly and accurately as he can.
236 **To relate the manner** = to tell specifically how. 237 **Were** = would be. **Quarry** = heap of killed game. **murder'd Deer**: the murdered innocents of Macduff's family. If I told you the details, you would die too.	
239 **Merciful Heaven**: praying.	239 Advising Macduff to vent his grief rather than burst by trying to hold it in.
241-242 **Give sorrow words** (speak your sorrow aloud); **the grief that does not speak** (grief that is not shared), **Whispers to the o'er-fraught** (overburdened) **heart, and bids it break.** Imagine a false friend whispering poisonous lies to make you feel bad.	240 **pull your hat**: This is an implied stage direction. Macduff has covered his face with his hat.
	243 **My Children too**: struggling to grasp the enormity of it.
244 **all that could be found** = They killed everyone in the castle.	
245 **from thence** = away from there. Cursing that he wasn't there to defend them.	
	246 **I have said**: not admonishing Macduff to pay attention, but unwilling to repeat it again unless he has to.

MALCOLM

247 Be comforted.

248 Let's make us Med'cines of our great Revenge,

249 To cure this deadly grief.

MACDUFF

250 He has no Children. ❡ All my pretty ones?

251 Did you say All? ❡ O Hell-Kite! ❡ All?

252 What, All my pretty Chickens, and their Dam

253 At one fell swoop?

MALCOLM

254 Dispute it like a man.

MACDUFF

255 I shall do so:

256 But I must also feel it as a man;

257 I cannot but remember such things were

258 That were most precious to me: ❡ Did heaven look on,

259 And would not take their part? ❡ Sinful *Macduff*,

260 They were all struck for thee: Naught that I am,

261 Not for their own demerits, but for mine

262 Fell slaughter on their souls: ❡ Heaven rest them now.

MALCOLM

263 Be this the Whetstone of your sword, let grief

264 Convert to anger: blunt not the heart, enrage it.

MACDUFF

265 O I could play the woman with mine eyes,

266 And Braggart with my tongue. ❡ But gentle Heavens,

267 Cut short all intermission: Front to Front,

268 Bring thou this Fiend of Scotland, and myself

269 Within my Sword's length set him, if he 'scape

270 Heaven forgive him too.

MALCOLM

271 This time goes manly:

272 ❡ Come go we to the King, our Power is ready,

273 Our lack is nothing but our leave. ❡ *Macbeth*

274 Is ripe for shaking, and the Powers above

275 Put on their Instruments: ❡ Receive what cheer you may,

276 The Night is long, that never finds the Day.

Exeunt.

What	Why
248-249 Let's make us Med'cines of our great Revenge: Let's take great revenge on Macbeth, and let that revenge be as a medicine **To cure this deadly grief.**	248 Steering Macduff to turn his grief into rage.
250 He (Macbeth) **has no Children**: Perhaps he means Macbeth doesn't know what it is to lose one's children, or perhaps meaning revenge isn't possible since Macbeth has no children to kill.	250 Experiencing a rapid succession of powerful reactions: **He has no Children** = raging; **All my pretty ones** = grieving; **did you say All** = disbelieving; **O Hell-kite** = raging; **All** = disbelieving again.
251 **Hell-Kite** = hawk from Hell.	
252 **Dam** = mother.	
253 **fell** = deadly.	
254 **Dispute it** = Struggle against succumbing to it (grief).	254 Rallying him.
256 **I must also feel it as a man**: I must feel the full impact of it before moving on.	256 Demanding a space of time for grief before turning to war.
257 **cannot but** = cannot help but.	
258-259 **Did heaven look on** (Did God just stand back and watch), **And would not take their part** (not fight on their side)**? Sinful *Macduff***: It was a sin for me to anger Macbeth and leave my family vulnerable.	
260 **for thee** = because of Macduff. **Naught** = nothing.	
260-262 Reordered: **Naught that I am** (because I am a worthless thing), **slaughter Fell on their souls** (they were murdered) **not for their demerits** (not because of any fault of theirs), **but for mine** (for my faults; because I abandoned them).	
263-264 **Be this** = let this be. **Whetstone** = sharpening stone. **blunt not the heart, enrage it**: Don't let this make your heart dull, but sharpen it with rage.	263 More rallying him.
265-270 **play the woman with mine eyes** = cry like a woman. **Braggart**: brag about the revenge he will take on Macbeth. **gentle Heavens** (dear God), **Cut short all intermission** (please shorten the time between now and then)**: Front to Front, Bring thou this Fiend of Scotland, and myself** (bring Macbeth and me face to face) **Within my Sword's length set him** (put where I can reach him with my sword). **'scape** = escape. I could cry or I could brag, but instead I just want to be face to face with Macbeth. If I fail to kill him, let **Heaven forgive him** (that's how certain I am of success).	265 Vowing revenge.
	269 **FORWARD**: Will Macduff get Macbeth within his sword's length? Can he kill him?
271 **This time goes manly**: Perhaps 'time' is a typo for 'tune'? Or perhaps he means Macduff is now speaking manly, as opposed to before?	271 Approving of Macduff's pledge.
	272 **go we to the King**: That done, moving on to the next business.
273 **Our lack is nothing but our leave**: There's nothing left to do but to say goodbye.	
274 **shaking**: destroying his rule. Imagine an earthquake shaking a castle down, or shaking the fruit out of a tree.	
275-276 **Put on their Instruments** = arm themselves. **Receive what cheer you may** = take the cheer that is available. **The Night is long, that never finds the Day**: If we don't find the day, we will be in everlasting night.	

ACTUS QUINTUS. SCENA PRIMA.

Enter a Doctor of Physic, and a Waiting Gentlewoman.

DOCTOR

1 I have two Nights watch'd with you, but can perceive no
2 truth in your report. When was it she last walk'd?

GENTLEWOMAN

3 Since his Majesty went into the Field, I have seen her rise from her
4 bed, throw her Night-Gown upon her, unlock her Closet, take forth
5 paper, fold it, write upon 't, read it, afterwards Seal it, and again
6 return to bed; yet all this while in a most fast sleep.

DOCTOR

7 A great perturbation in Nature, to receive at once the benefit
8 of sleep, and do the effects of watching. ¶ In this slumbry
9 agitation, besides her walking, and other actual performances,
10 what (at any time) have you heard her say?

GENTLEWOMAN

11 That Sir, which I will not report after her.

DOCTOR

12 You may to me, and 'tis most meet you should.

GENTLEWOMAN

13 Neither to you, nor any one, having no witness to confirm
14 my speech.

5.1.b -

Enter Lady Macbeth, with a Taper.

15 Lo you, here she comes: This is her very guise, and upon my
16 life fast asleep: Observe her, stand close.

DOCTOR

17 How came she by that light?

GENTLEWOMAN

18 Why it stood by her: she has light by her continually, 'tis her
19 command.

DOCTOR

20 You see her eyes are open.

GENTLEWOMAN

21 Ay but their sense are shut.

DOCTOR

22 What is it she does now? Look how she rubs her hands.

5.1.a Dunsinane palace (Macbeth has moved again, to the hill-fort of Dunsinane, where he can better defend himself against rebellion). Interior. Night.

Purpose: 1. To establish the gravity of the scene to come. 2. To make us eager to hear what Lady Macbeth will say when sleepwalking.

Drama: 1. Will the Doctor believe the Gentlewoman? 2. Will the Gentlewoman repeat what Lady Macbeth says in her sleep?

What	Why
1 **watch'd** = stayed awake.	1 Asking for proof. Apparently the gentlewoman has called him for help with Lady Macbeth's sleepwalking.
3 **into the Field**: on a military campaign.	3 Adding weight to her assertion with details. **FORWARD**: Will we see the sleepwalking?
4 **Closet** = bedroom.	
8 **effects of watching** = the things one does when awake. **slumbry** = sleepy. 9 **actual performances** = physical acts (as opposed to spoken).	8 In his professional capacity, formulating a diagnosis.
11 **which I will not report after her** = which I will not disclose against her.	11 Refusing to break the silence of a loyal servant.
12 **meet** = proper.	12 Urging her to break her vow by explaining why in this instance it would not be disloyal for her to divulge her secret.
13 **having no witness** = since I have no witness.	13 Again refusing. Protecting not Lady Macbeth but herself. This secret is no ordinary 'dirty laundry'.

5.1.b Purpose: 1. To take us inside Lady Macbeth's tortured mind, so we can personally experience the horrific truth, 'what's done cannot be undone' (page 162, line 53). 2. To paint a picture of the devastation of Macbeth's domain.

Drama: 1. Can Lady Macbeth get relief from her anguish of guilt? 2. How much will she reveal? 3. Can the doctor help her?

What	Why
15-16 **very guise** = usual practice. **upon my life** = I would bet my life on it.	15 Proving her assertion.
17 **How came she by that light**: How did she get that lit candle?	17 Gathering data for his assessment.
18 **continually**: she not only keeps a candle by her bed, she keeps it burning.	18 Helping the doctor with information.
	20 **eyes are open**: still gathering data.
21 **sense** = ability to sense. She can't see us.	
	22 **rubs her hands**: implied stage direction.

GENTLEWOMAN

23 It is an accustom'd action with her, to seem thus washing her hands:
24 I have known her continue in this a quarter of an hour.

LADY MACBETH

25 Yet here's a spot.

DOCTOR

26 Hark, she speaks, I will set down what comes from her, to
27 satisfy my remembrance the more strongly.

LADY MACBETH

28 Out damned spot: out I say. ¶ One: Two: Why then 'tis time
29 to do 't: ¶ Hell is murky. ¶ Fie, my Lord, fie, a Soldier, and
30 afear'd? ¶ What need we fear? Who knows it, when none can
31 call our power to accompt: ¶ Yet who would have thought
32 the old man to have had so much blood in him.

DOCTOR

33 Do you mark that?

LADY MACBETH

34 The Thane of Fife, had a wife: where is she now? ¶ What will
35 these hands ne'er be clean? ¶ No more o' that my Lord, no
36 more o' that: you mar all with this starting.

DOCTOR

37 Go to, go to: You have known what you should not.

GENTLEWOMAN

38 She has spoke what she should not, I am sure of that: Heaven
39 knows what she has known.

LADY MACBETH

40 Here's the smell of the blood still: all the perfumes of Arabia
41 will not sweeten this little hand. Oh, oh, oh.

DOCTOR

42 What a sigh is there? The heart is sorely charg'd.

GENTLEWOMAN

43 I would not have such a heart in my bosom, for the dignity
44 of the whole body.

DOCTOR

45 Well, well, well.

GENTLEWOMAN

46 Pray God it be sir.

What	Why
23 **accustom'd**: habitual.	
	25 **Yet here's a spot**: Noticing a spot of blood on her hand.
26-27 **set down** = write down. **to satisfy my remembrance** = to help me remember it.	
28 **One: Two**: The clock strikes two. 28-29 **time to do't**: i.e. to murder Duncan. 29 **Hell is murky**: perhaps she is in Hell? Fearing Hell? **Fie** = shame on you (to Macbeth). 30-31 **accompt** = account. **none can call our power to accompt** = nobody can defy our power and make us 'account for ourselves'. 32 **old man**: clearly, she means Duncan. 33 **mark** = note.	28 Washing her hands. In her mind, reliving all their crimes, one by one. 33 Realizing Lady Macbeth and her husband murdered Duncan, and is now reliving it.
34 **Thane of Fife** = Macduff. 36 **mar all with this starting** = ruin everything with these abrupt fits and starts. She's probably re-experiencing the banquet, when Macbeth saw Banquo's ghost.	
37 **go to**: a phrase of disapproval.	37 Realizing they also murdered Macduff's whole clan, but inappropriately pouncing on the gentlewoman because he can't think what else to do.
38-39 **I am sure of that**: I know at least this much. **Heaven knows what she has known**: If she reveals this much, God only knows how much more there is.	38 Defending herself.
41 **sweeten** = make it smell sweet.	
42 **sorely charg'd** = deeply burdened.	42 Empathizing.
43-44 **the dignity of the whole body**: the dignity (rank) of a Queen.	43 Pitying.
	45 **Well, well, well**: despairing of coming up with a helpful answer.
46 **Pray God it** will **be** well.	

DOCTOR

47 This disease is beyond my practice: ❡ yet I have known those which
48 have walk'd in their sleep, who have died holily in their beds.

LADY MACBETH

49 Wash your hands, put on your Night-Gown, ❡ look not so pale: I
50 tell you yet again *Banquo's* buried; he cannot come out on's grave.

DOCTOR

51 Even so?

LADY MACBETH

52 To bed, to bed: there's knocking at the gate: Come, come,
53 come, come, give me your hand: What's done, cannot be
54 undone. To bed, to bed, to bed.
Exit Lady Macbeth.

DOCTOR

55 Will she go now to bed?

GENTLEWOMAN

56 Directly.

DOCTOR

57 Foul whisp'rings are abroad: unnatural deeds
58 Do breed unnatural troubles: infected minds
59 To their deaf pillows will discharge their Secrets:
60 ❡ More needs she the Divine, than the Physician:
61 ❡ God, God forgive us all. ❡ Look after her,
62 Remove from her the means of all annoyance,
63 And still keep eyes upon her: ❡ So good night,
64 My mind she has mated, and amaz'd my sight.
65 I think, but dare not speak.

GENTLEWOMAN

66 Good night good Doctor.
Exeunt.

SCENA SECUNDA.

Drum and Colours. Enter Menteth, Cathnes, Angus, Lenox, Soldiers.

MENTETH

1 The English power is near, led on by *Malcolm*,
2 His Uncle *Seyward*, and the good *Macduff*.

What	Why
	47 **This disease is beyond my practice:** TURN. Pronouncing his conclusion. Offering a shred of hope: Perhaps she can die peacefully.
48 **who have died holily in their beds** = who have been restored to communion with God by the final unction administered by a priest on their deathbeds. 49-50 **Wash your hands:** remembering the night they killed Duncan, seeing Macbeth's bloody hands. **put on your Night-Gown**: to make it appear we were in bed. *Banquo's* **buried:** remembering Macbeth at the banquet raving about Banquo's ghost.	
	51 **Even so**: realizing this means she and her husband murdered Banquo too.
52 **knocking at the gate**: after Duncan's murder.	52 Hurrying her husband.
53-54 **What's done** (the murder of Duncan)**, cannot be undone**: there is no way to fix our mistake.	Note: in this line (**What's done, cannot be undone**), Lady Macbeth encapsulates the major theme of the play: regret.
56 **Directly** = immediately.	
57 **Foul whisp'rings** = dark rumors. 57-58 **unnatural deeds Do breed unnatural troubles**: Violating nature causes one's own nature to be disturbed. 59 **To their deaf pillows will discharge their Secrets** = will tell their secrets in their sleep (as we've just witnessed). 60 **Divine** = priest.	57 Piecing together the source of all of Scotland's strange mishaps.
61 **God forgive us all**: God please release us all from the consequences of her crimes.	61 Praying for divine mercy for the Queen and for Scotland.
62 **Remove from her the means of all annoyance**: (to the gentlewoman) Take away anything she might hurt herself with. 64 **mated** = confounded.	62 Giving doctor's prescription. **FORWARD**: The doctor suggests Lady Macbeth may attempt suicide. Will she?

5.2.a A road near Dunsinane. Exterior. Day.

Purpose: 1. To show the leadership of Scotland uniting behind Malcolm. 2. To show how Macbeth's grip, both on Scotland and on himself, is weakening. 3. To remind us of the Byrnam Wood prophecy.

Drama: What is the state of preparations for the fight against Macbeth?

What	Why
1 **The English power** = the English army.	1 Reporting good news.

3   Revenges burn in them: for their dear causes
4   Would to the bleeding, and the grim Alarm
5   Excite the mortified man.

ANGUS

6   Near Byrnam wood
7   Shall we well meet them, that way are they coming.

CATHNES

8   Who knows if *Donalbain* be with his brother?

LENOX

9   For certain Sir, he is not: I have a File
10   Of all the Gentry; ¶ there is *Seyward's* Son,
11   And many unrough youths, that even now
12   Protest their first of Manhood.

MENTETH

13   What does the Tyrant.

CATHNES

14   Great Dunsinane he strongly Fortifies:
15   ¶ Some say he's mad: Others, that lesser hate him,
16   Do call it valiant Fury, but for certain
17   He cannot buckle his distemper'd cause
18   Within the belt of Rule.

ANGUS

19   Now does he feel
20   His secret Murders sticking on his hands,
21   Now minutely Revolts upbraid his Faith-breach:
22   Those he commands, move only in command,
23   Nothing in love: Now does he feel his Title
24   Hang loose about him, like a Giant's Robe
25   Upon a dwarfish Thief.

MENTETH

26   Who then shall blame
27   His pester'd Senses to recoil, and start,
28   When all that is within him, does condemn
29   Itself, for being there.

CATHNES

30   Well, march we on,
31   To give Obedience, where 'tis truly ow'd:
32   Meet we the Med'cine of the sickly Weal,

What	Why
3-5 **Revenges burn in them** (they are burning for revenge)**: for their dear causes** (because their costly cause for revenge) **Would to the bleeding, and the grim Alarm** (to the bleeding and the trumpet blasts of battle) **Excite the mortified man** (inspire even a half-dead man to join).	
	6 **FORWARD**: they are going to Byrnam Wood. Will this figure in the fulfillment of the prophecy?
8 *Donalbain* is Malcolm's brother, and has fled to Ireland.	
9 **File** = list.	9 Wondering where the other prince is. Note: If Malcolm is killed in the battle, Donalbain is next in the line of succession.
11 **unrough** = unbearded; young.	11 Celebrating: Even the youngest are coming out to fight with us.
12 **Protest** = assert.	
13 **What does the Tyrant**: What is Macbeth doing?	
14 **Dunsinane** was a hilltop fortress north of the Firth of Tay.	14 Sharing more good news: Macbeth is debilitated by his temper.
15 **that lesser hate him** = who hate him less.	
16 **valiant Fury** = brave rage.	
17-18 **distemper'd** = rabid. **cause** = anger. **He cannot buckle his distemper'd cause Within the belt of Rule**: His anger is like a rabid dog, which can't be buckled into the collar of self-restraint.	
20 **sticking on his hands:** Imagine his hands sticky with the blood of his victims.	
21 **minutely** = every minute. **upbraid his Faith-breach** = punish him for his breach of faith.	21 Ridiculing Macbeth. Building up their faith that they can beat Macbeth.
22 **only in command**: only because they are commanded, not because they want to.	
23-25 **Now does he feel his Title Hang loose about him, like a Giant's Robe Upon a dwarfish Thief**: Being king is too big for him, the way a giant's robe is too big for a dwarfish thief.	
26-29 **Who then shall blame His pester'd Senses** (his moral sense, infested with his crimes like lice) **to recoil, and start** (for being jumpy), **When all that is within him, does condemn Itself, for being there.** Personifying Macbeth's senses - who can blame them for turning against him?	26 Piling on to the list of Macbeth's enemies: even Macbeth's own insides are now against him.
31 **where 'tis truly ow'd**: to Malcolm the rightful King.	31 Getting on with it.
32 **Meet we** (let's go meet) **the Med'cine** (Malcolm, who will heal like a medicine). **of the sickly Weal** (of Scotland, the ailing commonwealth). **Weal** = commonwealth.	

33 And with him pour we in our Country's purge,
34 Each drop of us.

LENOX

35 Or so much as it needs,
36 To dew the Sovereign Flower, and drown the Weeds:
37 ¶ Make we our March towards Byrnam.
Exeunt marching.

SCENA TERTIA.

Enter Macbeth, Doctor, and Attendants.

MACBETH

1 Bring me no more Reports, ¶ let them fly all:
2 Till Byrnam wood remove to Dunsinane,
3 I cannot taint with Fear. ¶ What's the Boy *Malcolm*?
4 Was he not born of woman? The Spirits that know
5 All mortal Consequences, have pronounc'd me thus:
6 Fear not *Macbeth*, no man that's born of woman
7 Shall e'er have power upon thee. ¶ Then fly false Thanes,
8 And mingle with the English Epicures,
9 The mind I sway by, and the heart I bear,
10 Shall never sag with doubt, nor shake with fear.
Enter a Servant.
11 The devil damn thee black, thou cream-fac'd Loon:
12 Where got'st thou that Goose-look.

SERVANT

13 There is ten thousand.

MACBETH

14 Geese Villain?

SERVANT

15 Soldiers Sir.

MACBETH

16 Go prick thy face, and over-red thy fear
17 Thou Lily-liver'd Boy. ¶ What Soldiers, Patch?
18 ¶ Death of thy Soul, those Linen cheeks of thine
19 Are Counselors to fear. What Soldiers Whey-face?

SERVANT

20 The English Force, so please you.

What	Why
33-34 with him pour we in our Country's purge, Each drop of us: We will also be part of the purgative medicine poured into the patient, our country, to make it purge (vomit) the poison Macbeth.	
36 dew the Sovereign Flower: water Malcolm, so that he may take root and blossom as King. **drown the Weeds** = kill Macbeth.	37 **FORWARD**: Byrnam again.

5.3 A room at Dunsinane. Interior. Day.

Purpose: 1. To bring us to experience for ourselves the bitterness of Macbeth's failure. 2. To make us hopeful that Malcolm's attack will succeed. 3. To show that, despite his weakened resources, Macbeth is still formidable in his rage. 4. To underline the question of Lady Macbeth's survival.

Drama: Can Macbeth maintain his resolve in spite of the overwhelming losses outside, and inside the castle, and in his own mind?

What	Why
1 **Reports**: reports of what's happening in the field. **let them fly all** = let all the thanes desert me.	1 At the news that his thanes are deserting, raging to prevent fear from bursting his bubble of invincibility.
2 **remove** = move.	
3 **taint** = be infected with. **What** is there in the **Boy** *Malcolm* for me to fear?	
4-5 **The Spirits**: the Witches. **mortal** = human (as opposed to heavenly).	4 **FORWARD**: reminding us of the key prophecy, 'no man that's born of woman'.
5 **Consequences** = inevitable results. **pronounc'd me thus** = pronounced to me in these words.	
8 **Epicures**: taken up with eating and drinking, and therefore ineffective.	
9 **sway** = rule.	
10 **sag with doubt** = droop with fear.	
11 **damn thee black**: put you so far into Hell that you are burnt to a cinder. **cream-fac'd**: he's white with fear. **Loon** = rogue.	
	13 **ten thousand**: fearing a terrible reprisal for delivering this bad news.
14 **Geese**: a symbol of timidity.	
16 **Go prick thy face, and over-red thy fear**: Stick a pin in your cheek and rub the blood in for rouge to hide your fear-induced pallor.	16 Repeatedly commanding him to speak, as the servant is tongue-tied.
17 **Lily-liver'd**: The liver was believed to be the seat of courage. If his liver was white as a lily, it was bloodless, hence cowardly. **Patch** = fool (fools wore patched clothes).	
18 **Death of thy Soul**: cursing him for being unable to speak. **Linen**: another word for pale.	
19 **Counselors to fear** = They teach fear. **Whey**: the watery part of milk.	

MACBETH

21 Take thy face hence. *[Exit Servant.]* ❡ *Seyton*, ❡ I am sick at heart,
22 When I behold: ❡ *Seyton*, I say, ❡ this push
23 Will cheer me ever, or dis-seat me now.
24 ❡ I have liv'd long enough: my way of life
25 Is fall'n into the Sere, the yellow Leaf,
26 And that which should accompany Old-Age,
27 As Honour, Love, Obedience, Troops of Friends,
28 I must not look to have: ❡ but in their stead,
29 Curses, not loud but deep, Mouth-honour, breath
30 Which the poor heart would fain deny, and dare not.
31 ❡ *Seyton?*
Enter Seyton.

SEYTON

32 What's your gracious pleasure?

MACBETH

33 What News more?

SEYTON

34 All is confirm'd my Lord, which was reported.

MACBETH

35 I'll fight, till from my bones, my flesh be hack'd.
36 ❡ Give me my Armour.

SEYTON

37 'Tis not needed yet.

MACBETH

38 I'll put it on:
39 ❡ Send out more Horses, skirt the Country round,
40 Hang those that talk of Fear. ❡ Give me mine Armour:
41 ❡ How does your Patient, Doctor?

DOCTOR

42 Not so sick my Lord,
43 As she is troubled with thick-coming Fancies
44 That keep her from her rest.

MACBETH

45 Cure her of that:
46 Canst thou not Minister to a mind diseas'd,
47 Pluck from the Memory a rooted Sorrow,
48 Raze out the written troubles of the Brain,

What	Why
22 **When I behold**: He was going to say, 'when I behold cowards', but then noticed nobody was listening. **this push** = this coming battle.	22 Protecting himself against this incentive to fear. **Seyton**: interrupting his own thought to yell for help.
23 **dis-seat** = dethrone.	
25 **Sere** = dry dead weeds. It's the late autumn of life.	25 Letting go of wishing to be loved and honored; accepting his new life, in which the best he can hope for is merely to be feared.
27 **As** = such as.	
28 **look** = expect.	
29 **Mouth-honour** = honors spoken but not truly felt. **breath** = words.	
30 **would fain** = would be glad to. His retainers speak deferentially to him only out of fear.	
	32 **gracious pleasure**: giving mouth-honor.
	34 **which was reported**: giving the minimum required.
	37 '**Tis not needed**: This is insubordination. An eager squire would leap at his king's command, needed or no. Seyton is resisting.
	38 **I'll put it on**: reprimanding him.
39 **skirt the Country round** = ride around the outskirts.	39 **more**: Folio has 'moe'
	40 **Hang those**: Note: This is not a sane command. Seyton would have to hang the entire population. **mine Armour**: erratically jumping from thought to thought. Note: Seyton still hasn't produced Macbeth's armor, even after being admonished.
41 **your Patient**: Lady Macbeth.	41 Note: He says 'your patient', not 'my wife'.
43 **As** = but rather. **thick-coming Fancies** = fantasies crowding into her mind.	43 Maintaining his professional demeanor as diplomatically as possible under the circumstances.
	45 **Cure her of that**: Folio has 'cure of that'
46 **Minister to** = care for; heal.	46 Refusing to seriously consider the difficulty — attempting to make the problem go away by imperial command.
47 **rooted Sorrow** = a sad memory that is stubbornly embedded.	
48 **Raze** = obliterate completely. **written troubles of the Brain** = permanent bad memories.	

49 And with some sweet Oblivious Antidote
50 Cleanse the stuff'd bosom, of that perilous stuff
51 Which weighs upon the heart?

DOCTOR
52 Therein the Patient
53 Must minister to himself.

MACBETH
54 Throw Physic to the Dogs, I'll none of it.
55 ❡ Come, put mine Armour on: give me my Staff:
56 ❡ *Seyton*, send out: ❡ Doctor, the Thanes fly from me:
57 ❡ Come sir, dispatch. ❡ If thou couldst Doctor, cast
58 The Water of my Land, find her Disease,
59 And purge it to a sound and pristine Health,
60 I would applaud thee to the very Echo,
61 That should applaud again. ❡ Pull 't off I say,
62 ❡ What Rhubarb, Cyme, or what Purgative drug
63 Would scour these English hence: ❡ Hear'st you of them?

DOCTOR
64 Ay my good Lord: your Royal Preparation
65 Makes us hear something.

MACBETH
66 Bring it after me:
67 ❡ I will not be afraid of Death and Bane,
68 Till Byrnam Forest come to Dunsinane.
Exit.

DOCTOR
69 *[aside]* Were I from Dunsinane away, and clear,
70 Profit again should hardly draw me here.
Exeunt.

SCENA QUARTA.

*Drum and Colours. Enter Malcolm, [Old] Seyward, Macduff, Seyward's
Son, Menteth, Cathnes, Angus, and Soldiers Marching.*

MALCOLM
1 Cousins, I hope the days are near at hand
2 That Chambers will be safe.

170   5.4.a   *Macbeth*

What	Why
49 **sweet Oblivious Antidote** = drug of oblivion. 50 **stuff'd bosom** = heart stuffed with sorrow. **perilous stuff** = dangerous memories.	
52 **Therein** = in this circumstance.	52 Gently delivering the bad news.
54 **Physic** = doctoring, as in 'physician'. **I'll** (have) **none of it.** 55 **Staff** = a fighting stick or a spear. 56 **send out** = starting to give an order but changing his mind mid-sentence. 57 **dispatch**: (to Seyton) Hurry with my armor. 57-58 **cast The Water**: It was a practice to examine the patient's urine to diagnose an illness. He says do this to Scotland to find what's wrong with it. 59 **purge:** give a drug to induce the patient to vomit out the offending substance. 60-61 **to the very Echo, That should ap-plaud again**: so loud that it echoes back from the mountains. 61 **Pull 't off**: chastising his armorer for getting it on wrong. 62 **Rhubarb, Cyme** = herbs used as purgatives. **Purgative drug**: a drug to make you vomit. 63 **scour these English hence** = scrub them off like food residue from a cookpot.	54 Vacillating between upbraiding his helpers and philosophizing with the doctor. 57 Fantasizing a way to get rid of the English without having to fight them.
65 **Makes us hear something**: we can tell by your preparation for battle. 66 **Bring it after me**: referring to some unfinished part of his armor. 67 **Bane** = thing that poses a lethal threat. 68 **Till Byrnam Forest come to Dunsinane**: forcing himself to believe that all will be well, because of the Witches' prophecy. 70 **Profit again should hardly draw me here**: no amount of money could lure me back here.	65 Being careful not to mention the rumors. 66 Mustering his courage. 68 **FORWARD**: Byrnam again.

5.4 A road near Dunsinane with a wood in view. Exterior. Day.

Purpose: 1. To accelerate us towards the impending battle. 2. To encourage us with the strength of Malcolm's army, but also remind us that Macbeth is still dangerous enough that the issue is in doubt. 3. To reveal that the Witches' Byrnam Wood prophecy was a mocking deception.

Drama: Will Malcolm be able to defeat Macbeth?

What	Why
	1 Rallying the troops, with confidence.
2 **Chambers**: rooms. Our homes will be safe.	

MENTETH

3   We doubt it nothing.

SEYWARD

4   What wood is this before us?

MALCOLM

5   The wood of Byrnam.

MALCOLM

6   Let every Soldier hew him down a Bough,
7   And bear 't before him, thereby shall we shadow
8   The numbers of our Host, and make discovery
9   Err in report of us.

SOLDIER

10   It shall be done.

SEYWARD

11   We learn no other, but the confident Tyrant
12   Keeps still in Dunsinane, and will endure
13   Our setting down before 't.

MALCOLM

14   'Tis his main hope:
15   For where there is advantage to be given,
16   Both more and less have given him the Revolt,
17   And none serve with him, but constrained things,
18   Whose hearts are absent too.

MACDUFF

19   Let our just Censures
20   Attend the true event, and put we on
21   Industrious Soldiership.

SEYWARD

22   The time approaches,
23   That will with due decision make us know
24   What we shall say we have, and what we owe:
25   Thoughts speculative, their unsure hopes relate,
26   But certain issue, strokes must arbitrate,
27   Towards which, advance the war.

Exeunt marching.

What	Why
3 **doubt it nothing** = doubt it not.	3 Assuring Malcolm they are confident.
6 **hew him down a Bough** = cut himself a tree branch. 7-9 **shadow The numbers of our Host** = hide the size of our army. **make discovery Err in report of us** = make Macbeth's scouts underreport our size.	6 Doing everything he can to ensure victory, even though they already have every reason to expect to prevail. **TURN: hew him down a Bough, And bear 't before him**: Finally we learn how Byrnam Wood will come to Dunsinane and fulfill the prophecy.
11-13 **no other, but**: this is surprising news. **endure** = allow. **setting down before 't** = surrounding it. We would expect Macbeth to sally out and prevent us besieging Dunsinane, but apparently he is overconfident and stays inside. 14 **his main hope** = his best chance. 15 **advantage to be given** = opportunity to escape. 16 **more and less** = noble and commoner. **given him the Revolt** = rebelled against him. 17 **constrained things** = people who are forced. 18 **hearts are absent** = hearts are not in it.	11 Puzzling aloud over why Macbeth would do this. 14 Explaining that, although ordinarily it would be suicide to allow yourself to be surrounded, Macbeth doesn't have a better choice.
19 **just Censures** = judgment. 20 **Attend** = wait on. **true event**: the outcome of the battle. 20-21 **put we on Industrious Soldiership**: Let's be hardworking soldiers.	19 Counseling them not to celebrate early, but to focus on the fight.
22-23 **The time approaches, That will with due decision make us know**: The time is coming that will in due course answer the question. 24 **What we shall say we have** (what we will be able to claim is ours), **and what we owe** (and what we have yet to do). 25 **Thoughts speculative, their unsure hopes relate** = Speculation can relate unsure hopes only (not reliable fact). 26 **certain issue** = the definite outcome. **strokes must arbitrate** = The actual battle (sword strokes) must decide.	22 Agreeing with Macduff, and amplifying on it. 26 **FORWARD: 'strokes must arbitrate'** brings the picture of the impending battle vividly closer.

Scena Quinta.

Enter Macbeth, Seyton, & Soldiers, with Drum and Colours.

Macbeth

1 Hang out our Banners on the outward walls,
2 The Cry is still, they come: Our Castle's strength
3 Will laugh a Siege to scorn: here let them lie,
4 Till Famine and the Ague eat them up:
5 ¶ Were they not forc'd with those that should be ours,
6 We might have met them dareful, beard to beard,
7 And beat them backward home. ¶ What is that noise?

A Cry within of Women.

Seyton

8 It is the cry of women, my good Lord.
Exit.

Macbeth

9 I have almost forgot the taste of Fears:
10 The time has been, my senses would have cool'd
11 To hear a Night-shriek, and my Fell of hair
12 Would at a dismal Treatise rouse, and stir
13 As life were in 't. I have supp'd full with horrors,
14 Direness familiar to my slaughterous thoughts
15 Cannot once start me. ¶ Wherefore was that cry?

Re-enter Seyton.

Seyton

16 The Queen (my Lord) is dead.

Macbeth

17 She should have died hereafter;
18 There would have been a time for such a word:
19 ¶ Tomorrow, and tomorrow, and tomorrow,
20 Creeps in this petty pace from day to day,
21 To the last Syllable of Recorded time:
22 And all our yesterdays, have lighted Fools
23 The way to dusty death. ¶ Out, out, brief Candle,
24 Life's but a walking Shadow, a poor Player,
25 That struts and frets his hour upon the Stage,
26 And then is heard no more. It is a Tale
27 Told by an Idiot, full of sound and fury
28 Signifying nothing.

5.5 A room at Dunsinane. Interior. Day.

Purpose: 1. To sharpen even further our sense of Macbeth's anguish, with two additional losses — his wife's suicide and the revelation that the Byrnam Wood prophecy was a ruse. 2. To conclude the story of Lady Macbeth. 3. To accelerate us towards the final battle.

Drama: 1. Will Macbeth stay in the castle or go out to fight? 2. How will he react to the death of his wife? 3. Will he be undone by the news of the approach of Byrnam Wood?

What	Why
1 **Hang out our Banners**: to signify defiance to the approaching enemy.	1 Reminding them they are still going to fight.
2-3 **The Cry is still, they come**: The official word is still, 'prepare for battle'. **Our Castle's strength Will laugh a Siege to scorn**: Our castle's strength will laugh at and scorn their siege. They have no chance of getting in. 3 **let them** (the enemy) **lie** (in wait). 4 **Ague** = fever.	
5 **Were they not forc'd with those that should be ours** = if they were not reinforced with soldiers that should be on my side.	5 Making an excuse for cowering in the castle instead of going out to fight.
6-7 **We might have** (gone out of the castle and) **met them** (in the field) **dareful** (bravely), **beard to beard** (face to face). **backward**: they would be retreating backward.	
10 **The time has been** = in the past. **my senses would have cool'd** = I would have felt a chill.	10 Noticing how far gone he is.
11 **a Night-shriek** = a shriek in the night. **Fell of hair** = mop of hair. 12 **dismal Treatise** = scary tale. 13 **As** = as if. Hearing a scary story, my hair would have stood up as if it were alive.	
14 **Direness** = horror. My thoughts are so full of horrors already that new horrors can't startle me.	***Re-enter Seyton***: Inferred. Not in Folio.
17 **hereafter** = later. 18 **such a word**: death. 19 **Tomorrow, and tomorrow, and tomorrow**: day after day after day.	17 Trying unsuccessfully to digest the death of his wife. She should have died later when we had time to deal with it.
20 **Creeps in this petty pace**: Time creeps along in this pace of insignificance. 21 **the last Syllable of Recorded time** = the end of time. 22 **lighted Fools**: Our yesterdays have been nothing more than beacons guiding fools to pointless death. 23 **brief Candle** = life, which is as brief and fragile as a candle flame. 24 **a walking Shadow** = of no more substance than a shadow. **a poor Player** = an incompetent actor. 25 **struts and frets** = struts around the stage and vexes himself. 26-27 **It is a Tale Told by an Idiot** (perhaps calling God an idiot?) 27 **full of sound and fury** (full of noise and motion, as if it had meaning). 28 **Signifying nothing**: life has no meaning.	20 Giving up all hope; but at the same time railing bitterly against the injustice of meaninglessness. Note: this is not mere frustration, but total existential despair.

Enter a Messenger.

29 Thou com'st to use thy Tongue: thy Story quickly.

MESSENGER

30 Gracious my Lord,
31 I should report that which I say I saw,
32 But know not how to do 't.

MACBETH

33 Well, say sir.

MESSENGER

34 As I did stand my watch upon the Hill
35 I look'd toward Byrnam, and anon methought
36 The Wood began to move.

MACBETH

37 Liar, and Slave.

MESSENGER

38 Let me endure your wrath, if 't be not so:
39 Within this three Mile may you see it coming.
40 I say, a moving Grove.

MACBETH

41 If thou speak'st false,
42 Upon the next Tree shalt thou hang alive
43 Till Famine cling thee:❡ if thy speech be sooth,
44 I care not if thou dost for me as much.
45 ❡ I pull in Resolution, and begin
46 To doubt th' Equivocation of the Fiend,
47 That lies like truth. Fear not, till Byrnam Wood
48 Do come to Dunsinane, and now a Wood
49 Comes toward Dunsinane. ❡ Arm, Arm, and out,
50 ❡ If this which he avouches, does appear,
51 There is nor flying hence, nor tarrying here.
52 ❡ I 'gin to be a-weary of the Sun,
53 And wish th' estate o' th' world were now undone.
54 ❡ Ring the Alarum Bell, blow Wind, come wrack,
55 At least we'll die with Harness on our back.
Exeunt.

What	Why
31 **I say I saw**: The Messenger is tongue-tied.	
35 **anon** = soon. **methought** = I thought.	
	36 **RESOLUTION**: Now Macbeth knows how Byrnam Wood can come to Dunsinane. **NEW DRAMA:** Does this mean Macbeth is now vulnerable?
	37 **Liar, and Slave**: reacting violently. This news destroys his last talisman save one.
	38 **Let me endure your wrath, if 't be not so**: scrambling to make Macbeth believe before he punishes him.
40 **Grove** = forest; grove of trees.	
43 **cling** = shrink till you starve. **sooth** = truth.	
44 **if thou dost for me as much** = if you do the same to me; if you hang me.	
45 **I pull in Resolution** = I rein in determination (because it's faltering).	
46 **doubt** = suspect. **Equivocation** = double-speak.	
46-47 **the Fiend, That lies like truth**: the Witch that tells truths that mislead.	
49 **Arm, Arm, and out**: Let's get our armor on and get outside.	49 **Arm, and out: TURN**: realizing he's going to die today, scrapping the plan to wait out the siege and deciding to go down fighting.
50 **this which he avouches** = this thing the Messenger swears is true.	
51 **nor flying hence, nor tarrying here**: it's not safe either to flee or to stay.	
52 **'gin** = begin. **a-weary of the Sun**: weary of being alive to see the sun.	
53 **wish th' estate o' th' world were now undone**: I wish the whole world would come down.	
54 **blow Wind, come wrack**: Let the storms come wreck everything. **wrack** = wreck.	
55 **Harness** = armor.	55 **At least we'll die with Harness on our back**: revising his ambition downward. Giving up hope of surviving, he now hopes only to die fighting.

SCENA SEXTA.

Drum and Colours.
Enter Malcolm, [Old] Seyward, Macduff, and their Army, with Boughs.

MALCOLM

1 Now near enough:
2 Your leafy Screens throw down,
3 And show like those you are: ¶ You (worthy Uncle)
4 Shall with my Cousin your right Noble Son
5 Lead our first Battle. ¶ Worthy *Macduff*, and we
6 Shall take upon's what else remains to do,
7 According to our order.

SEYWARD

8 Fare you well:
9 ¶ Do we but find the Tyrant's power tonight,
10 Let us be beaten, if we cannot fight.

MACDUFF

11 Make all our Trumpets speak, give them all breath
12 Those clamorous Harbingers of Blood, & Death.
Exeunt.
Alarums continued.

SCENA SEPTIMA.

Enter Macbeth.

MACBETH

1 They have tied me to a stake, I cannot fly,
2 But Bear-like I must fight the course. ¶ What's he
3 That was not born of Woman? Such a one
4 Am I to fear, or none.
Enter Young Seyward.

YOUNG SEYWARD

5 What is thy name?

MACBETH

6 Thou 'lt be afraid to hear it.

YOUNG SEYWARD

7 No: though thou call'st thyself a hotter name
8 Than any is in hell.

5.6 A plain before Dunsinane. Exterior. Day.

Purpose: To begin the final battle.

Drama: Can they draw Macbeth out to fight?

What	Why
2-3 Reordered: **throw down** the **leafy** branches that **Screen** us from the sight of the castle, and **show like those you are** , i.e. not trees but soldiers. 3 **worthy Uncle**: old Seyward. 4 **your right Noble Son**: young Seyward. 5 **Battle** = battalion. 6 **upon's** = upon us. 7 **order** = plan of attack.	2 Giving battle orders.
9 **Do we but find** (if we can only find) **the Tyrant's power** (Macbeth's army) **tonight.** 10 **Let us be beaten, if we cannot fight**: if we don't have the strength of character to fight vigorously, let the shame of defeat be our punishment. 11 **Make all our Trumpets speak** = sound all the trumpets. **give them all breath** = blow into them. 12 **clamorous** = loud and insistent. **Harbingers** = forerunners who announce the approach.	9 Giving a pep talk. 11 **give them:** Folio has 'give thee'. We believe that was a typo.

5.7.a Another plain before Dunsinane. Exterior. Day.

Purpose: To reinforce Macbeth's faith in his last remaining magic charm ('none of woman born'), in preparation for his meeting with Macduff.

Drama: Can Young Seyward kill Macbeth?

What	Why
1 **They have tied me to a stake**: Comparing himself to a bear at a bear-baiting, tied to a stake and set upon by dogs. 2-3 **What's he That was not born of Woman**: where's the man who was not born of woman?	3 Keeping faith in his final talisman to maintain his bubble of invincibility. **FORWARD**: 'not born of Woman' reminds us again of the prophecy. 5 **What is thy name**: Making sure he's fighting the right man. This is Young Seyward's first time in Scotland, so he doesn't know what Macbeth looks like. 6 **Thou 'lt be afraid:** taunting.
7 **hotter**: The worse someone was on Earth, the hotter their torments in Hell.	7 Refusing to be cowed.

MACBETH

9 My name's *Macbeth*.

YOUNG SEYWARD

10 The devil himself could not pronounce a Title
11 More hateful to mine ear.

MACBETH

12 No: nor more fearful.

YOUNG SEYWARD

13 Thou liest abhorred Tyrant, with my Sword
14 I'll prove the lie thou speak'st.

Fight, and young Seyward slain.

MACBETH

15 Thou wast born of woman;
16 ¶ But Swords I smile at, Weapons laugh to scorn,
17 Brandish'd by man that's of a Woman born.

Exit.

5.7.b -

Alarums. Enter Macduff.

MACDUFF

18 That way the noise is: ¶ Tyrant show thy face,
19 If thou be'st slain, and with no stroke of mine,
20 My Wife and Children's Ghosts will haunt me still:
21 ¶ I cannot strike at wretched Kernes, whose arms
22 Are hir'd to bear their Staves; either thou *Macbeth*,
23 Or else my Sword with an unbattered edge
24 I sheathe again undeeded. ¶ There thou shouldst be,
25 By this great clatter, one of greatest note
26 Seems bruited. ¶ Let me find him Fortune,
27 And more I beg not.

Exit.

Alarums.

5.7.c -

Enter Malcolm and [Old] Seyward.

SEYWARD

28 This way my Lord, the Castle's gently rendered:
29 The Tyrant's people, on both sides do fight,
30 The Noble Thanes do bravely in the War,
31 The day almost itself professes yours,

What	Why
	9 **My name's *Macbeth***: Trying to terrify him.
	10 **The devil himself:** defying him.
	12 **more fearful**: trying to scare him.
13-14 Reordered: **I'll prove the lie thou speak'st** (I'll prove you are lying) **with my Sword** (by killing you).	14 Again defying him. Note: in the Renaissance, a vestige of medieval thinking was the idea that a question of law could be fairly decided by a duel: God could be trusted to let the just man kill the cheater.
	15 **FORWARD:** 'Thou wast born of woman' reminds us again to wonder, who will appear who was not born of woman?
16-17 Here's the sentence, reordered: **I smile at Swords** and **laugh** in **scorn** of Weapons, that are **Brandish'd** (waved threateningly at me) **by man that's of a Woman born.**	16 **TURN:** Macbeth victorious. Laughing at the youth he killed.

5.7.b Purpose: 1. To urge forward the final confrontation of Macduff and Macbeth. 2. To show that killing Macbeth is Macduff's only goal.

Drama: Can Macduff find Macbeth?

What	Why
19 **If thou be'st slain, and with no stroke of mine**: if you are killed by someone else. 20 **still** = always. 21 **wretched** = pitiful. **Kernes** = Irish. 22 **hir'd:** They are mercenaries. **Staves** = fighting sticks (plural of staff). **either** I will use it to kill **thou *Macbeth.*** 23 **unbattered edge**: unused. 24 **sheathe again undeeded** = put back in its sheath unused. 25 **great clatter**: great noise. **one of greatest note** = the most important person. 26 **bruited** = announced with noise. Macbeth must be in the loudest part of the battlefield.	18 Searching for Macbeth. 21 Avoiding harming anybody but Macbeth. Note: We feel Shakespeare included this to show Macduff is a decent man, unlike Macbeth, who says "Whiles I see lives, the gashes Do better upon them".

5.7.c Purpose: To begin the overall resolution: The battle is almost won.

Drama: Will Malcolm's people win the battle?

What	Why
28 **gently rendered** = surrendered almost without violence. 29 **on both sides**: many of Macbeth's people are fighting on our side. 31 **itself professes** = calls itself. You've almost won.	28 Reporting wonderful news: The victory so far is easier even than we had hoped.

32 And little is to do.

MALCOLM

33 We have met with Foes

34 That strike beside us.

SEYWARD

35 Enter Sir, the Castle.

Exeunt.

Alarum.

5.7.d -

Enter Macbeth.

MACBETH

36 Why should I play the Roman Fool, and die

37 On mine own sword? Whiles I see lives, the gashes

38 Do better upon them.

Enter Macduff.

MACDUFF

39 Turn Hell-hound, turn.

MACBETH

40 Of all men else I have avoided thee:

41 But get thee back, my soul is too much charg'd

42 With blood of thine already.

MACDUFF

43 I have no words,

44 My voice is in my Sword, thou bloodier Villain

45 Than terms can give thee out.

Fight: Alarum.

MACBETH

46 Thou losest labour,

47 As easy may'st thou the intrenchant Air

48 With thy keen Sword impress, as make me bleed:

49 Let fall thy blade on vulnerable Crests,

50 I bear a charmed Life, which must not yield

51 To one of woman born.

MACDUFF

52 Despair thy Charm,

53 And let the Angel whom thou still hast serv'd

54 Tell thee, *Macduff* was from his Mother's womb

55 Untimely ripp'd.

What	Why
33-34 **Foes That strike beside us** = 'enemies' that fight on our side.	33 Echoing Seyward - marvelling that Macbeth's army is melting away with only slight resistance.

5.7.d Another part of the field before Dunsinane. Exterior. Day.

Purpose: Resolution. The whole play has built towards this moment.

Drama: Can Macduff kill Macbeth?

What	Why
36 **Roman Fool**: recalling the ancient Roman practice of suicide by falling on one's own sword. 37 **lives** = live people. 38 **better upon them**: better them than me.	36 Deciding to keep fighting, even though he can see he has no hope of winning.
	39 **TURN**: Macduff finally finds Macbeth. Challenging Macbeth to fight.
40 **I have avoided thee**: I don't want to fight you. 41-42 **charg'd With blood of thine** = covered with the blood of your family. Also burdened with guilt. 43 **I have no words**: There's nothing to say.	40 Macbeth has two reasons to avoid Macduff: 1. the prophecy ('Beware Macduff'), and 2. they were friends. 41 **get thee back**: giving Macduff a chance to live. Macbeth still believes he is protected by magic, and anybody he fights will die. 43 Attacking.
45 **Than terms can give thee out** = than words can describe you.	
46 **Thou losest labour** = You waste effort. 47-48 Reordered: You may (**may'st thou**) slice (**impress**) **the intrenchant** (invulnerable) **Air As easy** (easily) **as make me bleed.** 49 **vulnerable Crests** = helmets that are susceptible to hurt. 50 **charmed** = protected by magic.	46 Easily fending Macduff off. 47 Advising Macduff to give up.
52 **Despair thy Charm**: Give up faith in your charm. 53 **the Angel**: Satan. **still** = always. 55 **untimely ripp'd**: pulled out prematurely; born by Caesarian section.	52 Triumphing over Macbeth. 55 **RESOLUTION**: Now we know that 'none of woman born' was no protection at all.

MACBETH

56 Accursed be that tongue that tells me so;
57 For it hath Cow'd my better part of man:
58 And be these Juggling Fiends no more believ'd,
59 That palter with us in a double sense,
60 That keep the word of promise to our ear,
61 And break it to our hope. ¶ I'll not fight with thee.

MACDUFF

62 Then yield thee Coward,
63 And live to be the show, and gaze o' th' time.
64 We'll have thee, as our rarer Monsters are
65 Painted upon a pole, and under-writ,
66 Here may you see the Tyrant.

MACBETH

67 I will not yield
68 To kiss the ground before young *Malcolm's* feet,
69 And to be baited with the Rabble's curse.
70 Though Byrnam wood be come to Dunsinane,
71 And thou oppos'd, being of no woman born,
72 Yet I will try the last. Before my body,
73 I throw my warlike Shield: Lay on *Macduff*,
74 And damn'd be him, that first cries hold, enough.
Exeunt fighting.
Alarums.
Enter Fighting, and Macbeth slain.
Retreat, Flourish.

5.7.e -
Enter with Drum and Colours, Malcolm, [Old] Seyward, Rosse, Thanes & Soldiers.

MALCOLM

75 I would the Friends we miss, were safe arriv'd.

SEYWARD

76 Some must go off: and yet by these I see,
77 So great a day as this is cheaply bought.

MALCOLM

78 *Macduff* is missing, and your Noble Son.

ROSSE

79 Your son my Lord, has paid a soldier's debt,

What	Why
56 **that tongue**: Macduff's. Curse you for telling me this.	56 **TURN**: Macbeth has just lost his last talisman. His bubble of invincibility is burst.
57 **Cow'd** = made to cower in fear. **better part of man** = manhood; bravery.	
58 **Juggling** = deceitful. **Fiends**: the Witches.	
59 **palter** = shift; dodge.	
60-61 **keep the word of promise to our ear, And break it to our hope**: make promises which in a sense prove true, but which break our hopes.	60 Refusing to fight. Putting down his sword.
63 **show, and gaze o' th' time** = on show, gazed at by the public.	62 **yield thee:** Goading him to fight. It's clear from the context that if Macbeth were to yield, Macduff would bring him in alive. But he wants to kill Macbeth, so he's painting the most unpleasant picture he can of Macbeth's future life, so Macbeth will fight and Macduff can honorably chop off his head.
64 **rarer Monsters**: Disfigured people sometimes appeared in 'freak shows' for the public's entertainment.	
65 **Painted upon a pole**: your picture on a board on a pole. **under-writ** = written beneath.	
	67 **I will not yield**: TURN: Macbeth decides to die fighting.
69 **baited with the Rabble's curse**: like a bear tied to a stake, with the rabble crowded around cursing him.	
71 **thou oppos'd**: though I am opposed by you, who were of no woman born.	
72 **try the last**: fight to the end.	
73 **Lay on**: Let's fight!	
	Stage direction: **Macbeth slain**: This is usually done offstage, so there won't be a problem of what to do with the body.

5.7.e Dunsinane Castle. Interior. Day.

Purpose: Resolution. This is the happy ending. The tyrant is replaced by a humane, humble, diplomatic and sure-handed King.

Drama: 1. How many of Malcolm's supporters are dead? 2. What sort of King will Malcolm be? (see Endnote 7, page 193)

What	Why
75 **the Friends we miss** = our missing soldiers.	75 Worrying about the fate of his friends.
76 **Some must go off** = Inevitably, some must die. **by these** = by the number of survivors here with us.	76 Comforting Malcolm.
77 **so great a day** = such an important victory. **cheaply bought** = The cost in lives was small.	
79 **a soldier's debt**: he died fighting.	79 Delivering the bad news, but also comforting Seyward by stressing how honorably his son fought.

80 He only liv'd but till he was a man,
81 The which no sooner had his Prowess confirm'd
82 In the unshrinking station where he fought,
83 But like a man he died.

SEYWARD
84 Then he is dead?

ROSSE
85 Ay, and brought off the field: your cause of sorrow
86 Must not be measur'd by his worth, for then
87 It hath no end.

SEYWARD
88 Had he his hurts before?

ROSSE
89 Ay, on the Front.

SEYWARD
90 Why then, God's Soldier be he:
91 ¶ Had I as many Sons, as I have hairs,
92 I would not wish them to a fairer death:
93 ¶ And so his Knell is knoll'd.

MALCOLM
94 He's worth more sorrow,
95 And that I'll spend for him.

SEYWARD
96 He's worth no more,
97 They say he parted well, and paid his score,
98 And so God be with him. ¶ Here comes newer comfort.

Enter Macduff, with Macbeth's head.

MACDUFF
99   Hail King, for so thou art.
100 ¶ Behold where stands
101 Th' Usurper's cursed head: ¶ the time is free:
102 I see thee compass'd with thy Kingdom's Pearl,
103 That speak my salutation in their minds:
104 Whose voices I desire aloud with mine,
105 Hail King of Scotland.

ALL
106 Hail King of Scotland.

What	Why
80 **He only liv'd but till he was a man**: He had only just reached the age of manhood. 81 **no sooner had his Prowess confirm'd**: as soon as he had proved his manhood. 82 **unshrinking station:** he did not shrink from the spot where he fought.	
85-87 **your cause of sorrow** (your grief) **Must not be measur'd by** (must not be as great as) **his worth, for then It hath** (because then it would have) **no end.**	85 Consoling him.
88 **before** = on his front, not on his back. He was wounded fighting, not running away.	
90 **God's Soldier**: He's a soldier in Heaven now.	90 Accepting his son's death.
93 **his Knell is knoll'd**: His funeral bell is tolled.	
94 **more sorrow** = more funeral rite. 95 **I'll spend for him**: I will give him a proper memorial.	94 Thanking Seyward for his sacrifice.
96 **He's worth no more**: not that he doesn't deserve a proper send-off, but that he's already had the best.	96 Declining the offer of a state funeral, since in his mind, to die fighting valiantly is the highest honor.
99 **so thou art**: since Macbeth is dead, you are now King. 101 **the time** = the country.	99 Hailing Malcolm, and presenting Macbeth's head as a trophy. 101 **Th'Usurper's cursed head:** This is an implied stage direction. Macduff has literally brought in Macbeth's severed head.
102 **compass'd** (surrounded) **with thy Kingdom's Pearl** (finest men). 103 **speak my salutation in their minds**: they are hailing you in their minds, as I am aloud.	104 Exhorting the thanes to hail Malcolm.

MALCOLM

107 We shall not spend a large expense of time,
108 Before we reckon with your several loves,
109 And make us even with you. My Thanes and Kinsmen
110 Henceforth be Earls, the first that ever Scotland
111 In such an Honour nam'd: ¶ What's more to do,
112 Which would be planted newly with the time,
113 As calling home our exil'd Friends abroad,
114 That fled the Snares of watchful Tyranny,
115 Producing forth the cruel Ministers
116 Of this dead Butcher, and his Fiend-like Queen;
117 Who (as 'tis thought) by self and violent hands,
118 Took off her life. ¶ This, and what needful else
119 That calls upon us, by the Grace of Grace,
120 We will perform in measure, time, and place:
121 ¶ So thanks to all at once, and to each one,
122 Whom we invite, to see us Crown'd at Scone.

Flourish.
Exeunt Omnes.

FINIS.

What	Why
107 **We shall not spend a large expense of time**: I will not let much time go by.	107 Commencing his reign with humility, generosity and vigor. Note: He is going to be a good King (see Endnote 7, page 193).
108 **reckon with** = make account of. **your several loves** = the services each of you has performed.	
109 **make us even with you** = repay you; settle our debts.	110 **Henceforth be Earls:** Granting them titles. The implication is that 'Earl' is better than 'Thane'. Perhaps this is to honor King Edward and the Earl of Northumberland, who just saved Scotland (see Endnote 7, page 193).
112 **Which would** (should) **be planted newly with the time**: as seeds should be planted in spring. In other words, it's important to do these things now and not wait.	
114 **Snares of watchful Tyranny**: the traps set by the tyrant's spies.	
115-116 **Producing forth** = catching and bringing forth. **the cruel Ministers** = the cruel ones who administered the commands **Of this dead Butcher** (Macbeth).	
117 **self and violent hands**: by her own violent hands.	
118 **Took off her life** = committed suicide.	
118-119 **what needful else That calls upon us** = what other needed tasks we are called upon to perform.	
119 **by the Grace of Grace** = by the blessing of God.	
120 **in measure, time and place**: appropriately, at the right time and place.	
122 **Scone**: where the kings of Scotland were crowned for fifty generations. It is at the mouth of the Firth of Tay.	

THE END.

ENDNOTES

Over the many years of producing this play and teaching it to students, there are some questions that come up repeatedly. Here are our thoughts about these questions. These are not intended to be definitive answers, but one way to explore Shakespeare, through our lens as theatre practitioners. What are your thoughts? Email us at info@philadelphiashakespearepress.com.

1. What is *Macbeth* about?

Before you can tell a story properly, you have to know what story you are telling. Is this a story of Ambition? We don't think so. Macbeth achieves his ambition in Act Two. If it were an ambition story, the following three acts would be denouement. Is it a story of Revenge? Again, not in our opinion. Although it's true that Macduff's revenge is indispensable to the story, this is not the story of Macduff. Or Malcolm. They are supporting characters in this drama. Is it Fate vs. Free Will? Good vs. Evil? Dark Magic? Psychosis? Bad Advice? Bad Wife? The Corrosive Power of Falsehood? All these themes come into play in *Macbeth*, but in our opinion, these are satellite themes, arranged to illuminate the main theme.

In our view, the heart of the play is the sequence of introspections by Macbeth and Lady Macbeth — 'Macbeth does murder Sleep'; 'Nought's had, all's spent'; 'Out damned spot'; 'Life's but a walking Shadow'. These are the moments that make this play so gripping; the lines that stay with us years after seeing a production. And the story they tell is captured by Lady Macbeth: 'What's done, cannot be undone'. We believe that line is the very soul of *Macbeth*. It is a story of **regret**.

2. Is Duncan a good king? (1.2.a, page 4)

We have heard it argued that Duncan is a weak king. Evidence: He sits safe in camp, while others risk their lives to do his fighting for him; he faces a rebellion, which seems to indicate that at least some of his subjects have found his leadership wanting; he faces a foreign invasion, which means either he failed to adequately prepare to defend his country, or failed to make his defenses sufficiently obvious to outsiders; and he trusts both the old Cawdor and the new Cawdor, both traitors, which may indicate that he is easily duped.

If this were a history, then yes, these would be valid points. But it's not a history. It's a drama. And 'Bad King Gets Supplanted By Other Bad King' is not good drama, in our opinion. 'Great King Supplanted By Vile King', on the other hand, is good drama. Moreover, Duncan is reverenced by his followers. He is a 'sainted-King', whose 'Virtues Will plead like Angels'.

That's why we say that the purpose of 1.2.a is to show that Duncan is a good and wise king.

3. Do the Witches cause Macbeth to kill Duncan? (1.3.b, p. 14)

This is a question that often comes up in discussion. How much power do the Witches have over Macbeth? Do they control him? Or are they manifestations of his own unconscious? Or something else?

In our opinion, although it's probably true that Macbeth would never have killed Duncan if he had never met the Witches, it's not true that they turn an innocent man into a murderer. That wouldn't be a good story: 'Hero Is Helpless Victim of Fate'. Nobody would care. The poignancy of this story is that Macbeth *causes his own downfall*. The Witches see a latent impulse in him, and arrange matters in just such a way that that latent impulse is awakened to action. And to make it even more poignant — to really salt the wound — Macbeth *almost doesn't go through with it*. He knows it's wrong to kill Duncan. He twice decides, for excellent reasons which he expounds most persuasively, to abandon the plan. But the Witches, by showing him just a tantalizing glimpse of the positive consequences and hiding from him the negative consequences, trick him into his own ruin.

4. Is Lady Macbeth nervous? (1.6.a, page 34)

When Lady Macbeth welcomes Duncan to Inverness, her speeches are quite fluent and confident. It could be argued that, at least at this point in the story, she is pathologically invulnerable to the kind of misgivings one might expect from a would-be murderer.

But again, we refer back to our guiding principle: Which interpretation makes the best story? 'Invulnerable' is boring. If Lady Macbeth is in no danger of losing her poise, there is no drama in this scene; it's just two people exchanging pleasantries. But if she is struggling to maintain her composure, there is something at stake, and we are eager to see how it turns out.

In addition, if she can barely muster the cruelty required for the murder, then her breakdown afterwards ('Nought's had, all's spent') makes more sense.

5. Is Macbeth moral? (1.7.a, page 38)

The 'If it were done when 'tis done' scene is especially complex. 'We still have judgment here'; 'He's here in double trust'; 'his Virtues Will plead like Angels'; 'tears shall drown the wind' — these lines all seem to indicate that Macbeth is deciding not to murder Duncan because of the guilt it would engender.

But a closer reading shows that the scene is about something else. Yes, he is fully cognizant of the magnitude of the crime he is contemplating. But his train of thought is not about whether it's a crime; it's about whether he can get away with it. 'We still have judgment here' is followed by 'This even-handed Justice Commends th'Ingredience of our poison'd Chalice To our own lips'. That's about practical consequences, not moral scruples. And he doesn't worry that Heaven's Cherubin will blow the horrid deed in *his own* eye, but in *every* eye, in other words everybody else — it will destroy his reputation. And finally, 'I have no spur To prick the sides of my intent, but only Vaulting Ambition': The context makes it clear that by 'spur', he means not 'reason' but 'excuse'.

But this is not to say that he has no scruples: he makes it abundantly clear that he is keenly aware of the moral consequences of murdering his beloved king. Rather, he has decided that it would be an acceptable price to pay if he could get away with it. He later learns that this was a mistake — 'Macbeth shall sleep no more'.

6. How does Lady Macbeth change her husband's mind, and persuade him to go through with the murder of Duncan? Is she to blame for the murder? (1.7.b, page 40)

This is one of the most important — and most debated — moments in *Macbeth*. At the beginning of the scene, Macbeth is resolved not to kill Duncan ("We will proceed no further in this Business"). At the end of the scene, he has changed his mind. In between, his wife works on him with a variety of strategies. So the question is, how does she do it? Does she henpeck him? Dare him? Use her sexuality?

As we discussed in the Introduction, we have seen quite a wide variety of productions: Lady Macbeth as dominatrix; as seductress;

as insufferable nag. These are not without foundation — she does try all these strategies in her effort to change his mind.

But there are two reasons to look elsewhere for the root of her success. First, all her attempts to pressure him fail. His answer is merely, 'Prythee peace'. But when she suggests that they make it look like the chamberlains did it, he does a complete about-face: 'Bring forth Men-Children only'. It is not pressure that changes his mind, but logic. She presents him with a scheme for getting away with the crime, and he is converted. This is the 'aha' moment when his mind is changed.

Second, the downfall of a great man is a better story than the downfall of a weak man. Macbeth is not a simpering henpecked husband or a slave to his wife's sexual manipulations; this is the peerless kinsman, who with his bare arm won two wars and saved Scotland in a single day. For the audience, to see a bad man do badly is sad; but to see a powerful, intelligent, brave man do badly hurts us to the core. That's why this play stays with us. That's why we're still talking about it four hundred years later.

As for Lady Macbeth, it's important to note that she does not make her husband kill Duncan. She provides only the means, not the motive. The motive is his own creation, and thus the consequences are his own to bear.

7. Will Malcolm be a good king? (4.3.a, p. 138, 5.7.e, p. 188)

Another question we often get about this play concerns Malcolm's fitness to govern. In 1.1 we learn that in the Macdonwald fight Malcolm had to be rescued by the bleeding sergeant; in 2.4 when he learns his father's been murdered, he decides to run away; and in 5.6 he sends his cousins into the battle ahead of him. It could be said that all these are blots on his character, and that he will be a feeble king.

As always, our first concern is, What makes a better story, given the evidence in the script? 'Evil King Killed, But Successor Probably Won't Be Much Better' is not a particularly compelling story. 'Noble Son Avenges Father and Saves Scotland', on the other hand, is. Macbeth has a happy ending. A really happy ending is a lot better than a semi-happy ending.

And besides, Shakespeare takes pains to make us love Malcolm. 4.3.a is the longest scene in the entire play, and the only thing that happens is a conversation between Malcolm and Macduff. In that conversation, Malcolm reveals himself to be kind and steadfast like his father, but unlike his father, keenly astute in the ways of men. Malcolm also shines in 5.7 when, after becoming king, his first concern is the care of his supporters. And the evidence cited against him can also be interpreted in his favor: The fact that he needed rescuing in the Macdonwald fight means that he rushed into a doubtful situation, more concerned with beating the rebellion than with his own safety. His flight after his father's murder shows that his judgment prevails over his passion. And when he takes a back seat to his uncle in the fight against Macbeth, he is deferring to Seyward's superior soldiership. These are all virtues.

Carmen Khan and Jack Armstrong co-founded The Philadelphia Shakespeare Theatre in 1996. Together they have mounted sixty productions, fifty of which were Shakespeare's plays.

Carmen Khan is the Artistic/Executive Director. She holds a Bachelor of Education from St. Mary's College, University of London, England, and a Master of Fine Arts in Acting from The Catholic University of America, in Washington, D.C.

She has been a professional actor, director and producer for the last twenty five years. She co-founded The Laughing Stock Theatre, an all-comedy theatre, and was Artistic Director of The Red Heel Theatre, devoted to the little-known classics of the Jacobean era, both in Philadelphia.

Jack Armstrong: In addition to writing or editing most of the theatre's proposals and strategy papers, he has also written two novels, two screenplays, several stage plays and scores of essays and poems on a wide range of topics.

As the technologist of Reliance Graphics, Jack invented the Election Views ballot typesetting software, and has created the ballots for tens of millions of votes, across thousands of elections.

Jack loves climbing, hiking, paddling and sailing, taking photographs, building furniture, playing and composing music, and studying languages.